Critiquing Postmodernism in Contemporary Discourses of Race

Critiquing Postmodernism in Contemporary Discourses of Race

Sue J. Kim

CRITIQUING POSTMODERNISM IN CONTEMPORARY DISCOURSES OF RACE
Copyright © Sue J. Kim, 2009.

Sections of chapter two were originally published as "*Apparatus*: Theresa Hak Kyung and the Politics of Form." *Journal of Asian Studies* 8.2 (2005): 143–69. © 2005 The Johns Hopkins University Press. Reprinted with permission of The Johns Hopkins University Press.

Sections of chapter four were originally published as " 'The Real White Man is Waiting For Me': Ideology and Morality in Bessie Head's *A Question of Power.*" *College Literature* 35.2 (Spring 2008): 38–69. Reprinted with permission of *College Literature.*

First published in 2009 by
PALGRAVE MACMILLAN®
in the United States—a division of St. Martin's Press LLC,
175 Fifth Avenue, New York, NY 10010.

Where this book is distributed in the UK, Europe and the rest of the world, this is by Palgrave Macmillan, a division of Macmillan Publishers Limited, registered in England, company number 785998, of Houndmills, Basingstoke, Hampshire RG21 6XS.

Palgrave Macmillan is the global academic imprint of the above companies and has companies and representatives throughout the world.

Palgrave® and Macmillan® are registered trademarks in the United States, the United Kingdom, Europe and other countries.

ISBN: 978–0–230–61874–9

Library of Congress Cataloging-in-Publication Data

Kim, Sue J.
    Critiquing postmodernism in contemporary discourses of race / Sue J. Kim.
        p. cm.
    Includes bibliographical references.
    ISBN 978–0–230–61874–9 (alk. paper)
    1. Postmodernism (Literature) 2. Other (Philosophy) in literature. 3. Marginality, Social, in literature. 4. Race in literature. I. Title.

PN98.P67K5 2009
809'.9113—dc22   2009009730

A catalogue record of the book is available from the British Library.

Design by Newgen Imaging Systems (P) Ltd., Chennai, India.

First edition: December 2009

10 9 8 7 6 5 4 3 2 1

Printed in the United States of America.

For Key Young & June Kim

Contents

Acknowledgments

A s is often the case with first books, this project has been in development for so long, in so many forms, that there are many, many people to thank. The numerous faults with this book, however, are entirely my own doing.

First, I simply could not have completed this book without a number of generous grants and fellowships. Cornell University's Sage Dissertation Fellowship enabled me to lay the groundwork in my dissertation. At the University of Alabama at Birmingham, a considerable Faculty Development Grant from the Office of the Provost (2004–05) afforded me the time needed to develop this project. Two faculty development grants from the Dean of the School of Arts & Humanities (2003–04 and 2008–09) and one from the Office of Equity and Diversity (2006) also provided the means to complete this book. I am extremely grateful for this crucial support.

The initial research for this book was conducted at the Library of Congress, using the general collections as well as the African and Middle Eastern Division Reading Room, in Washington, DC; Cornell University's extensive library collections in Ithaca, NY; and the Theresa Hak Kyung Cha archive at the Berkeley Art Museum and Pacific Film Archive in Berkeley, CA. At UAB's Mervyn H. Sterne Library, I thank Heather Martin, Reference Librarian Extraordinare for the Schools of Arts & Humanities, and Eddie Luster, Head of Interlibrary Loan. You should both know that I am your number one fan!

The editors and external reviewers I have been lucky enough to work with provided critical guidance and feedback: at the Journal of Asian American Studies, former editor George Anthony Peffer and the external reviewers; and at College Literature, editor Kostas Myrsiades, the ever-helpful (and speedy!) editorial assistant Elizabeth Alex Lukens, and the external reviewers. Palgrave Macmillan has been fantastic from start to finish, particularly my editor Brigitte Shull and my lifesaver, editorial assistant Lee Norton. The external reviewer for this book was incredibly generous with insights and suggestions; I tried to make this book more of what you said it could be.

The students I have worked with at UAB have taught me as much—probably more—than I have taught them. I thank the students that, in the past six years, I have had the pleasure to work with in my literary theory course and/or on thesis projects, particularly Cassie Caldwell, Sherman "Vic" Camp, Carl Chang, Junsong Chen, Nathan Cook, Tressa Cook, Sally Culpepper, Daniel Davis, Lucy Dorn, Rebecca Duncan, Michael Ferguson, James "Ron" Guthrie, Jessica Heine, Heather Helms, Ben Holley, Elizabeth Gaines Marsh, Natalie McCall, Shane McGowan, Katie Movelle, Carolyn Myers, Russell Norris, "Uncle" Jim Owens, Jake Patrick, Paul Pickering, Whitney Reed, Adrianne Roberts, Nathan Shepura, Abigail Short, Rob Short, Matt Smith, Jennifer Stack, Andrea Thomas, Tabitha Wade, and Kate Wood. I particularly thank my research assistants Chris Mahan, who helped me research chapter three and edited early versions of chapters two and four, and the inimitable Rob Short, who hunted down crucial information for the later stages of this book.

My colleagues in the English Department at UAB are amazing; every day I feel fortunate to come to work. I particularly thank the members of the Junior Faculty Reading Group (2003–05): Alison Chapman, Ann Hoff, Cynthia Ryan, Daniel Siegel, Gale Temple, and Jacqueline Wood. Chapters two and four saw the light of publication day thanks to your input. I also thank my mentoring committee, William Hutchings, Bruce McComiskey, and Rebecca Bach; Marilyn Kurata and Peter Bellis; and my partner in academic crime, Linda Frost. Daniel Siegel patiently listened to more versions of this book's direction(s) than I'm sure either of us want to remember. The seeds of my research on Theresa Hak Kyung Cha's Dictee stretch back to my undergraduate senior thesis work with my beloved mentor, Brenda Silver, whose wise counsel still guides my life and scholarship. My esteemed graduate committee at Cornell University somehow agreed to unleash me on the universe: Committee Chair Biodun Jeyifo, Chandra Talpade Mohanty, Gary Okihiro, and Sunn Shelley Wong.

I feel incredibly fortunate to count among my best friends three of the smartest people I have ever met: Gina Caison, Priya Gopal, and Gloria Son. And by "smart," I don't mean just intellectually, but also emotionally, politically, existentially smart. I also thank my Facebook support network (you know who you are!) for getting me through the last few months of revisions.

Finally, I thank my loving and sanely insane family. Connie, Eddie, and Sophia Chang have always provided me a haven, while Dorothy Joo pelted me with pomo donuts. Doctors Shin and Kim Oh, my Birmingham "parents," have nurtured and supported me in a land far from my hometown. My actual parents, Key Young and June Kim, have filled my life with wisdom, humor, love, and golf; you are what I want to be when I grow up! My brothers John and Jay and my sister and partner-in-crime Emily Sargo entertained, encouraged, and sustained me during what seemed like the endless years of this project. Last but not least, to the cheezpets—Mozzarella, Muenster, Monterey "Monty" Jack, Nacho, and Cheddar—you are the best writing buddies a girl could ask for.

Introduction

In *Critiquing Postmodernism in Contemporary Discourses of Race*, I critique the epistemology and politics of what I refer to as "otherness postmodernism," or the group of critical tendencies based on the privileging of difference and alterity—particularly in regards to race and gender—in contemporary literary criticism and theory. This tendency is manifested variously in poststructuralist, postmodernist, and even antitheoretical positions; although it takes different guises, otherness postmodernism, I argue, is ubiquitous in academic and public conversations about race in particular and alterity and marginality in general. I contend that otherness postmodernism constitutes what Slavoj Žižek, in *The Sublime Object of Ideology* (1989), terms an ideological fantasy, or the notion that ideology functions primarily through belief rather than practice. The ideological fantasy of otherness postmodernism includes the belief, for example, that the postmodernist believes that he/she resists racism and other kinds of exploitation by "seeing through" the ideologies that the credulous essentialist presumably believes. On the contrary, I argue that despite the insights of postmodernism, literary criticism and theory continue to perpetuate essentialisms, obscuring the institutional, political, and economic structures that shape issues of race and marginality.

I focus on otherness postmodernism as manifested in critical conversations around three notable "postmodern" literary texts: Theresa Hak Kyung Cha's *Dictee*, Thomas Pynchon's *Gravity's Rainbow*, and Bessie Head's *A Question of Power*. The reception of each text has been key in establishing the hegemony of philosophical postmodernism across the literary studies landscape. Critical readings of *Dictee* and *Gravity's Rainbow* served to promote, institutionalize and, normalize the assumptions of postmodernism, while readings of *A Question of Power* have been informed by and ultimately hampered by those assumptions. And while contemporary methods of reading almost uniformly privilege heterogeneity and difference in a variety of ways, I argue that analyses of these novels remain limited by essentialist determinations based on the author's identity and narrow notions of the ideological valences of narrative form. A wider consideration of political, aesthetic, critical, and other historical contexts and genealogies complicates those essentialist assumptions. Moreover, the texts themselves—dealing with the same political, ethical, and epistemological issues as the theories applied to them—in many ways offer subtler and more complex understandings of ideology, culture, and identity than the narrow terms of otherness postmodernism allow.

Otherness postmodernism encompasses a number of critical tendencies. It repeatedly pits sameness against difference, unity against heterogeneity, and singularity against multiplicity in a variety of ways—in terms of signification, determination, identity, social formations, literary form, and so on. The critical proclivity for the sameness/difference dichotomy produces a number of interlinked problems. First, otherness postmodernism fails to account for the structures and processes that produce the situation in which certain terms are articulated as "Same" or central, while others are "Other" or marginal. This failure to render structures and processes of power explicable runs the risk of naturalizing and thereby reinforcing them. Second, the overly simplified sameness/difference binary ends up consistently privileging difference, particularly because a *perfectly* unified, totalized, or homogenous social phenomenon never really exists. But without ways to account for mediations between, say, total unity on one hand and heterogeneity on the other, the default choice becomes that of difference. Third, when formalized, the sameness-versus-difference dichotomy fails to provide the grounds for evaluation between social articulations by appeal to, for example, ethics, reference, or metanarratives. Because otherness postmodernism offers no guides for evaluating cultural practices and productions other than that sameness/difference dichotomy, postmodernism itself becomes the only means for progressive politics and theoretical sophistication. Therefore, the hermeneutics of difference ironically ends up flattening differences into sameness, or rendering the diversity of significations and possibilities only in terms of sameness *or* difference. In other words, otherness postmodernism fails to live up to the truth of its own tenets.

For example, this privileging of difference ironically lumps all marginal writers into a flat, static category. In literary criticism, otherness postmodernism often correlates narrative form to politics, assuming that difference from literary realism constitutes political resistance because of the presumed correlation between realism and bourgeois ideology and subject formation. Narrative interruption, therefore, constitutes political resistance and the formation of new subjectivities. These narrow critical parameters, however, often lead to the underconsideration of the various, actual historical contexts that impact a writer and his/her texts; the complex aesthetic form of the texts that can themselves provide commentaries on and theorizations of those historical moments; and the ideological valences of those texts. In contrast to the tendencies of otherness postmodernism, I argue that the central concerns, aesthetic style, and implications of an author's texts should not be determined primarily by his or her identity, but rather by a constellation of considerations that can be applicable to all writers. The predominant critical methodologies available to us today have not sufficiently accounted for some major narrative tendencies in "postmodern" fiction. The narrow sameness/difference paradigm has prevented us from reading, for example, across political, ethnic, and historical identities; through such foreclosure, otherness postmodernism ends up undermining its advocacy of difference.

My aim is to connect discourses that are usually separate in order to examine common underlying assumptions and structures, so this book is comparative in several senses. I bring together issues from cultural studies fields such as U.S. ethnic studies, "mainstream" or Euro-American poststructuralist theory, and postcolonial studies, which are related but often quite separate. My approach is syncretic in that while I am a Marxist, I agree with Sartre's argument in *Search for a Method* that historical materialism must take seriously the multileveled complexities of a situation (person, event, thing) before locating it in a larger system. I believe that many of the approaches and epistemologies commonly associated with postmodernism have produced insights that are not only useful but also true. It is in subscribing to notions of truth and ethics, however, that I depart from postmodernism in general. My goal is to check some of excesses of postmodernism in order not to lose its insights to irrelevancy.

In the first chapter, "The Ideological Fantasy of Otherness Postmodernism," I outline the basic characteristics of otherness postmodernism, drawing on the recent critique of poststructuralism's rejection of referentiality by Rey Chow. I also examine the historical and theoretical bases for otherness postmodernism, or why it arose when it did and why it may be limited now. I look at influential retheorizations of the social in the mid-1980s, primarily Ernesto Laclau and Chantal Mouffe's *Hegemony and Socialist Strategy* (1985) and Michael Omi and Howard Winant's *Racial Formation in the United States* (1986), which posed not only new articulations of the social, but also attendant prescriptions for "radical democracy" through the politics of difference. Despite the insights provided by these texts, they also laid the groundwork for many of the problematic assumptions of otherness postmodernism, including binaries between utter sameness and difference and an emphasis on insuperable alterity. The failure to account for the mediations between sameness and difference—the messy in-betweens that constitute most actual social processes—results in the constant privileging of difference. Furthermore, otherness postmodernism's unwillingness to identify a common ground to evaluate between social elements and interpretations leads to postmodernism itself becoming the de facto political litmus test; the only way to be a political radical is to be a postmodernist. In these ways, otherness postmodernism promotes a sense of superior knowledge as the key to puncturing ideology, while failing to account for gaps between belief and action enforced by social, political, and economic structures. Revisiting the work of Laclau and Mouffe and Omi and Winant—their contents, contexts, and institutionalization—offers insight into the reasons for our current critical tendencies, as well as some ways to move beyond it. To remedy this situation, I concur with those such as Chow, Masao Miyoshi, Madhu Dubey, Frederick Luis Aldama, and others that we must allow referentiality, ethics, metanarratives, and even traditional Marxist critique to interrupt our current ways of thinking.

Chapter two, "Theresa Hak Kyung Cha and the Politics of Form," questions one of the central tenets of otherness postmodernism: that experimental texts by minority and/or female writers constitute political resistance by contravening realist narrative forms. As several critics have noted, such readings of Theresa Hak Kyung Cha's experimental text *Dictee* marked a turning point in Asian American Studies' embrace of postmodernism. I point out, however, that the interpretive methodologies of the criticism and the narrative elements that such criticism highlights in the text do not differ greatly from mainstream postmodernist reading modes. Implicitly, then, her work appears to be more oppositional than that of other modernist and avant-garde artists because she is a Korean American woman. In order to think beyond this dead-end, I situate Cha's work in its complex context of aesthetic and political ideas. Through an examination of Cha's earlier anthology on film theory, *Apparatus: Cinematographic Apparatus*, I argue that Cha's work, including *Dictee*, responds as much to modernism and postmodernism as it does to realism. Locating her work within the politically ambivalent avant-garde aesthetic context—including New Wave film and psychoanalytic film theory—demonstrates that it is oppositional not only because its form is unconventional, but also because it calls into question an increasingly depoliticized formalism and a problematic notion of a passive subject-viewer in modern/postmodern art and art theory. To do so, Cha's work reasserts the importance of history and human agency, coupling experimental formal strategies with pointed emphases on reclaimed histories and contexts. At the same time, such historical and aesthetic contextualization recasts the politics of Cha's work in more complicated lights.

The third chapter, "Not Three Worlds but One: Thomas Pynchon and the Invisibility of Race," critiques the postmodern fascination with the "sublime"—technological, historical, ethical, epistemological, et cetera. I argue that the concept is used, in Pynchon's terms, to "approach and avoid" difficult issues of ethics, history, technology, race, and the structures that shape them. I examine the curious absence of issues of race and imperialism in Pynchon criticism, although these are central issues in Pynchon's work. Whereas the work of Cha and Bessie Head are always tied to the ethnic and gendered identity of the author, Pynchon's work rarely is, beyond his status as a cult figure. My contention is that, in fact, Pynchon's whiteness and maleness license a literary universality that underlies the critical reception of his work, demonstrating the essentialism that underlies even the most theoretically sophisticated postmodernist approaches. If, as with Cha's text, we examine the context of Pynchon's writing, we can see the genealogy of the issues of race and imperialism in *Gravity's Rainbow* extend to the literary and political movements that shaped Pynchon. I read Pynchon's early work as a reaction to American modernist, Beat, and counterculture appropriations of difference, particularly blackness and colonial views of the other. Pynchon's early stories, articles, and his first novel *V.* struggle with identification and alterity in ways that cannot be understood through a blanket notion of the sublime. I contend that *Gravity's Rainbow*, in exploring differences and similarities in the situations of three central characters—Slothrop, Enzian, and Tchitcherine—suggests that race and colonialism must be understood within global economic and political structures. In other words, Pynchon invokes and challenges the Three Worlds theory in ways that harmonize with Aijaz Ahmad's argument that we live not in three worlds but *one*. The lacuna regarding race in Pynchon criticism brings us back to the idea that even as "incredulous" poststructuralists, we still think in terms of essentialism, whether discussing "difference" race or "sameness" whiteness.

The fourth chapter, "Analyzing the Real: Bessie Head's Literary Psychosis," calls into question the methods of readings that reduce Bessie Head's novel *A Question of Power* to a manifestation of psychosis, an example of the impossibility of articulation, or a cultural specimen. Older readings of Head's novel, some of which tend toward the patriarchal, racist, and condescending, have interpreted it as straight autobiography or simply a portrait of a mental breakdown. With the postmodern

turn, scholars read the novel as an example of the impossibility of signification, of universals, and of coherent subjectivity—in other words, the
usual terms of otherness postmodernism. Even praise for Head's novel
usually treats it as an expression of culture, in David Treuer's sense of a
cultural artifact, rather than as a complex literary product from a complex individual drawing on various aesthetic traditions. In contrast, my
reading demonstrates that, through subtle, masterful manipulation of
aesthetic form, the novel constitutes a challenging examination of the
various ideologies at work in the historical moment Head was writing.
Whereas Cha and Pynchon's work demand that we mine their political
and aesthetic histories to understand them, I argue that Head's *A
Question of Power* narrative itself offers a challenging, compelling historical framework. I read the three hallucinatory characters—Sello the
Monk, Sello of the brown suit, and Dan—as figures of the competing
ideological metanarratives at work in the 1960s and 1970s, interlinked
by descendence yet simultaneous and conflicting. Critics have not
treated Head's novel as a serious philosophical-artistic endeavor because
otherness postmodernism constantly reproduces the essentialism and
paternalistic racism it claims to have overcome. As with the work of Cha
and Pynchon, Head's text is far more complex than the usual heuristic
contours of otherness postmodernism acknowledge.

In the concluding notes, I examine how some of the tenets of otherness postmodernism have migrated beyond literary studies and theory;
its assumptions have been mobilized by both liberals and conservatives
to justify ideologically problematic positions. The Right's appropriation
of postmodernism particularly demonstrates the danger of its ethically
blind, formalistic approach to knowledge and being. The ideological
fantasy of otherness postmodernism can be counteracted partially by
attention to history and by reference to the world, even as we treat this
information critically and understand that it is always already interpreted. I argue for a reconsideration of referentiality, or what we might
think of as an ethics of reading—literature and the world—that includes
at least the attempt to account for more than what is given within the
hegemonically articulated field of the existing social. Nonfoundationalist
notions of "truth" with a small "t," or, as Sandra Harding puts it, a
"strong objectivity" can seriously consider processes of signification and
interpretation while attempting to produce increasingly accurate
accounts of the world ("Rethinking Standpoint" 69–74).

Before continuing, I want to make a note about terminology.
"Otherness postmodernism" is an ugly, clunky term, but that is as it
should be. The repetitive theoretical approach it refers to is not only

tired, it has limited how we read literature, people, and social formations. I add the tag "otherness" to emphasize this particular strand of
postmodernism; the proliferation of the meanings and uses of the term
"postmodern" makes it almost useless. It has been used to refer to an
epistemology (or rather, anti-epistemology), ontology, aesthetics, social
conditions (such as the organization of late capitalism), models of subject and identity, and notions of power and resistance. It has been called
a form of Western imperialism as well as inherently subversive, particularly in relation to marginal groups. The various definitions of
postmodernism sometimes conflict; the philosophical claims of postmodernism are sometimes identified with poststructuralism, while
sometimes they have been clearly differentiated. Moreover, postmodern
aesthetics do not always correspond to philosophical postmodernisms;
this disjunction is one of the claims I make in this book. But I choose
to use "postmodernism" because it is more widely known than the term
"poststructuralism." While many of the claims I explicitly deal with are
poststructuralist, and while there are many differences between specific
poststructuralist theorists and the general notion of postmodernism,
I would argue that there are still identifiable critical tendencies that
draw on both poststructuralism and postmodernism and have produced
a common set of theoretical assumptions and methodological moves.
This set of critical tendencies, clustered around the issues of otherness
and marginality, are what I interrogate in this book.

There Is No Such Thing as the Vulcan Mind Meld

My favorite metaphor when I'm teaching literary theory—although I
somehow manage to incorporate it into almost every class—is that there
is no such thing as the Vulcan Mind Meld. I ask students if they know
what that is, and usually one or two students do. (A disconcerting number of students are too young to even have watched *Star Trek: The Next
Generation*!) In the original *Star Trek*, Mr. Spock had the amazing
ability to become *one* with a member of any alien species simply by
putting his hands on his/her/its head or equivalent. They share their
memories, thoughts, emotions, experiences—their total subjectivities.
I like to illustrate the Mind Meld by approaching some hapless student
and pretending to put my hands on his/her head and become seized by
shared consciousness.

Unfortunately (or fortunately) we mere human beings do not have
this ability; we can only communicate with one another through discourses, primarily language but also nonverbal cues. We can't even do

the Vulcan Mind Meld on ourselves! In order to think and, often, even to feel, we have to be able to articulate and interpret ourselves, but *no* word or sign can ever capture the full, complex subjects that we are, or can ever be truly equivalent to what we want to mean. As Lacan writes, "I think where I am not, therefore I am where I do not think" (142); even as we postulate ourselves in language, we are banished from self-presence. In fact, driven by the desire for presence and meaning, we strive for better and more words and signs to capture ourselves and the world, even as these things are constantly changing and thereby making our quest even more impossible.

Put in these terms—there is no Vulcan Mind Meld with others, ourselves, or any sign—students find the likes of Derrida and Lacan not just explicable but kind of banal. Descriptively, the notions of fundamental nonidentity, absence, overdetermination, indeterminacy, et cetera, make sense. But why, then, does simply registering this description itself become a political good? In other words, why, in one essay and book after another, does just the fact of recognizing this basic nonfoundationalism become a means toward liberation? And why does the reverse—whether accurately identified as essentialism (both philosophically and in terms of identity) or not—immediately become politically reactionary?

Many critical tendencies of otherness postmodernism have already been examined and critiqued. The tide of theory-with-a-capital-T has turned and the heyday of postmodernism has passed (although part of my thesis is that, even in theory's "heyday," many arguments that are not self-identified as postmodern or poststructuralist and that are even directed against those "Western" schools of thought, nevertheless implicitly reproduce the theoretical assumptions of postmodernism). This book participates in the project of articulating the strengths and weaknesses of past and current practices and trying to figure out a path for the future. A change in direction is palpable in recent scholarship and conferences, particularly a turn to greater attention to aesthetics and form, which is to the good. But even as we turn to more closely and complexly treating literary form beyond the realist/experimentalist divide, we have to balance this turn to form with even more weight to context and identity, not in essentialist ways, but in understanding that these still profoundly shape how we think and exist, despite claims of a "post-race" world.

CHAPTER ONE

The Ideological Fantasy of Otherness Postmodernism

It is important not simply to practice antiessentialist differencing ad infinitum but also to reconsider such a practice in conjunction with the rejection of referentiality that lies at the origins of poststructuralism. Exactly what is being thrown out when referentiality is theoretically rejected?

—Rey Chow

To right the situation, to null the transaction and be just to all on earth, we may have to relearn the sense of the world, the totality, that includes all peoples in every race, class, and gender.

—Masao Miyoshi

In his foundational work *The Sublime Object of Ideology*, Slavoj Žižek argues that ideology is not simply the fantasy that people believe about themselves and their society. The classical notion of ideology assumes it to be "false consciousness," so if people were simply informed about how the world works, they would change it. Against this notion, drawing on Lacan, Althusser contended that ideology constitutes the subject's "imaginary relations" to the real conditions of existence (109–112). In turn, Žižek argues that "ideology" is not only this Imaginary relationship to reality; rather, ideology itself is the notion that social reality relies on a fantasy: "the fundamental level of ideology, however, is not of an illusion masking the real state of things but that of an (unconscious) fantasy structuring our social reality itself" (*Sublime* 33). The ideological fantasy is that ideology can be separated from reality, whereas ideology is not only what people "think" or "know" but also—even primarily—what they *do*. Belief, Žižek continues, is not merely an individual or purely mental state; rather, it is "always materialized in our effective social reality: belief supports the fantasy which regulates social reality" (36). Therefore, ideological critique is not only a matter of figuring out how an ideological illusion relates to some reality constituted by its social relations (commodity exchange, value, labor), but also of identifying "the ideological fantasy efficient in social reality itself" (Žižek, *Sublime* 36). For example, Žižek demonstrates how, despite our understanding of the materiality (both physical and symbolic) of money, we treat it as a "real abstraction," or as universal value. Our "non-knowledge" is required for this; even if we "know" that money does not have inherent value, our actions constitute the social reality that in turn relies on the consistency of our actions with ideological directives, whether we "believe" or not.[1]

So if the "ideological" belief holds that people continue to do what they do because they do not know what they are doing, the ideological fantasy is that we believe that knowledge—including knowledge of the nature of signification via poststructuralism—would be enough to debunk ideology. The ideological fantasy is not—or, I would add, not only—that we have been interpellated in a particular way by power or that we do not have information; on the contrary, many people realize how global capitalism works or recognize that skin color does not determine essence. Rather, we continue doing what we are doing because the notion of false consciousness gives us an Other, assuring us that we are not dupes of false consciousness. In other words, if we think that ideology functions primarily by duping, then we may believe ourselves liberated by "seeing through" ideology.[2]

If, as Žižek writes, "rule is secured not by its truth-value but by simple extra-ideological violence and promise of gain" (*Sublime* 30), we might then be temped to think that traditional ideology critique is therefore less crucial; on the contrary, if we think of the political as beyond articulation and belief, traditional ideological critique—exposing the problems of society, particularly the deleterious effects of late capitalism, according to human-created and critical notions of justice and human rights—proves more important than ever. In other words, the cynic's rejection of ideological critique stems from the mistaken notion that ideological illusion is limited to "knowing," but because social reality is an "ethical construction," to act as if certain things are true *makes* them real, whether or not we really think they are "true" in a foundational, universalist sense. Practically, this means that ideology is not merely at the level of thinking or knowing but also of doing. Belief is not simply internal but external, embodied, materialized, and social. So false consciousness may take the form not only of people out there who may believe in foundationalist terms (essentialists, fundamentalists, etc.), but also those who "know" (postmodernists) because they differentiate themselves from those who do not know (essentialists). This faith in the Other of postmodernism masks the continuance of identity-based and essentialist assumptions. The problem, I contend, is less identity politics than the assumption that postmodernists see through ideology, replicating a fairly consistent theoretical argument of differentiating objects from some central term of sameness, while not being able to account for why structural inequalities continue.

Today, what I describe as otherness postmodernism constitutes such an ideological fantasy. This ideological fantasy includes the idea, for instance, that the postmodernist sees through the fantasy that the credulous essentialist believes; the postmodernist presents him/herself as resisting racism and other kinds of exploitation primarily by *disbelieving* the ideologies that the credulous essentialist presumably accepts. The postmodernist faith in this "seeing through" as not just *a* political litmus test but *the* most important determinant of epistemologically sophisticated progressive politics, as evidenced by controversies over postmodernism in the past few decades, is a form of the fantasy that ideology works primarily through our belief or intention rather than through our actions as shaped by institutional forces and the threat of violence or privation.[3] Otherness postmodernism obscures and reinforces the reality that problematic racializations—essentialist or not—remain endemic, structuring societies and the practices that constitute them, and that the poststructuralist turn has not shaken us out of our ideological fixity. Furthermore, our particular kind of ideological fantasy, this "seeing through" that is not a seeing-through, may foreclose pursuing other possibilities of meaning. In its turn away from referentiality and its embrace of oddly ossified thought structures, otherness postmodernism obscures and thereby enables the reality that racism and other exploitative processes structure our world and the practices that constitute it. Rather than truly shaking us out of our ideological and epistemological fixities, certain forms of postmodern thought forecloses other possible ways of reading the world, thereby exacerbating our ideological entrapment.

This book focuses how otherness postmodernism has limited readings of aesthetic form, of content, and of contexts. Otherness postmodernism suffuses literary and cultural studies today, not only informing the content of many arguments about otherness, but actually structuring the ways in which we have those discussions. Many readings of marginal texts display a surprising degree of consistency in their basic theoretical moves. A text's difference from some term of sameness, most often related to literary realism and unitary subjectivity, marks that text as resistant and oppositional, but the actual exegetical moves of such readings are not that different from interpretations of experimental texts by non-marginal writers. Moreover, because difference and sameness has been delineated in fairly narrow terms, a variety of contexts, forms, and contents have been neglected and underread. In practice, the actual term of difference turns out to be the identity of the writer, so despite the explicit anti-essentialism of such readings, the actual basis for them—and the ways that texts and writers are understood as individuals and as fields of study—are still delineated and hierarchized by race in fairly traditional ways. In this context, I do not argue for a "return" to essentialism or for some new, truly anti-essentialist theory; rather, my claim is that we need to shift the framework by which we analyze texts and understand historical articulations of difference and exclusion. At heart, my argument is for an ethics of reading, specifically about literature in this study, but applicable to areas beyond the literary.

In this chapter, I first explore and critique the notion of otherness postmodernism. Then I discuss some alternatives, such as reconsidering referentiality, ethics, and metanarratives. In the last section, I provide a transition to the next three chapters by discussing how literary criticism in particular has demonstrated otherness postmodernism, or this constant positing of a disruptive difference that ironically ends up reinforcing the same, and why this repetition is a problem for understanding both the texts we read and the world in which we read them.

Otherness Postmodernism

The basic theoretical configuration of what I am calling otherness postmodernism has been eloquently described by Rey Chow in a 2002 essay, in which she examines the application of poststructuralist theory in areas of study dealing with marginal groups. Chow focuses on criticism that claims to be "resistant" to Western theory while also replicating its basic problematic assumptions, particularly the articulation of a term of "difference" and its eventual and problematic recuperation into sameness; this critical move is what I am terming otherness postmodernism. In the essay, Chow outlines how "theory," or "the paradigm shift introduced by poststructuralism," has ingrained in us a deep skepticism about not only our ability to conduct research from a point of externality or total objectivity, but also about the very "notion of an object of study" (174). That is, objects—subjects, signs, texts—are never metaphysically "present" because they are constantly other than themselves in time and space. In such a state of "permanent differentiation and permanent impermanence," stable objectification or signification is impossible (179). This critique of essentialism goes hand in hand with an emphasis on the specific and the local and a deep distrust of metanarratives, totalities, and other universals. And because the objects of Western study have so often been Other, Chow notes that quite reasonably this "poststructuralist metalanguage of differencing"—that is, that things (subjects and objects) are different from one another and from themselves—has become prominent in fields that deal explicitly with Otherness as "multiculturalism, postcoloniality, and ethnicity" (177).

But what has evolved is a repeated maneuver by which a critic ends up "gesturing toward and resisting Western theory at the same time" (Chow 179):

> The critic makes a gesture toward Western theory, but only in such a way as to advance the point that such theory is inadequate, negligent, and Eurocentric. As a consequence, what legitimates concern for the particular group, identity, or ethnic culture under discussion . . . is its historical, cultural, gendered difference, which becomes, in terms of the theoretical strategies involved, the basis for the claim of opposition and resistance. Epistemologically, what is specific to X . . . is imagined to pose a certain challenge to Western theory. (Chow 171)

Critics thus repeat the theoretical move of proclaiming difference against the established terms of sameness. This move is made again and again, for example, in literary criticism, in which formal realism and/or poststructuralist theory are identified as Western/male hegemonic formations against which an Other is posited. Repeatedly, against some term of sameness, otherness is posited as "'ambivalence,' 'multiplicity,' 'hybridity,' 'heterogeneity,' 'disruptiveness,' 'resistance,' and the like" (Chow 184). But the repetition of this claim of difference ironically ends up losing its specificity in the framework of poststructuralist otherness. The Other term is articulated and recuperated as a sign of difference that ironically ends up flattening and dehistoricizing difference into sameness.

So this critical move poses a conundrum:

> When scholars of marginalized groups and non-Western subjects rely on notions of resistance and opposition (to Western theory) in their attempts to argue the specificity of X [in which X is an object of study], they are

unwittingly reproducing the epistemological conundrum by which the specificity of the object of study is conceived of in terms of a differential—a differential, moreover, that has to be included in the chain of signification in order to be recognized. However, by virtue of its mechanism of postponement and displacement, this kind of logic implies the eventual dissolution of the objection without being able to address *how X* presents not just a condition (exteriority) that has always already existed but more importantly an active politics of exclusion and discrimination. Within the bounds of this logic, the more resistive and oppositional...*X* is proclaimed to be, the more inevitably it is to lose its specificity...in the larger framework of the systematic production of differences, while the circumstances that make this logic possible...remain unchallenged. (183–4)

In other words, if I claim the disruptive "otherness" of a subject, object, group, text, event, or any "*X*"—and this otherness can be passive or active, structural or ideological—I am claiming its specificity in its difference from the norm. In today's critical discourse, this articulation may take the form of either embracing or rejecting poststructuralist theory, but whatever the argument's explicit relation to some Western body of theory, either way I replicate the assumptions about the value of disrupting the chain of signification by this Other term *X*. Therefore, the various forms of difference become flattened and recuperated into the dominant discourse as a general difference. Or, as Chow puts it, "the attempt to define *X* seems doomed to destroy its own object in the process of objectification" (179).

Such repeated claims of Otherness-as-disruption pose two key problems that are interrelated. First, the theoretical rejection of referentiality does not enable us to understand *why* the Other term is excluded, outside, or other, or what structures and processes produced those terms of Sameness and Otherness. As Neil Larsen points out, "Beyond this formal refusal of the essentialist fallacy, 'hybridity' offers no purchase whatsoever on the emancipatory question itself" (96). Second, not attending to the reasons for the very terms of sameness and difference ends up reinscribing exclusion in "a rather conventional anthropological attitude toward the other's otherness—which is often unproblematically held up as a fact" (Chow 179). The failure to make structures of hierarchy, marginalization, and oppression explicable runs the risk of naturalizing those structures and thereby implicitly reinforcing them. As Chow writes, "The reference that is social injustice—itself a type of differential but a differential hierarchized with value—cannot be as easily postponed or displaced, because the mechanisms of postponement and displacement do not by themselves address the hierarchical or discriminatory nature of the differential involved" (184). Actual resistance, Chow concludes, requires that we "let referentiality interrupt, to reopen the poststructuralist closure on this issue, to acknowledge the inevitability of reference even in the most avant-garde of theoretical undertakings" (185). So rather than endlessly replicating the positing of an "outside" Other, which ultimately gets recuperated into an ironically homogenous category, Chow argues that we must reexamine referentiality.

I would add to Chow's call for a reconsideration of referentiality an attempt to articulate some kind of ethics—beyond difference—to evaluate between different social-historical articulations.[4] For example, how do we know that different cultures are to be celebrated while economic disparities are not? The qualitative distinction between such differences only make sense through reference to the messy unraveling of historical circumstances and a collective ethical evaluation about what, say, a human being should be free to do (write literature, create culture) and not have to suffer (deprivation, racism, sexism, etc.). In other words, without reference and some kind of evaluative ethics, we are left not only without a means to understand why and how the terms of sameness and difference have come about, but also without a way to evaluate between, say, two terms that are different from the same. Chow argues that in this sense, referentiality poses the unthought or truly disruptive difference from poststructuralism, not merely as a formal difference but as an impetus to radically formulate how we structure our thought: "Referentiality . . . may in the end require us to accept it precisely as the limit, the imperfect, irreducible difference that is not pure difference but difference thoroughly immersed in and corrupted by the errors and delusions in history" (185). For example, rather than difference as that which is outside the chain of signifiers (embracing/acknowledging the Other as unknowable Other in the manner of poststructuralist ethics), or as recuperated into the chain of signifiers as formally disruptive difference (studies of X), we might conceive of chains of signifiers within various discourses and non-coincident terms disrupting one another, mutually pointing out the limits of each particular discourse/chain of signifiers. In the realm of literature, for example, discourses about specific texts may be disrupted by reference both to nonliterary contexts as well as to other fields of literature. Comparative work, then, becomes crucial to understanding any particularity. I will discuss such possibilities further in the following sections of this chapter.

Furthermore, due its theoretical configuration of sameness versus difference, most otherness postmodernism reduces arguments to an overly simplified and often simply false binary. This binary manifests in many ways: as the unbreachable distance between the Self and Other; in discussions of the social sphere, as either unity or heterogeneity; in discussions of subjectivity or identity, as a self-present, unified being versus a heterogeneous and overdetermined one; in considerations of meaning in general, as platonic, fundamental truth versus instability, multiplicity, and provisionality. Because such arguments are based on inaccurately opposed dichotomies, they fail to account for the levels of mediation or complications that may exist between those two binaries. Just as Shu-mei Shih points out that not all differences are the same, neither are all samenesses the same ("Global" 27).

And when these oversimplified binaries of sameness and difference are combined with a lack of means to evaluate between social articulations and antagonisms, the de facto political litmus test becomes postmodernism differencing itself. In other words, if the terms of the debate become reduced to, on the one hand, truth and unity, and on the other, difference and heterogeneity, difference will always be the choice. It is not hard to demonstrate that an ethnic community, a nation, a political credo (e.g., feminism), a linguistic communication, or any social element cannot be consistent, unified and static; any endeavor involving the active productivity of human beings cannot be final due to human multiplicity and history. As a result, the "difference" term is privileged repeatedly, while many kinds of particularities, similarities, in-betweens, and even samenesses are overlooked or suppressed. Thus the truly "progressive" or "radical" politics becomes that which is most postmodern.

Such issues have been examined by critics who simply point out that which fails to fit into the limited logic of different-as-interruption. For example, in the seminal *Immigrant Acts*, Lisa Lowe argues that Asian American cultural production forms a site of resistance because it shows the impossibility and failures of American discourses of citizenship. But, as Viet Thanh Nguyen points out, Lowe does not account for neo-conservative Asian Americans and, even more complexly, Asian Americans who accept the ideal of the liberal subject (633). Nguyen cites Asians (in the diaspora and in Asian nations) who participated in capitalist ventures historically as translators and mediators, and how immigrants have been "as equally apt as these corporations to exploit their fellow immigrants as subcontractors and labor importers" (633). In fact, Nguyen contends that Asian American studies articulates itself as resistance because "different" but romanticizes its own unity. Sau-ling Wong has likewise been a staunch critic of the tendencies of otherness postmodernism; against an emphasis on hybridity and heterogeneity, Sau-Ling Wong cautions against the postnationalist tendencies in Asian American studies arising from more global paradigms (capitalism, diaspora, cosmopolitanism) and postmodern approaches that stress difference over any master narrative of sameness. Despite more complex understandings of global processes, subject formations, and communal ties, and despite the risks of romanticization, as Nguyen and Wong note, Asian American nationalism is still important and useful, particularly in ways outlined by Yen Le Espiritu in *Asian American Panethnicity* (within particular institutions in the United States, such as electoral politics and the census).

In African American studies, both bell hooks and Madhu Dubey have pointed out the limits of the sameness/difference paradigm of postmodernism. In the pivotal essay "Postmodern Blackness," bell hooks characterizes 1960s black nationalisms that premise a group homogeneity and unity as "modernist," while the postmodern "politics of difference" purports to recognize the margins and greater diversity within the community (24). hooks goes on to demonstrate that Euro-American postmodernism forms its own "master narrative" that, in appropriating racial difference, collapses minority experiences into the great "Same" of postmodernism. Madhu Dubey responds to hooks' paradigm by demonstrating that the situation is even more complicated than the progression from sameness-modernity to difference-postmodernism; black nationalism posited itself as Other to expose Western universalist humanism's hypocrisy and promoted an "ideal of culture rooted in racially specific experience" (33).

In postcolonial studies, in an astounding apotheosis of otherness postmodernism, Denis Ekpo argues that because modern African thought on European modernism, all of it—nationalism, pan-Africanism, identity, culture—should be rejected and replaced with postmodernism ("Towards a Post-Africanism"). Elsewhere, he argues that the failure of both Marxist and reactionary Afrocentrisms necessitate a new postmodern anticolonialism ("How Africa Misunderstood the West"). It has been and continues to be another odd contradiction of postmodernism that despite its insistence on difference, otherness postmodernism tends to be intolerant of other methodologies and epistemologies. As a result, the de facto political litmus test becomes postmodernism itself. In contrast, Adéèkó points out that in the complex world we live in, "I am not prepared, yet, to abandon the influence of nationalist and ethnocentric will on black intellectual reactions to slavery and colonialism" (12).

Even some critiques of the philosophy of difference have fallen into the trap of the terms of otherness postmodernism, such as failing to account for *why* such terms of centrality and marginality, sameness and difference, came about. In such conversations, we see clearly that such debates cannot take the form of theoretical, abstract valences of sameness or difference or even essentialism; rather, we have to examine the histories and structures of power that construct the terms of the debate. For example, in a 2000 special issue of *New Literary History* titled *Is There Life after Identity Politics*, Walter Benn Michaels argues against the privileging of difference. He describes a "complete saturation of the field of conflict by sameness and difference," in which there is a "consensus about the value of the opposition between difference and sameness, the other and the self. It does not matter whether what is valorized is the other or the same; what matters is only that, whatever is valorized, it is valorized as the other or the same" ("Political" 658). In both this essay and his later book *The Shape of the Signifier* (2004), Benn Michaels argues against a politics based on identity and the mere privileging of difference. He argues that ideological disagreement is lost in the valorization and almost fetishization of difference, because politics then focuses solely on identity and differing interests. Relinquishing disagreement and its implication of universals leaves us essentially in a brute contest for survival because we cannot have debates about what should be changed and what those things should be changed into ("Political" 655).

While I agree with his critique of the fetishization of difference, I am less sanguine that we can simply "get beyond" the politics of identity and difference without reckoning with structures of economics and politics that shape discourse—in other words, the *reasons* for sameness and exclusion. As David Palumbo-Liu points out in that same issue, we cannot really move beyond identity because identity cannot be thought of apart from social structures of power and "assumptive narratives of identity." Palumbo-Liu argues that calls for a "postethnic" society, even—and particularly—by liberals and progressives, often simply elide the continuing reality of cultural (both positive and negative) traditions. Identities are not simply voluntary and cannot be easily plucked out of narratives that shape our views of the world *before* actual encounters with other human beings. Identity politics is not simply a knee-jerk reaction to other interests; rather, identity politics grew out of, indicates, and challenges the ways that individual identity is more often than not already refused to minorities, who are already seen as types or expressions of a "group."

Therefore, Palumbo-Liu argues, going beyond difference "will be far from easy, not because minorities and women obstinately cling to identity [and difference], but precisely because the narratives that have been put into place to deny them identity are deeply rooted, and the psychic form of racism is thoroughly entangled in institutional forms" (778). The difficulty in contemporary politics is not the separatism or identity-fixation of minority groups, but the continuance of such assumptive narratives that attribute a particular "essence" to members of a group (774). A pathological Other minority identity is contrasted with an assumed "normal" or "common" one—usually heterosexual, white, male, middle-class, First World—and both these identifications assume an implicit series of actions that will follow from that identity. Such narratives posit a conclusion from an identity, regardless of whether that identity is claimed. Even "identity politics" or "essentialist" is a kind of identity, Palumbo-Liu argues, used to characterize a certain kind of simplistic political animal who must therefore practice a simplistic and reactionary kind of politics.

Palumbo-Liu argues that we are not ready to "go beyond" race because we still have trouble "getting to" race, which is usually embedded in "specific institutional practices that are often as not shielded from sight, bureaucratically rationalized on the basis of assumed identities" (777). Responding to David Hollinger's *Postethnic America*, Palumbo-Liu writes, "Hollinger asks us to drop our weapons and shake hands with a historical institutional situation that is armed to the teeth" (777). In other words, identity politics is never wholly voluntarist, but rather a product of various situational and institutional pressures. Both critics of identity politics like Benn Michaels and proponents of otherness postmodernism miss this point. One can neither simply reject the complex pressures of identity nor pretend that one's claim to identity is not an actual claim of identity (such as a "strategic" or provisional or fundamentally negative one) that, in claiming an identity, constitutes that identity.

Along the same lines, calls to go "beyond race" reflect the recognition that simply to claim the Other's difference ad infinitum ultimately leads to a dead end. But when the conversation remains cast as one of interruption of discourse rather than of power structures and institutional practices, it fails to move beyond the pitfalls of otherness postmodernism. A prominent example of the desire simply to *will* a movement beyond race is Paul Gilroy's *Against Race: Imagining Political*

Culture Beyond the Color Line (2000). It epitomizes otherness postmodernism's ideological fantasy that simply "seeing through" hegemonic ideology is the key to politics. While the spirit of his book—against narrow identity politics, for a more universal notion of human rights—is laudable, Gilroy's failure to consider the political and economic structures that create race leads him to a solution that falls woefully short: he prescribes that people adopt an anti-hegemonic articulation of the social (that is, postmodernist), without accounting for how/why any particular group would have hegemony.

Paul Gilroy ends his seminal *Black Atlantic* (1993) with an inspiring vision for a "politics of a new century in which the central axis of conflict will no longer be the colour line but the challenge of just, sustainable development and the fronts which will separate the overdeveloped parts of the world (at home and abroad) from the intractable poverty that already surrounds them" (223). To bring about this shift in politics, Gilroy seeks to forge a "response to racism that doesn't reify the concept of race" (*Black Atlantic* 223). In *Against Race*, Gilroy critiques what he calls "raciology," or any race-based thinking, which has been reified as "a central political and historical reference point" by a wide variety of political interests, from revolutionary to fascist. These movements, or rather, ideologies seek to define a racial type as "coherent, rational, and authoritative" (31). He wants to replace raciology with a "planetary humanism" that would emphasize and celebrate hybridity, diaspora, fluidity, syncretization, and movement. Although I agree with Gilroy's general impulse toward "humanism," and I agree that cultural productions need to be seen as syncretic productions "to be evaluated on their own terms as complex, compound formations" rather than indicators of authenticity (117), Gilroy ultimately only offers a cultural, discursive solution to the problem of raciology, instead of other ways to understand a racialized world in, say, terms of political-economic historical structures or agency. Although *Black Atlantic* treats the dialectic of modernity with care, *Against Race* is curiously nondialectical in its privileging of hybridity, syncretization, diaspora, movement, and even pure will. Gilroy writes,

> By emphasizing diaspora, theories of identity turn instead toward contingency, indeterminacy, and conflict. With the idea of valuing diaspora more highly than the coercive unanimity of the nation, the concept becomes explicitly antinational. This shift is connected with transforming the familiar unidirectional idea of diaspora as a form of catastrophic but simple dispersal that enjoys an identifiable and reversible originary

moment—the site of trauma—into something far more complex. Diaspora can be used to instantiate a "chaotic" model in which shifting "strange attractors" are the only visible points of fragile stability amid social and cultural turbulence. (128)

Gilroy prescribes a shift from nationalist or culturalist models to one of "diaspora," contingency, and indeterminacy. Gilroy wants us to embrace the fundamental absence at the heart of each social articulation, as if it were the lifejacket that is going to save us from drowning. His treatment of the "trauma" of diaspora is telling; if diaspora as one-way departure from the homeland is traumatic, simply reconceiving it as multidirectional or "chaotic" is not necessarily going to remove that trauma. If, for example, the migrant recognizes that one can never "go home" because home no longer exists as it does in the memory—and probably never actually did—and the migrant or diasporic person gives up the idea of "home," that still does not change the reasons that may have forced that migrant to move: poverty, political persecution, occupation, violence, ethnic strife. (Furthermore, the valorization of the migrant also does not account for how home does not really exist, in fact, for anyone, except in the practice of creating such a concept.) In other words, simply changing one's mindset to a postmodern one (strategically or not) is not necessarily going to change others' minds or the situations of the world. Everyone may function on the basis of a heteroglot, discursive construction of the world, but those discourses will have histories and materiality by the time any one person enters the fray. As Carole Boyce Davies points out, Gilroy's political prescriptions are ultimately culturalist, emphasizing "style and performance, not on active practices of power," and "leaves the state and its practices intact while its black population is singled out for the most attack" (*Against Race*). By the same token, in response to Gilroy's polemic against the notion of victim as identity and the related arguments for compensation, Palumbo-Liu writes, "that leaves us with the unrelenting, indelible historical fact—these people were aggrieved because of racial thinking on *another's* part, not (necessarily) their own" (*"Against Race"* 54).

Gilroy recognizes the stalemate of the sameness-difference binary, but his solution fails to move beyond it. While previous racisms have pitted the "particular, singular, and specific against the general, universal, and transcendent," Gilroy seeks to "break up these unhappy couples" (*Against Race* 29). He recognizes that the simplistic opposition between a single universal humanism versus a relativist scattering of cultures separate from one another is untenable. Nevertheless, he ends up advocating the same radical politics of difference.[5] He argues for this resistant postmodern articulation of the social without accounting for how or why a particular articulation would be hegemonic. His alternative to raciology, "planetary humanism," he writes, "cannot be reached via any retreat into the lofty habits and unamended assumptions of liberal thinking, particularly about juridical rights and sovereign entitlements" (*Against Race* 30). Rather, the "failures, silences, lapses, and evasions" of those institutions must become central; "they can be reinterpreted as symptoms of a struggle over the boundaries of humanity and then contribute to a counterhistory" of all-inclusive humanism (*Against Race* 30). Gilroy's "planetary humanism," therefore, is the ultimate privileging of hybridity and difference to, ironically, irreducible and universal values.

Otherness postmodernism, then, is the hegemonic idea that, by describing the anti-hegemonic in a formal way as difference, recuperates it back into the hegemony. It fails, moreover, to explain *why* the hegemonic-versus-anti-hegemonic or sameness-versus-difference axes are articulated in particular ways; other than an anti-postmodern will to totalize, it offers no explanation for historical, political, aesthetic, social, and other reasons for exclusion and sameness. Therefore, it fails to provide a concrete means to move beyond that sameness-difference binary. In doing so, otherness postmodernism reinforces false, overly simplistic binaries that end up reinscribing the Other's otherness and flattening all difference into sameness. Without a means to evaluate between different social articulations and antagonisms, otherness postmodernism provides no "way out" other than itself; the only way to be truly progressive is to be postmodern.

Articulations and Antagonisms

The historical development of postmodern ideas has been discussed many times,[6] but it is illuminating to revisit that history in a slightly different way by examining two seminal texts that are rarely discussed together. Ernest Laclau and Chantal Mouffe's *Hegemony and Socialist Strategy* (1985) and Micheal Omi and Howard Winant's *Racial Formation in the United States* (1986) helped rearticulate the theoretical basis for contemporary ideas about subjectivity, identity, social articulation, politics, and cultural production. Both texts make an intervention at a particular historical moment, emphasizing the radically non-totalizable nature of the social field. But they share the problem of shifting from the *description* of articulations of social antagonisms to the *prescription* that progressive political movements should be premised on radical notions of difference. They also provide the theoretical frameworks for the incorporation of difference into sameness, both as hegemony (the hegemonic power seeks to articulate everything in its own terms) *and* as resistance (difference from the hegemonic "Same" constitutes resistance), as described by Chow. Both texts emphasize this difference because of the exigencies of their historical moment, but they also evidence the problems of otherness postmodernism, such as the lack of means to evaluate between articulations through ethics or reference. But most of all, I find it telling that despite the resonance of their ideas, the texts operate in almost totally separate fields. In this section, I examine these two key texts in the development of the ideas undergirding otherness postmodernism to shed light on its internal and external limits.

The familiar narrative of progressive political movements, theory, and the relationship between them in the post-1960's West has been rehashed many times. Briefly, it runs as follows: After the apparent failures and frustrations of the various leftist and national movements in the 1960s and 1970s, progressive theorists in the 1980s and 1990s sought to reconceptualize the basis for united democratic movements through, apparently paradoxically, an emphasis on radical difference. For postmodern progressives, "radical difference" meant each social element's difference from another as well as difference from him/her/itself. Such a conceptual move was necessary to account for hegemonic discourses without universalizing, and to recognize partial, provisional, multiple, and shifting political meanings. As Stuart Hall states in another key text, the collection *Marxism and the Interpretation of Culture* (1988), "we know now . . . that there is no unitary logic of inference or deduction" from "material interests" and "position in social structure" (45). New politics are born of feminism, psychoanalysis, poststructuralism, postmarxism—"the cultural revolutions of the 60s" and the "theoretical revolutions of the 60s and 70s" debunked economic determinism and opened up the field of signifiers. "Class is not the only determinant of social interest (e.g., gender, race)," Hall writes, "More important, interests are themselves constructed, constituted, in and through the ideological process" (45). The overly narrow political reductions of previous movements such as Marxism and cultural nationalism led to the fragmentation of the left, so theorists sought to rearticulate the grounds for a "radical democracy" that incorporated different political identities, which often form the basis for political mobilization, while avoiding essentialism and its pitfalls. New social movements arose simultaneously with the epistemological/ontological movement variously referred to as postmodernism, poststructuralism, "posthistoricism," et cetera. The Left's retheorization of the social took place in the face of the neoconservative backlash of the Reagan and Thatcher years as well as what would later be referred to as the Washington Consensus, or the putative agreement about the social, political, and economic benefits of economic neoliberalism and globalization. Some have argued that the postmodern turn signaled the retreat of Left intellectuals from politics, but there are many reasons to read this philosophical turn more generously.[7] Some of the insights produced by otherness postmodernism are not only politically important but also true, but it is precisely in rejecting notions of truth and reality that it proves problematic.

Ernesto Laclau and Chantal Mouffe's seminal *Hegemony and Socialist Strategy* explicated the theoretical basis of this new politics. They define the political as a field of shifting, unfixed antagonisms; they point out "the impossibility of establishing in a definite manner the meaning of any struggle, whether considered in isolation or through its fixity in a relational system" (170). That is, there is no final determinant or transcendental signifier that "fixes" all the other signifiers because "each of these elements and levels is no longer the expression of a totality which transcends it" (190–1). Without the metonymic link to a "meta" totality, each antagonism therefore becomes a "floating signifier." These local contradictions are not less "real" or important to we who live them; rather, Laclau and Mouffe redefine each moment of the social sphere as irreducible to one signification. The hegemonic articulations of the social are determined by power, and power is not unidirectional but nevertheless maintains dominance through hegemony.

In reconceptualizing the social sphere to capture the ever-complex, multileveled, dialectically developing social sphere(s) of our world, Laclau and Mouffe define key terms such as articulation, discourse, and moments:

> We will call articulation any practice establishing a relation among elements such that their identity is modified as a result of the articulatory practice. The structured totality resulting from the articulatory practice, we will call *discourse*. The differential positions, insofar as they appear articulated within a discourse, we will call *moments*. By contrast, we will call *element* any difference that is not discursively articulated. (105, emphasis in original)

The identity of an element in the signifying field is determined in various, interconnected ways. First, all identity is relational, and even systems of differences cannot be fixed or stable; this is the "post-" to structuralism. No sign has meaning that can be finally determined or have "final suture," because each moment is subverted and exceeded by the field of discourse that "overflows" it. So the articulation of "elements" into "moments" can never be complete. Elements are floating signifiers and cannot be wholly articulated to a signifying chain; they can never be fully fixed or stable. This instability "penetrates" or is shot through every discursive identity. In other words, there is not a "poverty of signifieds" but a "polysemy," or multiplicity of every signifier, that "disarticulates" the discursive structure and makes it uncloseable. Because the field is overdetermined, without fixed meaning but with many possible meanings and undergoing constant change, "every nodal point is constituted within an intertextuality that overflows it"; so, they conclude, "the social *is* articulation insofar as 'society' is impossible" (114). This description of the social makes sense, but it becomes more problematic when it becomes politically prescriptive.

Laclau and Mouffe thus argue that discourse becomes central for politics not only in the more conventional usage of "discourse" as semiotics and cultural production, but more generally because the "social" *is* discourse. In other words, what is discursively articulated constitutes the social. Furthermore, "to articulate" here means not simply to define one thing or moment, but rather to establish a relation among elements and modifies their identity. Therefore, the terrain of struggle against domination is also the terrain of struggle over the hegemonic articulation of that field of struggle. Of course, any articulation, even an antihegemonic one, can never be complete or fully comprehend every element and level of the social, which always subverts the articulation in its excess (111). Still, such contingent articulations are necessary for political organization; social struggles are struggles to articulate the social, and particular struggles will produce particular contingent but necessary articulations. So since the social sphere is neither fixed nor wholly indeterminate, we can conceptualize the social as constituted by varying levels of provisional articulation and fixity, with areas of instability and contestatory articulations.

Crucial to their notion of articulation is Lacan's notion of the *point de capiton*, or "nodal point," or "privileged signifiers that [temporarily and partially] fix the meaning of a signifying chain" (112). This temporary stoppage of the signifying chain is necessary for predication, because a total inability to affix meaning results in "the discourse of the psychotic" (112). This temporary "nodal point" is the signifier that "fixes" or, as Slavoj Žižek puts it in *The Sublime Object of Ideology*, "quilts" the terrain of floating signifiers by interpreting or inflecting those antagonisms through itself. "Nodal points" are those privileged points constructed by any discourse that arrest the field of different floating signifiers. This notion of the *point de capiton* is distinct from a dialectical understanding of mutual interiority and exteriority between signifiers; rather, a nodal point is an arbitrarily fixed point that articulates the rest of the field. For political progressives, articulating the social—which must always take place for any element to exist as a moment to our understanding—relies on the provisional nodal points, a necessary compromise even for those who understand the basic inability to "fix" meaning. This compromise is necessary because, write Laclau and Mouffe, "any discourse is constituted as an attempt to dominate the field of discursivity, to arrest the flow of differences, to construct a centre" (112). The struggle over the articulation of the social, in other words, takes places over the determination of this nodal point.

The basis of a radical democratic practice, therefore, must be the understanding that such provisional articulations take place in a state of impossibility of any final or total articulation. The provisional articulations are necessary, however, in order to struggle over the social and contest hegemonic articulations. So Laclau and Mouffe clearly recognize the need for some mediation between total multiplicity and total uniformity, total meaninglessness and total determinations, but the only real mechanism they offer to evaluate the mediations or "quiltings" of the field of signifiers is its hegemonic status, or relationship to "power." But since "power" itself will be a product of articulation, the question remains: how can we evaluate between different articulations? Which nodal point is better or worse?

This conundrum leads Laclau and Mouffe, in contrast to those who bemoan the fragmentation of the New Left after the 1960s, to encourage the proliferation of differences and different identities and celebrate a form of otherness postmodernism. They argue that the proliferation of cultural differences suggests an implicit understanding of the polysemic nature of the social field: "there is an identifiable tendency towards the valorization of 'differences' and the creation of new identities which tend to privilege 'cultural' criteria (clothes, music, language, regional traditions, and so on)" (164). In fact, Laclau and Mouffe see this explosion not as fragmentation but as a new wave of struggle on a new basis for solidarity. Social identities, as the malleable products of discourse, become the battleground of the social field: "*the form of antagonism as such*...always consists in the construction of a social identity—of an overdetermined subject position—on the basis of the equivalence between a set of elements of values which expel or externalize those others to which they are opposed" (164–5, emphasis in original). In other words, political struggles over social identity are struggles against a hegemonic discourse that creates, includes, and excludes through the interpellation of subjects. New political subjects are formed in political movements such as ethnic nationalist movements, feminism, the green movement, and other new social movements (166). Laclau and Mouffe see these "new antagonisms" as resisting "commodification, bureaucratization and increasing homogenization of social life" through "a proliferation of particularisms" and "a demand for autonomy itself" (164). Oddly, Laclau and Mouffe are as optimistic about the inherent benefits of "liberal democracy" as are the pro-market economists and politicians that I discuss in the Concluding Notes of this book. They claim that the reorganization of the social field emerges logically from the postwar expansion of "democratic revolution" into new social arenas and an "egalitarian imaginary constituted around the liberal-democratic discourse" (166, 165). In other words, liberal democracy and neoimperialism, whatever their various intentions and processes, rely on and encourage notions of democracy, participation, individualism, and difference. Therefore, when neoconservatives such as Samuel Huntington identify the proliferation of differences and identities in the 1960s and 1970s as too much democracy, threatening to make the people ungovernable (165–6), Laclau and Mouffe agree.

This proliferation of antagonisms, none of which can be final, rejuvenates the notion of the subject. As they write, "Renunciation of the category of the subject as a unitary, transparent and sutured entity opens the way to the recognition of the specificity of the antagonisms constituted on the basis of different subject positions, and, hence, the possibility of the deepening of a pluralist and democratic conception" (166). Everyone's different, multiple identities provide the bases for an increasingly dispersed social field. Such a celebration of difference in terms of culture and identities seems odd, given that global capitalism relies on the notion of the "individual" as free consumer and promotes the proliferation of identities tied to consumer products.[8] At the same time, sometimes resisting or lacking access to the dominant interpellation of the subject does pose an important problem for hegemony. But again, we are left with the question: what is the basis for distinguishing and evaluating between two contending articulations of the same social element?

Laclau and Mouffe's notion of a new radical, open-ended democratic politics developed simultaneously with, but separately from, that of sociologists Michael Omi and Howard Winant in *Racial Formation in the United States: From the 1960s to the 1990s*, indicating the convergence of historical exigencies of the Left during the political backlash of the 1980s, as well as the developing academic institutionalization of oppositional movements (New Left, ethnic nationalist movements, feminism). Since its initial publication in 1986, *Racial Formations* has informed most contemporary discussions of race in U.S. ethnic studies. Drawing more on Foucault than Lacan, Omi and Winant also theorize the social as radically constituted by articulation, and they also struggle with balancing radical social articulation, mediation, and evaluation. But the contrast in the contents and contexts of these two works speaks to the structural and institutional forces for which neither study can fully account.

Racial Formations traces the transformation of racial rule from one based on force to one based on consent and self-regulation, or hegemony. For Omi and Winant, racial groupings constitute neither essentialism nor illusory false consciousness. Through these hegemonic "racial projects," individuals are constituted as subjects in a system that is already thoroughly racialized, although any such system is overdetermined, non-homogenous, and constantly developing. Furthermore, they explain, not all racial projects are "racist"; rather, racism is a racial project that *"creates or reproduces structures of domination based on essentialist categories of race"* (71, emphasis in original). So racism is not simply any grouping or categorization based on race, but rather "essentialist representations of race" used for "structures of domination." This accounts for the various ideological valences of racial categorizations and identifications. Like sexuality and constructions of the body, the subtle dynamics of racial power suffuse every aspect of our existence. Politics is not just "politics, economics, or culture," but also "lived experience" that "suffuses each individual identity, each family and community, yet equally penetrates state institutions and market relationships" (Omi and Winant 96). Therefore, Omi and Winant assert the "centrality of race in American society" (138).

In Laclau and Mouffe's terms, then, in the U.S. "race" constitutes one major "nodal point." In a generally overdetermined, unfixed social field of signs (there is no necessary shape or order for social structure or discourse), "race" does not have intrinsic or self-present meaning but nevertheless structures the field of signifiers as a partially hegemonic determination. As Omi and Winant write, "Racial difference and racial identity are unstable. They are continuously being disputed, transformed, and eroded" (157). Racial formations constitute the sites of struggle in a social field in which discourse, structure, and power are inextricable. Thus race is "an unstable and 'decentered' complex of social meanings constantly being transformed by a political struggle . . . *race is a concept which signifies and symbolizes social conflicts and interests by referring to different types of human bodies*" (55, emphasis in original). As such, although race is only one factor among many possible articulations and multivalent determinations, the history of the United States testifies to the centrality of "race" as a privileged signifier, which is both "discursive" in the usual sense of cultural representation as well as in the articulation of structures of power that constitute our reality.

In articulating racial formations in this way, Omi and Winant seek the middle ground between determinism and naive notions of "free will" that do not sufficiently consider structures of power. Race is not an essence and does not serve dominant institutions in any simple, reflective way, but at the same time race cannot be understood as a wholly arbitrary grouping or categorization. Like Laclau and Mouffe, Omi and Winant respond to what they see as overly narrow articulations of the social by previous social movements. In the 1960s and 1970s, radicals disillusioned with the civil rights and integrationist models created "class-based and nation-based paradigms" that they saw as "a more thoroughgoing restructuring of the social order" (130). Ultimately, however, radical cultural nationalists and Marxists "failed to consolidate a new political project of 'radical democracy' which could expand beyond the issue of race and aspire to majoritarian status" (Omi and Winant 139). Therefore, "this fragmentation resulted in an absence of unified radical politics and an inability to define a coherent political subject," and by the 1980s were exhausted, outmaneuvered, and/or co-opted by the Right (Omi and Winant 139). At the same time, they argue that the fluidity of identities celebrated by looser forms of postmodernism neglect both the structures of power that provisionally dictate some kinds of racial categorizations, as well as the history of cultures that are complexly related to racial organization. In fact, often those problematic racial categorizations are reclaimed and rearticulated into the basis of not only oppositional political organizing but also rich, unique cultural traditions. Furthermore, the development of such theories was inseparable from the increasing institutionalization of oppositional movements "from below," such as ethnic studies, postcolonial studies, and women's studies, and "from within," particularly poststructuralism and postmarxism.

So, like Laclau and Mouffe, Omi and Winant counter what they see as an overemphasis of unity from both the Right and the Left with the opposite: difference. They argue that the basis for a progressive democratic movement must be a politics of articulation based on difference. They write, "race, class, gender all represent *potential* antagonisms whose significance is no longer given, if it ever was"; such things "constitute 'regions' of hegemony, areas in which certain political projects can take shape" (Omi and Winant 68, emphasis in original). That is, such concepts that we have tended to use uncritically actually refer to a field of possible contradictions, which are organized together by power but which often form the grounds for resistance. In other words, the social field is not determined by any one or a priori consideration; rather, all factors such as race, class, and gender constitute possible areas of contradiction, oppression, and resistance, not simply false consciousness.

In examining these parallel responses to the historical situation, we can see the groundwork for many of the theoretical commonplaces today. The nonessential, constructed nature of social antagonisms and the political identities mobilized to address those antagonisms must be recognized as specific and local. This general particularity of differences can then become the basis for a new unified radical democratic vision and movement. This may seem paradoxical, but on the contrary, critics argue, the presumptuous totalizations of class- and nation-based political ideologies of previous decades were so inflexible they actually divided the Left, leading to a political paralysis and hegemony of the left-right neoliberal consensus. For these theorists, then, the impossibility of final suture becomes the basis for radical politics; Laclau and Mouffe write, "there is no radical and plural democracy without renouncing the discourse of the universal and its implicit assumptions of a privileged point of access to 'the truth,' which can be reached only by a limited number of subjects" (191–2). Similarly, Omi and Winant point out that the failure of 1960s and 1970s Marxists and cultural nationalists to consolidate a "unified radical politics" resulted from their inability to understand that "racial difference and racial identity are unstable" (139, 157).

But while Omi and Winant's work was crucial in mediating between essentialist and other reductive understandings of race in the United States, like *Hegemony and Socialist Strategy*, it also leaves unclear how we adjudicate between articulations. In their discussion of "racial projects," Omi and Winant suggest that we can identify and evaluate racial articulations by understanding how they work within social structures.

If we are neither determined by one factor nor completely free of any determinant, there are mediations of fluid racial articulations that contend with one another. We can identify different articulations mobilized within the power structure, but, as with Laclau and Mouffe, we are still not sure about how to differentiate articulations. Omi and Winant state that they want to militate against politically irresponsible forms of freeplay postmodernism, but because their primary concern at that historical moment was to argue against essentialisms, they focus more on the power of social articulation than of social structures. One could say the same for Laclau and Mouffe; the historical imperative at that moment seemed to be militating against too much totalizing and sameness after what many perceived as the failure of the New Left. Put another way, we might say that the articulation of antagonisms took precedence because of the particular antagonism of articulations at that historical moment.

But while stressing a politics of articulation, both texts imply that the evaluations between articulations would be made by an appeal to power structures. But if we accept that even the definition of "power" must be articulated, how do we know which "power" is ethically problematic? In other words, the postmodernists determine political valency through power (Which articulation is hegemonic? Which articulation troubles that hegemony?), but since power itself will be a product of human creation and articulation, how will we know which meaning of power to use, even if provisionally? In other words, as Biodun Jeyifo asks, how can we tell when a hegemonic discourse, a nodal point structuring the field of signifiers, is useful or just hegemonic? Because power is wily and flexible, any discourse can become a "master discourse":

> What gives a particular critical discourse its decisive effectivity under these circumstances is the combination of historical, institutional and ideological factors that make the discourse a "master" discourse which translates the avowed will-to-truth of all discourse into a consummated, if secret, will-to-power. In other words, this "master" discourse becomes the discourse of the "master," in its effects and consequences at least, if not in its conscious intentions. (34)

Although such questions have been raised since the 1980s, they remain relevant and largely unanswered. The problem becomes evident in considering not only the content of these two theoretical texts, but also their rhetoric and contexts. Although *Hegemony* and *Racial Formations* coincide on many points of social articulation and politics, a noticeable difference between the rhetoric of *Hegemony* and *Racial Formations* is that the former assumes its universality, not limiting its context, while the latter remains grounded in specific histories and contexts. Laclau and Mouffe, despite their critique of universalism and foundationalism, nevertheless write an epistemology of overdetermination, or what Spivak calls a "politics of overdetermination" ("Theory in the Margin" 167), not for any particular society but all societies. Omi and Winant, in contrast, situate their argument, first, within discourses of race (nationalism, essentialism, etc.), and second, within the context of post-1960s U.S. politics. This contrast arises partly due to their different disciplines and methodologies. Laclau and Mouffe emerge from the same European philosophical tradition and poststructuralism that also produced, despite internal variations and differences, Lacan, Derrida, and Foucault. All of these thinkers, despite situating themselves nominally within the West, produce theories of knowledge, power, language, and subjectivity that are presumably universally applicable. In contrast, while also drawing on poststructuralist theory, Omi and Winant are produced by and participating in producing U.S. ethnic studies, which tends to be scrupulously conscientious about context and history.

Put very bluntly, minority is perceived as minority (although "nonwhite" constitutes the vast majority of the world's population), while white is universal. The insights of minority (nonwhite, non-Western, nonmajority) studies are generally seen as pertinent to that particular community, while nonminority (i.e., white) has universal application. This situation is exacerbated and produced by the postmodernist valorization of the local and specific, delinked by any universals or commonalities except the insights of postmodernist itself. Again, my point is *not* that some insights of Laclau and Mouffe—and of Omi and Winant—might not be universally applicable (or applicable beyond its immediate context), or that Omi and Winant's arguments—as those of Laclau and Mouffe's—do not arise out of and speak to particular contexts. Rather, the difference in the content, forms, and contexts of these arguments speak to larger social structures, hierarchies, and formations that they, in their emphasis on articulation, do not fully account for.

This rhetorical difference speaks to the different ways that nonethnic/ nonminority and minority texts, theories, and discourses still function in cultural studies, which imagines itself to be fairly liberated compared to the rest of the world. Despite the resonance of the basic ideas of these two texts—*Hegemony and Socialist Strategy* and *Racial Formations*— they are seldom discussed in the same context. Although some fields of cultural criticism have been partially decolonized, great disparities still exist within and between fields. For example, E. San Juan has pointed out that postcolonial/Third World theories that receive institutional recognition are those that draw from poststructuralism, while more specific, sociological, or factual studies are seen as simplistic and/or not intellectually rigorous. Such disparities between, on one hand, Euro-American, nonminority theory and, on the other hand, ethnic and post-colonial studies are even more evident on the ground at individual institutions, particularly community and junior colleges, where the "decolonization" of the university is extremely uneven. Institutional changes to reflect and further disciplinary development often give way to providing the basic literacy skills that broken public school systems have failed to provide students. The politics of difference may allow a degree of theoretical freedom, but its lacunae hinder us from account-ing for or even addressing problematical structural inequities in and among fields and institutions.

The irony is that these texts themselves do implicitly offer means to analyze the hegemony of otherness postmodernism and possible alter-natives. Laclau and Mouffe and Omi and Winant argue for a radical politics of plurality against a hegemony that seeks not only to "resolve" smaller antagonisms but also to configure the very ways in which we articulate these antagonisms. In supporting this politics of pluralism and overdetermination, otherness postmodernism implicitly flattens sameness and difference into formal categories with inherent meaning. But *Hegemony* and *Racial Formations* both also argue that any such articulations of the social are not final or fixed. For example, Laclau and Mouffe write that "the forms of articulation of an antagonism . . . far from being predetermined, are the result of hegemonic struggle. . . . these new struggles do not necessarily have a progressive character" (168). They continue, "All struggles . . . have a partial character, and can be articulated to very different discourses. It is this articulation which gives them their character, not the place from which they come. There is therefore no subject . . . which is absolutely radical and irrecuperable by the dominant order" (171). That is, no social articulation, including difference, has inherent political valence. Hegemonic articulations are formed by, first, "the presence of antagonistic forces," and second, "the instability of the frontiers which separate them" (136). Their argument relies on the notion of "antagonistic forces" and other social elements that remain before, beyond, or outside the current social articulations. "Reference," in such cases, may indicate not a singular or fixed signified for a material signifier, but rather the pressures that social antagonisms and contending articulations put on current hegemonic articulations.

Seen in this light, the problem with otherness postmodernism is that it leaves out *both* articulations that are not reducible to or identical with the hegemonic articulation, *and* antagonisms that may lie outside the limits of the hegemonically determined limits of the field of elements that are to be articulated.

Antagonisms may exist that are not articulated or even articulateable in the dominant discourse, or what Jameson refers to as the "cultural dominant." And what has become hegemonic—at least within studies of marginality, identity, and literature—is postmodernism itself.

In other words, otherness postmodernism cannot adequately account for such social elements because they are constituted not simply through discourse but through structures that may exceed the set of discourses in contention. That is, while it is true that elements of human society must be discursively articulated—you have to know what a rock is to kick it—in a particular conversation, the discourses in play may be inadequate. In literary and cultural studies, where many of the most dynamic theorizations of race, identity, and politics take place, the predominance of otherness postmodernism has led us to neglect the larger structures (political, economic, educational, etc.) and the possibilities for ethics, referentiality, and metanarratives that are necessary to understand what is happening in our world.

Referentiality, Metanarratives, Ethics

What would it mean, then, to "let referentiality interrupt" (185)? It may mean that, rather than positing the term of "difference" as being outside the chain of signifiers or as recuperated into a chain of signifiers as disruptive difference, we might think of various discourses disrupting one another and revealing each other's limits. This possibility makes more sense in practical terms; for example, formal and contextual literary criticism of a particular text may "interrupt" one another, allowing configurations beyond the Sameness/Other configuration.[9] It may also mean reconsidering a fairly simple notion of reference (to the world, to texts, to history) to check the accuracy and inaccuracy of our claims. Also implicit in the critique of the valorization of difference is the reconsideration of "sameness," whether in terms of metanarratives, totalities, or comparative contexts. Bracketing off local differences from one another robs us of the comparative grounds to understand larger structures, the logic and structure of hierarchizing, marginalizing, and exploitative processes. Furthermore, I would argue that the reconsideration of the sameness/difference ideological litmus test of otherness postmodernism necessarily forces us to articulate the ethics by which we evaluate signs, events, social configurations, texts, and so on. And all these elements would be mutually inextricable; for example, any ethics we articulate relies on referentiality and some overarching framework in which to comprehend singularities. In this section I discuss some possibilities for alternatives to otherness postmodernism, focusing on issues of referentiality, metanarratives and comparative contexts, and ethics.

Otherness postmodernism is both a form of and a reaction to the kind of culturally dominant postmodernism Fredric Jameson excoriates. Because my focus in this book is a hegemonic critical tendency in literary and cultural studies, it will be worthwhile to examine the concept of otherness postmodernism in relation to Jameson's rationale for the importance of identifying a cultural dominant. He points out that the concerns about "periodizing hypotheses" include the obscuring of actual differences into some homogenous, consistent whole. Rather, drawing on Raymond Williams' notion of emergent, residual, and dominant cultural formations, Jameson argues for the necessity of a "cultural dominant," against which to measure the meaning of other cultural formations; he argues that "it [is] only in the light of some conception of a dominant cultural logic or hegemonic norm that genuine difference could be measured and assessed" (*Postmodernism* 6). That is, while not all cultural productions are postmodern, "the postmodern is, however, the force field in which very different kinds of cultural impulses . . . must make their way. If we do not achieve some general sense of a cultural dominant, then we fall back into a view of present history as sheer heterogeneity, random difference, a coexistence of a host of distinct forces whose effectivity is undecidable" (*Postmodernism* 6). In other words, for Jameson a notion of the cultural dominant is necessary in order to interpret culture.

But to return to the beginning of this chapter, the limitations of Jameson's formulation of the cultural dominant and his interpretations of culture in relation to that dominant are, ironically, that he falls back into the sameness-difference binary, which, rather than making a space for heterogeneous and anti-hegemonic articulations, recuperates everything back into the dominant term. He writes,

> Yet the totalizing account of the postmodern always included a space for various forms of oppositional culture: those of marginal groups, those of radically distinct residual or emergent cultural languages, their

existence being already predicated by the necessarily uneven development of late capitalism, whose First World produces a Third World
within itself by its own inner dynamic. In this sense postmodernism is
"merely" a cultural dominant. To describe it in terms of cultural hegemony is not to suggest some massive and uniform cultural homogeneity
of the social field but very precisely to imply its coexistence with other
resistant and heterogeneous forces which it has a vocation to subdue and
incorporate. (*Postmodernism* 159)

But as applied to otherness postmodernism, Jameson's model is mis-
leading in several ways, both over- and underestimating the extent to
which Other cultural forces are assimilable to the dominant. On one
hand, in the passage above, James reduces "the Third World" into
merely a symptom of the First World; that which is marginal "already
predicated" by the internal antagonisms of Western capital. This reduction reminds us of how Sartre reduces the postcolonial struggle to a
historical by-product of the development of capitalism, for which Frantz
Fanon, in *Wretched of the Earth*, admonishes him and asserts the
existential "fact of blackness" itself. Instead of reducing the Otherness
of the Third World to a product of the internal contradictions of the
First World, *or* claiming the inherent resistance posed by the alterity of
the Third World, Fanon posits "blackness" and the Third World as that
which may lie beyond the bounds of First-Worldist discourse. Here,
Fanon references social elements that put pressure on and disrupt
Sartre's discourse.

On the other hand, Jameson arrays too neatly the range of cultural
forces against the dominant. That is, while Jameson claims that his
conception of the cultural dominant (postmodernism) is not homogenous, that it makes room for and can incorporate otherness, this schema
still assumes a fairly static central term of Sameness arrayed against and
ultimately recuperating discrete, separate objects of Otherness. Jameson's
argument risks falling back into the same pitfalls that Chow describes,
of recuperating Otherness into Sameness, albeit in a different configuration. As Jameson points out, the modus operandi of the cultural dominant is to incorporate those other terms—that is its reason for
being—but put in terms of a cultural dominant discrete or separate
from other resistant forces, the only alternative to assimilation seems to
be assertion of Otherness against that dominant. But because Jameson
rejects the simple multiplication of heterogeneity, he effectively advocates that the terms of difference ultimately simply become recuperated
into Sameness.

In fact, that is exactly what Jameson has done a number of times, particularly in relation to the Third World. Aijaz Ahmad famously excoriated Jameson for the reduction of all postcolonial texts to "national allegories." Nevertheless, Jameson repeats this move in his 2003 book *A Singular Modernity: Essays on the Ontology of the Present*:

> Everyone knows the formula by now: this means that there can be a modernity for everybody which is different from the standard or hegemonic Anglo-Saxon model. Whatever you dislike about the latter, including the subaltern position it leaves you in, can be effaced by the reassuring and "cultural" notion that you can fashion your own modernity differently, so that there can be a Latin-American kind, or an Indian kind or an African kind, and so forth. Or you can follow Samuel Huntington's lead and recast all this in terms of essentially religious varieties of culture: a Greek or Orthodox modernity, a Confucian modernity, and so on to a Toynbeean number. But this is to overlook the other fundamental meaning of modernity which is that of a worldwide capitalism itself. The standardization projected by capitalist globalization in this third or late stage of the system casts considerable doubt on all these pious hopes for cultural variety in a future world colonized by a universal market order. (12–13)

I agree that the facile notion of a multiplying of cultures, or the privileging of "difference," does discount and often serves to obscure the central dominating drive of late capitalism; capitalism and multiculturalism are extremely compatible. As an advertisement in the *Economist* puts it, "Culture is the power of globalization." But Jameson's vast oversimplification is problematic not only for its singularity but also because—just in terms of simple reference—it does not look at the rest of the world. Jameson's cavalier dismissal of the Latin-American, Indian, and African modes of modernity is appalling, particularly given that his study does not include any texts or theorists from the Third World or feminism or U.S. ethnic studies or hemispheric studies. He discusses Adorno, de Man, Lúkacs, Luhmann, Foucault, Heidegger, Habermas—in fact, the only non-male artist or theorists he mentions is Virginia Woolf, and there are no non-Westerners or nonwhites. Referentially speaking, this particular book fails to support the claim that he makes in his preface and in the title itself, *A Singular Modernity*.

So there are two ways to interpret the problem of Jameson's singular modernity. The first way would be the path of otherness postmodernism, rejecting the notion of a single contradiction driving the world on the grounds of its totalizing tendency. An alternative would be to treat critically both Jameson's claim and the formalistic rejection of any totality in itself. The evaluations would have to arise from the information we can glean about our contexts, from the metanarratives we choose to adopt, and the ethics we choose to hold and practice.

Some viable alternatives to otherness postmodernism would include some key characteristics or considerations. First, it is important to retain a notion of reference or knowability—or degrees of better and worse knowability—about the world around us, even as we understand that our understanding of that world is dialogic, constituted by us and constituting us. As Madhu Dubey writes,

> [T]he recognition that all knowledge is textual need not provoke a disheartened retreat from any effort to know and understand the world. I am convinced that it is necessary to posit some notion of the real in order to make any claims about social life, while remaining fully aware that because human knowledge of reality is always discursively mediated, it is also always fallible and reversible. (13)[10]

In this sense, Chow's call for us to "let referentiality interrupt" is both banal and radical. On one level, we function on the basis of referentiality all the time, every day (for example, we know that wealth is distributed unequally because we assign value to money); on another level, the theoretical distress caused by reference to "reality" indicates the degree to which the assumptions of otherness postmodernism are instilled in us.

Second, it is important to recognize the ultimate failure of any homogenous dominant—*not* out of the formalistic rejection of totality, but because human practice makes homogeneity impossible—and thereby remove it as a straw man. As E. San Juan has observed, while pointing out the failure of homogeneity, unity, and/or totality may be correct and, as such, useful, it has limited efficacy as a political critique: "it is untenable to posit a homogenous culture dominating a complex society. Instead of fixing on the abstract and large cultural configuration at play in any society, we should conceive of historically specific cultures that stand to one another in relations of domination and subordination, in struggle with one another" (335). Like Jameson, San Juan suggests Raymond Williams' notion of dominant, residual, and emergent cultures as more useful mediating terms between the poles of sameness and difference. Methodologically, Raymond Williams' concept of the dominant, emerging, and residual cultural formations remains helpful, but even these terms assume a chronological relationship that may lead us to underestimate the degree to which hegemonic and resistant forces are coterminous, intertwined, and inconsistent. Here, the multivalence of the social articulation of signs is preferable not because difference is inherently better but because the multivalent way of reading more accurately describes the object in question.

Third, even as we recognize the polyvalence of even the dominant term, the notion of a hegemonic or dominant cultural formation can be useful as long as that totality is understood to be in motion or in process. For example, Žižek observes that the "recourse to multitude," in the manner of Hardt and Negri's text of that name, "is false not because it does not recognize a unique, fixed 'essence' of modernity," but because it denies the central antagonism of capitalism as the driving force of modernity ("Ongoing" 296). That is, the notion of a dominant or a hegemony is important not simply as a central "Same" term, but as a way to identify its ongoing relationship to other elements of the world around it.

To offset the isolationist tendencies of particularity, Masao Miyoshi reimagines "totality" in several ways. The relationship between the totality and the particularity has to be thought of dialectically and dialogically. Masao Miyoshi advocates such a conception:

> An individual, a group, or a program requires a totality in which to position itself. Conversely, a totality is not always a monolithic system for the suppression of all differences and marginalities. Specifics and particulars negotiate at all levels with the context and with other specifics and particulars. Likewise, all concepts and ideas may be bound to a specific locale in time and place, but a specific locale in time and place does not produce uniform and identical concepts and ideas. (42)

Miyoshi's conception here of dialectically related, developing particularit(ies) and totalit(ies) is especially apt for studies that have to do with marginal communities and individuals, enabling us to understand both the complex dynamics of an individual life (including individual aesthetic development drawing on many different contexts), a historically constituted group, and the multifaceted, ongoing relations to various larger structures, such as the state, capitalism, aesthetic movements, and so on. Miyoshi thus attempts to balance the benefits of the "philosophy of difference" with context:

> Such precise identification is a beneficial calibration in the face of crude generalizations that obliterate the distinctions that exist in any category. It helps to fight marginalization and erasure. Yet if the strategy of division and fragmentation is not contained and moderated with the idea of

a totality—its context—it may very well lose its initial purpose and end up paradoxically in universal marginalization. (41–42)

Miyoshi reminds us that the "strategy of division and fragmentation" must be balanced with some notion of totality or "context." Miyoshi's argument resonates with Chow's in calling for the reconsideration of those concepts that poststructuralism and postmodernism have led us to reject, even if implicitly.

I want to emphasize that this is *not* to say that we should throw out the lessons of poststructuralism and postmodernism and return to a brute empiricism, but it *is* to say that because the tendencies of otherness postmodernism have sometimes obfuscated structures of power, we need to take those lessons and rethink, critically, referentiality, information, "facts." That these will not always fit our extant categories or desires, that they should force us at times to reshape our views, is a good thing. An analogy for this would be letting a close reading of a text shape one's arguments about a text; we understand that texts are mediated by language, ideology, subjectivity, form, production and distribution, and many other factors, and these should all constitute part of our understanding of a text, yet we also understand that within these discourses and contexts, we can make arguments about the meaning of a text based on, as we like to tell our students, "what is on the page." Of course, these will not be simple or unanimous; in fact, contention is important—both about the shape and nature of the social structures in which we live and the meta-discourses we use to analyze them.

I cannot stress this enough: while the need for metanarratives, totalities, and comparative contexts is vital, we must also avoid falling back into the recuperation of difference into sameness that, for example, Jameson is prone to. Neither sameness nor difference is preferable in itself, and debates that revisit this dichotomy ad infinitum are missing the point. It is easier to imagine what this means in literary studies: an ethics of reading that balances the need for specificity and heterogeneity with a willingness to let referentiality, in and to multiple contexts, interrupt our extant categories. In the next section, I will discuss the particular contours of otherness postmodernism in literary studies and the possibilities for alternatives.

Reading Literature

As Madhu Dubey writes, "Indeed, a synthesis of aesthetic indeterminacy and racial essentialism, allowing us to have our cake and eat it too, may be defining of postmodern approaches to racial representation in literature" (10). In literary studies, otherness postmodernism "swallows politics into aesthetics" by equating literary realism with the central term of Sameness and centralized power (patriarchy, the state, reactionary nationalisms, et cetera), and concomitantly links "formal experimentation and political contestation"; as Dubey puts it, we have "to snap the[se] enduring links" (10). This critical tendency in literary studies arises from the theoretical bases of otherness postmodernism, the repeated privileging of difference with insufficient regard to *how* and *why* certain signs are "Same" and others are "Different."

The suspicion of literary realism is tied to the supposed formal imperative of realism to hide its artifice and hide its ideological functions. From Bakhtin's criticism of Tolstoy's monologic narrator to Lukács' well-intentioned but off-putting valorization of the normalizing foundation of nineteenth-century bourgeois realist fiction, the "sameness" of literary realism has been opposed to the "difference" of nonlinear, experimental art forms since the early twentieth century, or what Andreas Huyssen refers to as "the historical avant-garde." The argument usually runs as follows: formal realism not only mimics and expresses but also naturalizes ideological narratives; our acceptance of the "reality" of the novel reflects the successful ideological interpellation of each of us in the extratextual, ideological political realm. The challenge to realism takes a variety of forms, such "mainstream" (e.g., "white" or Euro-American) postmodernism, women's writing, ethnic writing, postcolonial fiction. Hence the debate about realism has taken a variety of forms. For example, as I will discuss further in chapter two, theorists have argued that cinematic realism not only tries to hide its difference from reality through realist content (coherent characters, "cause and effect" plotlines) and form (narratively consecutive scenes), but also through the cinematic apparatus itself (the viewer pretends to be "the same" as the illusorily unified camera eye, but each frame is in fact a different picture; the filmic technology "represses" this difference to create the illusion of a singular film). Many race and narrative theories rely on an implicit allegory between text/discourse production and social and personal processes. The reader/viewer is passive, and the disruption of this process to "wake" the reader or start some process of intellection correlates reading, politics and subjectivity. This familiar argument emerges even in theories that do not claim affiliation with poststructuralism or psychoanalysis. Aesthetic experimentation and the critique of normative narratives are often assumed to be correlated.

But despite repeated disclaimers that form is not necessarily tied to any particular politics, contemporary experimental works by marginal writers repeatedly become recuperated into otherness postmodernism in a variety of ways. Sometimes ethnic literature *is* postmodern because it is not Western, linear, realist, or masculine. Others argue that ethnic literatures are *not* postmodern because postmodernism is yet another Western metanarrative or universalizing conceptual frame, and postcolonial and ethnic texts cannot be judged by the same criteria. This form of otherness postmodernism contends that while mainstream postmodern literature, such as works by Pynchon, DeLillo, and Coover, may be ideologically ambivalent, experimental texts produced by marginal writers are politically resistant. In such readings, two aspects belie otherness postmodernism's claims to be distinct from "regular" postmodernism. First, the actual methodology of reading minority texts are often not all that different from the ways "mainstream" texts are read. Poststructural and postmodern critical tools for textual analyses have so thoroughly suffused literary and cultural studies that they are reproduced constantly whether one is aware of them or not. Second, if the actual mechanics of reading and the processes of the text are the same for minority and mainstream writers, what is it that differentiates works by those writers? In most cases, the implicit difference is the identity of the author. Thus, despite otherness postmodernism's claims to greater sophistication and complexity than readings driven by identity politics or "no politics" (formalisms), they end up replicating the same results. Experimental forms disrupt the rational languages of the West, but the truly socially progressive texts are the ones by minorities and/or women.[11]

For example, Kwame Anthony Appiah, in his seminal essay, "Is the Post- in Postmodernism the Post- in Postcolonial?" delineates two stages of postcolonial literature along the sameness/difference axis. The first stage is nationalist and celebratory, and the exemplary text of this first stage is Chinua Achebe's *Things Fall Apart*. This stage envisions a unitary nation and prefers a realist aesthetics. The second stage consists of what he terms "novels of delegitimation," which register disillusionment after decolonization, questions cultural nationalism and even the concept of the state, and corresponds to the postcolonial theories of Spivak and Homi Bhabha. In *Reclaiming Difference*, Carine Mardorossian takes this progression a step further, claiming that the work of postcolonial women writers of the Caribbean constitute a "third phase" to Appiah's second stage literature, which tends to treat identity categories such as race, gender, religion, and ethnicity as "discrete and preexisting categories" (3). This third phase, in contrast, "revise[s] the second stage's reconceptualization of culture and identity and take us beyond settled spatial, linguistic, discursive, and literary configurations" (2–3). Mardorossian argues, "the writers of the third phase of rewriting transform such approaches to identity (and correlatively our reading strategies) by making them more attuned to the contingent workings of difference" (3). But rather than having sameness on the one hand and difference on the other, historical realities and real texts incorporate both. For example, in Appiah's second stage, former nationalists' disillusionment with the state arose not only because the state failed to be unified, but also because global capital and the superpower nations (particularly during the Cold War) manipulated postcolonial states, from without (as with Cuba) or within (any number of nations from Liberia to Nigeria), using both the logic of difference (pitting groups against one another) *and* sameness (the surprising consistency of the capitalist logic of profit and the depressingly familiar histories of postcolonial states exploited by dictators shored up by the West) to make economic self-sustenance and political stability impossible. Likewise, in the "third stage," social flux may consist of some stabilities and some changes, not simply difference upon difference.

In narratology, critics such as Margaret Homans have taken up the question of realist narrative. While psychoanalytic feminist critics "take it as axiomatic that the structure of narrative itself is gendered and that narrative structure is cognate with social structure" (5), other feminist and minority critics point out that narratives do not have any inherent politics but rather, their politics are contextual (7). Homans concludes that we need to examine the social structures that produce the desires structuring narrative. Counter-narratives and anti-narratives, she writes, "both resist linear narrative as the continuation of a destructive past" (12). Narrative is "potentially polyvocal" (Friedman qtd. in Homans 8), and "its gendered meanings defined not by any intrinsic qualities but by its social uses" (Homans 8). For instance, Jinqi Ling demonstrates that certain Asian American realist texts, such as Louis Chu's *Eat a Bowl of Tea*, challenges that normalizing national ideology as exclusionary and destructive. Ling's study focuses on texts that exemplify what Homans means by "alternative" realisms that cannot be so simply dismissed as ideologically problematic. While I agree with Homans' conclusions, I question her acceptance of the ideological valence of narrative realism by, presumably, white male writers. Homans draws a triad between white male narrative realism, women's experimental (nonrealist) narrative, and realist narratives or "counter-narratives" by people of color. By taking seriously Homans' call to analyze the social structures producing narratives, I argue that we can denaturalize or question all three points of that triad.

Realist narrative does not necessarily do what many critics assume it does. As Madhu Dubey puts it, "there is no straight line from form to politics and...aesthetic innovations do not inevitably produce politically subversive effects" (10). Any sweeping characterizations of either literary realism or its ideological work will oversimplify the situation. On the one hand, even structuralist narratology of "normal" realist narratives demonstrates that realism's apparent consistency is illusory. For example, Gerard Genette demonstrates the simultaneity between mimesis and diegesis in even realist narratives; in such cases, an apparently monologic voice is destabilized. Furthermore, when people read realist fiction (and watch realist films), they do not necessarily "believe" what is happening in them. The readings of experimental aesthetics argue that narrative disruptions can spark and constitute political disruptions of ideological narratives, equating formal disruption or experimentation with political disruption.

Authors and their works should not be reduced to their identity; rather, texts need to be understood in all their historical, aesthetic, cultural, and political contexts. A kind of dogged devotion to notions of greater referentiality—not *perfect* truth, but *better* information—can help in the endeavor to do justice to a text and its author. For example, David Treuer demonstrates in his excellent *Native American Fiction: A User's Manual* (2006) that simply researching the actual conditions of a text's production, including all the influences on the author, reveals flaws in the dominant ways that text has been read. He begins with the bold claim that Native American literature does not exist because it is treated as "culture" rather than literature. In other words, literature by Native writers are treated as cultural artifacts—like shards of pottery or ossified bones—instead of human-produced literature complexly positioned in complex and sometimes ambiguous traditions of both "Western" (Euro-American) and minority or "non-Western" (i.e., non-Euro-American). Treuer passionately argues that literature by American Indian writers should not be read as passive products of culture, as if, because writers like Leslie Marmon Silko, Louise Erdrich, and Sherman Alexie are Native, they could not have written in any other way. Rather, he argues that these writers—like all writers—utilize the aesthetic tools of their choice, including the conventions of the novel, a "Western," or at least originally European, genre. For example, in the chapter "Smartberries," he roundly critiques the tendency to read Erdrich's *Love*

Medicine as epitomizing the multiple and nonlinear narratives of the "Other." Literary critics argue that in Eldrich's work, "multiple narrators confound conventional Western expectations of an autonomous protagonist, a dominant narrative voice, and a consistently chronological linear narrative" (31). On the contrary, Treuer argues, there is no tradition of multiple speakers in the Native traditions Eldrich is drawing upon; he calls this "the myth of polyvocality" (39). Rather, Erdrich's manipulation of voice and point of view comes from her use of the usual tools of fiction; "the impetus for Erdrich's prose project does not differ from that of many other twentieth-century writers" (46). Treuer, himself a novelist, argues that Erdrich makes brilliant use of "Western literary tactics" because *they belong to her as much as to anyone else.*

Neither aesthetic form nor identity has any inherent political valence, and the political valence of a text should certainly not be based on the author's identity. This tendency, more than anything else, betrays the essentialism that otherness postmodernism believes itself to be free of. Despite the sophisticated critical readings of text, often the *way* a text is read depends on the author's identity. In the following chapters, I will argue that while otherness postmodernism's focus on race and gender as ahistorical "Other" categories have occluded various aspects of Theresa Hak Kyung Cha's and Bessie Head's work, serious considerations of race and gender are almost never applied to Thomas Pynchon's work. Instead, his work is universalized; in the identity politics of privilege, white male identity means one (and one's work) is free from being determined by identity. As a result, the racial, gendered, and national characteristics of Cha and Head almost cloud consideration of their aesthetics, while reception of Pynchon's work seems to be absent of identity and almost entirely about form. These writers' works have been central in theorizing otherness postmodernism, and as such an examination of their critical receptions can tell us a lot about our contemporary literary critical structures of practices and feelings.

CHAPTER TWO

Theresa Hak Kyung Cha and the Politics of Form

> Literary forms have to be checked against reality, not against aesthetics—
> even realist aesthetics.
>
> —Bertolt Brecht

Theresa Hak Kyung Cha's 1982 experimental novel, *Dictee*, has become a key text in Asian American studies, particularly as the locus for contemporary methodologies in the field. Korean American filmmaker, writer, and performance artist Cha developed her work in the California and New York avant-garde art communities of the late 1960s through the 1970s, then studied semiology in France before returning to the United States to teach and continue her work (Roth 151–60). In 1981, she published the film anthology, *Apparatus: Cinematographic Apparatus*; including pieces from theorists and artists ranging from Dziga Vertov and Maya Deren, to Roland Barthes, Christian Metz, and Cha herself, the anthology examines the ideological processes of the filmic apparatus. Following her tragic death, her novel *Dictee* was published in 1982. After nearly a decade of neglect by scholars in Asian American Studies, as Shelley Wong notes, in the early 1990s, the poststructuralist turn in the field enabled and was spurred on by the novel's interrogation of form, subjectivity, and ideology (Wong 103–6). Since then, numerous studies of the political significance of *Dictee* have appeared. While some readers choose to emphasize the cultural specificity of the text, many critics focus on the ways in which the narrative disruptions of the novel constitute political disruptions of ideological narratives and formations.

Lisa Lowe's influential book, *Immigrant Acts*, best exemplifies the argument that *Dictee*'s formal disruptions interrogate the multiple, sometimes contradictory configurations of the ideological apparatuses of state, church, neo-imperialism, patriarchy, and other structures of power. If mimetic realism ideologically "resolves" social contradictions by convincing readers of the ability to equate "the name and the thing," in contrast, the "discontinuity, fragmentation, and episodic unfluency" of *Dictee* undercut this ideological function (Lowe 152). She writes, "*Dictee* makes explicit that every social formation includes a multiplicity of social contradictions—of race, national origin, ethnicity, gender, or class—arising from heterogeneous origins and conditions, with certain conditions taking priority over others at particular historical moments" (147). Such readings emphasize that the novel challenges not only certain representations, such as Orientalist historical texts, hagiography, patriotic legends of martyrdom, and the interpellative processes of U.S. citizenship, but also the ideological innocence of any process of signification, including narrative, translation, dictation, collective identification, reading, and writing.[1] In such "reading framework[s]," Sue-Im Lee explains, *Dictee* is celebrated as "suggestive of a new form of Asian American subject representation, a postmodern, anti-realist subject whose empirical substantiality is not generated through the 'intelligible whole' of plot nor whose social identity is categorizable within ascriptive terms of the majority culture" (242). Other critics, while acknowledging the novel's formal resemblance to other postmodern texts, argue that *Dictee*'s primary political significance lies in its recovery of specific histories, contexts, and experiences. In her contribution to the 1994 collection of essays on *Dictee*, *Writing Self, Writing Nation* (which also included an early version of Lowe's essay on Cha), Elaine Kim notes that Cha "foregrounds a highly specific cultural context, inserting Korea, Korean women, and Korean Americans into the discourse" ("Poised" 8); in a more recent essay, Kim numbers *Dictee* among important Korean American texts that recover "subjugated knowledges" ("Myth" 91). Likewise, Helena Grice argues that although the novel undoubtedly employs postmodern narrative strategies, Cha's "primary project" is "creating a Korean (American) national identity which is gendered" (44). In response, others characterize such claims of "cultural ownership" as "highly irritating" (Twelbeck 227).

Analyses foregrounding form or content are not mutually exclusive; rather, critical readings tend to emphasize one aspect or another. But while readers generally agree that the formal disruptions of the text constitute some kind of political resistance, there is fundamental difference about where to place the emphasis: is it *Dictee*'s challenging form, or is it Cha's Korean American identity? Critics believe that privileging the former—nonmimetic form—can avoid the pitfalls of identity politics, but if we emphasize the political resistance value of aesthetic *strategies*, then why and how is Cha's experimentalism distinguished from Euro-American postmodernism, which is sometimes castigated for universalizing its assumptions and "colonizing difference itself" (Wong 135)? On the other hand, if the difference lies in her identity as a Korean American woman, this risks renewing a form of identity politics. This conundrum explains the ambivalence or confusion on the part of some critics about the status of Cha's context and life in relation to the form of her work. But if we historicize her use of form and relate it dialectically to content and context, then we can understand Cha's historical position *and* concerns, as evidenced in *Dictee*, as new and progressive without reifying the postmodernist aesthetic forms that she uses.[2]

A current of formalism becomes apparent upon examining characterizations of aesthetic realism in discussions of *Dictee*. Mimesis, realism, clarity, and linearity are seen as inherently problematic; Jinqi Ling characterizes this division between realism and experimental forms as "a hypothetically assumed, though rarely admitted, opposition between 'traditional' and 'contemporary' Asian American articulations" (v). The notion that realism necessarily resolves cultural and ideological contradictions often assumes a passive subject-viewer/reader, who can be awakened through the disruption of form. The argument goes: whereas mimetic realism, in teaching the subject to naturalize and resolve, helps inculcate ideological subjects, experimental aesthetics challenge the reader to become active and break out of fixed meanings. But this is not the only way literature and art can work. For example, Ling argues that Louis Chu's 1961 novel *Eat a Bowl of Tea* problematizes the narrative of American citizenship through realist narrative form (53–78). Such differentiation between realism and experimentation serves as the basis, implicitly or explicitly, for numerous readings of not only *Dictee* but also other experimental works by women and women of color. The history of the forms and theories Cha engages in *Apparatus* and *Dictee*, however, suggest a more complicated picture.

The reason for this tacit debate is confusion about terms of the debate. As with any art, politics lies not in form, content, or context alone, but the developing dialectical relationship between these elements. An examination of *Apparatus* assist us in historicizing Cha's use of form, because, as Ling argues in his reconsideration of Asian American literary realism, we need to be attuned to the contemporary contexts and tools artists critically utilize for their own needs. Cha's selection of certain theoretical essays and artistic pieces indicates her historical, aesthetic, and political contexts and orientations, and demonstrates Cha's active engagement with these theories. While her work clearly intends to disrupt various ideological narratives (of subjectivity, citizenship, history, etc.), it also shares in some of the ideological pitfalls of avant-garde and postmodernist aesthetics.[3] Since much has been written about *Dictee*, I will discuss *Dictee* itself only briefly; my focus will be on its intertexts, the political and aesthetic conversations in which the novel intervenes. In *Dictee*, I argue, Cha responds to an increasing reification of form that limits politics to aesthetics and a problematic conception of the passive subject-viewer. As such, Cha's work responds not only to Asian American realism, but also to a wider field of avant-garde and modernist art and theory that is very self-consciously and fitfully engaged with the relation between art and politics. Reorienting Cha's work in this way may help us to reconceive the terms of the debate about the political valence of *Dictee* as well as experimental works by writers from marginalized groups.

Cinematographic Apparatus

In her preface to *Apparatus*, Cha writes that the anthology seeks "to turn backwards and call upon the machinery that creates the impression of reality whose function, inherent in its very medium, is to conceal from its spectator the relationship of the viewer/subject to the work being viewed" (i).[4] This is done through the "semio-psychoanalytic" film theory of Roland Barthes, Jean-Louis Baudry, and Christian Metz, which moves beyond the traditional focus of film criticism on content, to the process of signification itself.[5] These essays share an ideological analysis of the filmic apparatus through a Lacanian reading of the processes of meaning-production in/by the subject-viewer. Similarly, filmmaker Maya Deren criticizes the "linear logic" of traditional criticism and art manifestos, and she castigates "realists," "sur-realists," and "romantics" for simply debating content, rather than engaging in substantive discussion about forms or methods of art in "semio-psychological" terms.[6] The other filmmakers in the anthology—Gregory Woods, Danièle Huillet, and Jean-Marie Straub—also share this orientation.[7]

Although the theorists and artists vary in specifics, they arise out of the rejection of the same things: nineteenth-century bourgeois realism;

what Andreas Huyssen refers to as the "programmatic" attitude toward art, life, and the relationship between them of the early-twentieth-century leftist avant-garde (a particular pet peeve of Deren); the socialist realism espoused by the French Communist Party; the 1950's canonization and celebration of High Modernism by the culture-industry wing of the Cold War; and the pop/mass culture created, appropriated, and promulgated by increasingly corporatized publishing houses, film, television and recording companies, and art and educational institutions, all manifestations of and driving forces for the commodification of art, taste, pleasure, and desire. According to the contributors to *Apparatus*, these various tendencies share an overemphasis on the content, context, or referent in art and criticism, and this emphasis on referentiality must be rejected. Thus, the writers and artists in *Apparatus* can be seen as part of a larger movement in literary and cultural theory, sharing a critique of logocentrism, a concern with the post-1960s "crisis of the left," and an investment in the innovations in and the implications of postmodern art. As such, we can examine the anthology as an example of and metonym for the general aesthetic and critical trends that, although still marginal in 1980, today have become commonplace in literary studies in general and Cha criticism in particular.

That the concerns of *Apparatus*, however, remain tied to a socialist past is signaled by the early appearance of Dziga Vertov, the "most radical" of the early-twentieth-century Russian neo-constructivists.[8] Cha's inclusion of Vertov, a generational anomaly among the contributors, reflects his influence on politicized artists and theorists of the 1960s and 1970s; Vertov's *The Man with a Movie Camera*, as Michelson notes, was "the key film-text for the generation of filmmakers who called into question the grounds and claims of cinematic representation through the political uprisings of 1968" (xxvii). Influenced by the constructivists and futurists, in the early twentieth century, Vertov's *Kinoks* sought both to liberate cinema from merely recording bourgeois melodramas and to foster active mental participation during and after screenings. They sought a revolution in both the production and the distribution of films. Revolutionary newsreels, montage, and "unstaged" films that used ordinary workers in lieu of actors were utilized to unmask the ideological dimensions of "staged" films and their conventions. But formal innovation was not sufficient in itself. In order to take these new types of films to the people, particularly the peasants and working classes, the Kinoks arranged "agit-trains," special traveling cinemas and discussion groups to villages without cinemas (Petric 3). In these ways, the *Kinoks* and Vertov believed that it was possible, in a revolutionary context, not only to focus on the everyday (particularly of the worker) but also to actually *enter* the everyday, while simultaneously advancing art on a international scale. For Vertov, as he writes in *Apparatus*, "liberation" fundamentally means being "liberated from capitalist slavery," and political revolution can enable, is enabled by, and interacts with a revolution in artistic means (technology, especially sound), methods (montage, slow-motion), subject matter ("unstaged" events), *and* distribution (17).

Vertov, like Brecht, treats the relationship between form and content, the text and the world, form and politics, dialectically. In contrast, another innovative filmmaker, Jean-Luc Godard, whom Cha quotes in the inscription to the preface, signals the general direction of the contributors to *Apparatus*. Upon being asked to discuss the distinction between "making a political film" and "making a film politically," Godard offers the following reply: "Yes, these two things are completely different. As Brecht already said, it's not important to know what are the real things but rather how things are real. The relation is in that reality" (i). Godard's language signals a subtle but fundamental shift from a dialectical understanding of the relationship between content ("what are the real things") and form ("how things are real"), to almost a sole emphasis on form.

This deceptively small shift in emphasis manifests its practical and surprisingly significant impact in the history of Godard and *Groupe Dziga Vertov*. In his essay, "Godard, The *Groupe Dziga Vertov*, and the Myth of 'Counter-Cinema,'" Steve Cannon recounts how the *Groupe's* increasing focus of political analysis on form edged the concrete audience out of the picture, replacing it with abstract "subject-positions," and led to its depoliticization. Inspired by the collaboration between artists, students, and workers in May 1968, Godard, Jean-Pierre Gorin, and other filmmakers formed the *Groupe Dziga Vertov*. The collective's professed goal was to create a new kind of cinema through a revolution in its processes of production (Cannon 76–77; Loshitsky 29–32). Invoking Brecht, the *Groupe* argued that the first priority was to break the induced identification with character, narrative, et cetera, and thereby intervene in the naturalized process of viewing film that undergirds the ideological work of mainstream films. Traditional left documentary, in claiming to be able to give the spectator direct access to "the truth," participated in this problematic naturalization. As Cannon points out, the *Groupe* assumed that realism lulled the working class into a state of dream-like passivity, a continuation, despite 1968, of the theory of the "passive audience" (82). Concerned primarily with this passive audience, they neglected to establish/maintain links with any "concrete audience," which would have required different or more complex understandings of the audience, the subject, and politics (i.e., beyond the text) (Dixon 116; Loshitsky 32; Monaco 215, 219).

The "failure" of the *Groupe Dziga Vertov* had several important results, many of which were not unique to the *Groupe* and its associates. Disillusioned participants rejected radical politics, turning their full attention to art and theory. As Loshitsky notes, "The greatest impact of the revolutionary spirit of the organization was registered in the arena of film theory" (25). In other words, disillusionment pushed the focus from politics to political aesthetic theory, from art for/of revolution to a revolution in art. And again, this development was not limited to Godard and film theory. Peter Wollen, author of the oft-cited analysis of Godard's "counter-cinema," points out that, in film criticism, "as poststructuralism developed, materialism and scientificity were quickly thrown out the window and replaced by discourse theory, deconstruction, and refusal of the extra-textual" (211). Or, put another way, the problem with Godard and the *Groupe Dziga Vertov*, and the general direction they reflected in avant-garde film theory, was that they came to see the political as formal, rather then understanding form as dialectically related to content and the social, extratextual realm.

Cha's invocation of Godard signals the direction *Apparatus* takes, including, unfortunately, this tendency to formalism. This problem becomes pronounced when, with the advent of Lacanian psychoanalysis, "the Real" becomes explicitly problematic. The works in *Apparatus* reflect the shifts made by Godard and the *Groupe*: the talk of revolution recedes, and the formal, particularly in what Baudry calls "semio-psychoanalysis," takes precedence. Unfortunately, this trajectory turns out to be not only bad politics but also bad (i.e., incomplete) psychoanalysis. Because Cha's conception of the relation between art and politics clearly draws on these theories, I want to examine them before turning to the ways in which Cha's work both reflects and responds to them.

"Projection Mechanism" and the Subject of Cinema

Cha begins and ends *Apparatus* with two images that suggest the anthology's desire to theorize more rigorously the ideological function of film, particularly in the processes of subject formation. The frontispiece of the anthology is a photo of an empty theater, and the final image of the anthology shows the same theater filled with spectators. The theorists and artists of the anthology attempt to reinsert the subject into consideration of the filmic apparatus via semio-psychoanalysis, but to various extents they rely on a narrow conception of the individual as abstract, passive "subject." This notion of the subject is intimately tied to the kind of formalism that Godard's political aesthetic evidenced. Furthermore, many contemporary readings of *Dictee* share some of the fundamental assumptions of these theorists.

A number of essays in the anthology demonstrate the semio-psychoanalytic approach of Baudry, Metz, Bertrand Augst, and Thierry Kuntzel. Because critical focus has hitherto been almost exclusively on "the effects [films] have as finished products, their content, the field of what is signified," Baudry writes, "the technical bases on which these effects depend and the specific characteristics of these bases have been ignored" (26). Instead of dealing only with already-constituted signs, critics must engage with the interrelation between the filmic apparatus and the processes of the subject in producing meaning. The filmic apparatus, Baudry explains, relies on the illusion of continuity created from discontinuous elements, thus requiring difference as well as its negation. At the level of the mechanical apparatus, difference is marked as frames in a reel and as moments in time and space, but, at the same time, projection minimizes and represses difference through the rapid succession of images. This "projection mechanism," or "*le défilement*," as Kuntzel calls it, suppresses the heterogeneity of the elements so that only their relationship remains. Thus, this formal or mechanical continuity in the filmic apparatus enables a narrative continuity based on the repression of difference. The apparent continuity in the constitution of meaning creates a false continuity of/for the viewing subject, and this, of course, yields ideological ramifications.

This imaginary continuous subject is likened to the Lacanian Mirror-Stage in the Theater. The Imaginary Order posits itself on the basis of a fundamental misunderstanding of the wholeness of the self and its continuity with the world. The "impression of reality" created by film is not the Imaginary per se, but a repetition of the desire for that state. Whereas in the mirror-stage, the subject imagines a unification of the fragmented body, in film, the transcendental subject of the camera unites into a meaningful whole the discontinuous fragments of phenomena, "lived experience," or, at the simply mechanical level, individual frames. In other words, viewers primarily identify not with what is represented (the spectacle, the content, etc., which is recognized as fictional), but with the unified transcendental subject of the camera, or "what stages the spectacle, makes it seen, obliging him to see what it sees" (34). So, in cinema, the false "reality" is not the image onscreen but "a simulation of the condition of the subject, a position of the subject, a subject and not of reality" (60). The cinematographic apparatus thus brings about a "state of artificial regression" (56). The relative narcissism of the experience, and the resemblance to a state in which reality envelopes, and in which the separation of the body and the world has not yet been defined, help to explain the intensity of attachment to the images of the film and the process of identification created by the cinema (50, 55). In other words, viewers accept this ideological control because it feeds their unconscious desires. Augst explains that "behind any fiction there is a second fiction: the diegetic events are fictional, that is the first; but everyone pretends to believe they are true, and that is the second" (253). According to Kuntzel, the part of the viewer that does believe is the unconscious. The "credulous person" is the unconscious part of the self, beneath the incredulous viewer, who wants to believe.

The subject's unconsciously chosen credulity is problematic because it helps produce the ideologically malleable unitary subject. The cinema collapses the plural, heterogeneous, complex, analyzable subject, into the unanalyzable collective subject "necessary to the dominant ideology" (34). For example, the ideological output of Hollywood films far exceeds that of Eisenstein's because commercial films allow the filmic apparatus to function on the subject at optimum capacity. Here we see parallels to the characterization of literary realism's ideological work in resolution, identification, naturalization, and so on. Theorists in *Apparatus* see this process as the primary ideological mechanism of film. Baudry writes, "the forms of narrative adopted, the 'contents' of the image, are of little importance so long as an identification remains possible" (34). Resistance therefore lies in "disturbing cinematic elements" to make such processes visible, by means such as that of Vertov's "The Man With a Movie Camera." While Baudry claims the "system of repression" to which he refers is "primarily economic," he argues that "the ideological mechanism at work in the cinema seems thus to be concentrated in *the relation between camera and subject*" (34, my emphasis)

The ideological process of the cinematic apparatus works similarly to that of Žižek's ideological fantasy. The identification that drives the film process is based on a misrecognition: the viewer does not suspend disbelief, but he/she does repress the discontinuity of the individual screens and shots to accept the continuity of the film. The subject accepts the fundamental fantasy of "the transcendental subject of the camera," primarily through repression of difference, out of a desire for continuity and meaning. In other words, the subject accepts the "interpellation" of the camera as capital-S Subject. In both cases, the ideological fantasy is fundamental to the functioning of an ideological reality. The surface belief or disbelief does not matter so much as the structures that shape a subject's constitutive actions.

Baudry is right to identify the heterogeneous, complex individual subject as the desired and/or actual state, but a wholly collective, abstract, ideologically malleable subject arguably does not actually exist. The fallacy of the passive subject-viewer leads to several others. First, it supposes that mimetic realism necessarily produces this ideologically malleable, falsely unified, unifying passive subject-viewer, and is therefore inherently problematic. While perhaps sometimes, in some cases, it may do so, this also assumes that realism can have little or no positive ideological function. Furthermore, this focus on awakening the passive subject assumes that the viewer/critic of non-mimetic work cannot be manipulated ideologically or be constituted as an imaginary subject; the imagined membership into an elite group who can "view" properly (the critic who "sees"?) can just as readily become the Imaginary or a central, specular, and interpellating Subject for critic/viewers who believe themselves sophisticated. Another fallacy is the assumption that *any* viewer is passive. This position ignores the possibilities for and the historical evidence of audiences who were not passive with either conventional films or ideological hegemonies but in fact created resistances (talking back to the screen, leaving the theater, creating different readings and/or different creations), individual and collective.[9] In other words, we forget that human beings *choose*, and that every subject is complex and individual, as well as collective and ideologically malleable. Finally, this odd formalism, which sees the *primary* site of ideological work as the formal aesthetic processes constituting a certain kind of subject, leads to the privileging of experimental art as *the* site of political resistance. Therefore, the "disruption" of formal-ideological processes, particularly of the subject, and the identification of such disruptions, become the primary task for ideological criticism. But, as Huyssen pointed out over twenty years ago, the insistence on the power of resistance, by breaking linguistic codes in the face of cultures in which every advertisement features a domesticated form of modernist aesthetics, betrays the poststructuralists' overestimation of art's transformative function for society (Huyssen 210).

Blinking, Flickering, Flashing Semiotics

Marc Vernet, like Augst in the tradition of Bellour, Baudry, and Metz, contributes the essay, "Blinking, Flickering, and Flashing of Black-and-White Film." The fiction film does not just tell a story (content), he writes, "it tells the story of itself as well" (368). It does so not necessarily through self-reflexivity (taking itself as object diegetically), but through the workings of the apparatus form itself. But Vernet's essay also does not just tell a story about the filmic apparatus' staging of its own crises in order to hold onto the spectators; it also stages its own crisis. Like his contemporaries, Vernet desires to get away from content-fixation and lay bare the ideological apparatus of film. He does so by showing that cinema is premised upon the spectator's fundamental desire for repetition of a prior state of identity of self and world, not so much by content but by the false impression of wholeness and identity given by the subject-camera. This impression of wholeness of the subject fulfills the desire of the viewer, who, because having one's desires fulfilled is pleasurable, gives him/herself up to the celluloid image on the screen and stays immobile in both mind and body. In doing so, I argue, Vernet and others fulfill *their* desire—not primordial but very overt—to get away from content, but in the process, the viewer and viewed, the "plural, heterogeneous, complex," "analyzable individual subject" that Baudry wants to recover, disappears, along with the presumable reason for making ideological critiques in the first place. In other words, in trying to get away from an ideologically problematic use of the "truth" or "real," they dispense with the "real" altogether.

Vernet's essay begins with a reading of a photo taken from Barthes' *Roland Barthes*. In the background of a family photo is the maid, and according to Vernet, the only caption reads, *"Me fascine, la bonne"* ("fascinating me, the maid"). Vernet also makes this phrase the heading for this section of the essay. In a footnote, however, the translator notes that Vernet's attribution of the phrase is a "slip of the pen," because the original caption reads *"me fascine, au fond, la bonne." "Au fond"* positions the maid "in the background" of the photo. The phrase could therefore be read as "fascinating me, in the background, is the figure of the maid," although the translator notes that Richard Howard's translation reads "What fascinates me here: the maid" (357). The translator finds the omission strange considering that Vernet's essay is centrally concerned with "the whole question of the position of the fetish object" (357). Interestingly, "au fond" also means "basically," "actually," or "really." We could let this slide as an interesting but accidental coincidence, if we really believed in accidental coincidences.

What fascinates not only Barthes but evidently Vernet as well is the maid, or rather, the figure of the maid, or rather, his own reading of the figure of the maid. The photograph is "almost empty," representing neither a figure nor a scene, because the female family members in the foreground are neither identified nor doing anything particularly interesting. Vernet concludes, "there is nothing here to provoke the imaginary, except in the corner, in the background, the maid pointed out by Barthes" (357). Vernet finds this fascinating as his own eye was not caught by the figure of the maid. Therefore he undertakes to find out what there is about this figure that could have fascinated Barthes. He describes what is not a person but an image, a "solid white mass of apron against the darkness of the corridor," a face that is not real but is coming into existence, like a photograph being developed. It is a "silhouette," a "feminine form," a "hollow form filling a hollow form."

His faithfully semiotic reading of the image slips a little as Vernet engages in a little creative, empathetic personification of the figure; the figure hovers in the doorway, "torn as she is between self-effacement and curiosity" (357). He gets back on track, however, in the next sentence: he realizes that the figure resembles Barthes in another photograph (dressed up in white for a play and frozen with stage fright). The maid is also the double of the photographer, because her position "is symmetrical with the photographer's." She is "taken in" by the camera's eye, but in the same moment she takes him in with hers. She is "a containing content, an observed spectator, a watching sight," and in this capacity she reflects the "man standing in the doorway in the background of Velasquez's *Las Meninas*, who is turning around to look at the scene he seems to be leaving." And as viewer/spectator taking in the scene, she doubles not only the photographer but also "the person looking at the photograph."[10]

Given the function of this image in the photo, and in the experience of viewing the photo, Vernet suddenly has the insight: "The maid—a white mass against a black background, framed by the white of the doorway, white in black, black in white—it's a photograph in the photograph" (359). For while the maid "belongs to the bourgeois environment," "she does not enter its representation," either to itself or to others. When she does appear, "it is on the outskirts" (358, 359). Then why does she figure so prominently here? As a detail in the photo, the maid is "a white spot watching me and who draws my eye towards the edge of the photograph and into the depths of space, to the back of the depth, only to send it immediately back to me like a mirror." In other words, the image of the maid not only gives a third dimension to a two-dimensional photograph, it also "leads me back to where I am standing—in front of the photograph and outside it." As such, the maid occupies "what is called in perspective the 'principal point' or 'point of view,' which is the projection of the eye onto the plane of the picture, and where, in central projection, the parallels converge." But this process, as with the filmic apparatus, takes place in neither the image of the maid or the viewing of the photo *alone*, but in the meeting of the viewer's eye with the "point symmetrical with the eye of the spectator." At this point, "representation is at the same time founded and annihilated," "a spot blinking, flickering, flashing in the background of the scene."

Vernet's reading signals the triumph of form and the apparatus over the human. For Vernet, the image of the maid ultimately leads him back to himself, the processes of viewing, and the abstract viewer who responds to the photo in a particular way according to particular, yet generalized, psychoanalytic readings. Even a psychoanalytic reading suggests that Vernet imagines a unity that leads back to himself. The ideological interpretation—which the *Apparatus* contributors all more or less claim to be doing—should lie between the semiotic analysis and the critique of the "bourgeois environment." But, as evidenced in the history condensed into the anthology, the description of the "viewer" moves from Vertov's revolutionary worker to the abstract, passive analysand in nearly complete serial isolation. "Content" and history disappear, and by the time we reach the end of the anthology and the cutting edge that it represents, the human being has completely dropped out while the analysis of the filmic apparatus has become extremely sophisticated, and the place of a particular type of analyst/critic doing a particular kind of analysis/criticism has become central.

Whereas critics of *Dictee* repeatedly point out that the political work of the novel entails taking the reader beyond the text into social realities, the theorists collected in *Apparatus* privilege the disruption of subject formation. This leads to a question: If the subject-viewer is passive and ideologically malleable, who is the resisting subject-viewer who can see through the ideological machinations of realism? And is a mere change in form sufficient to change the reader/viewer? Not only the contributors to *Apparatus* but also many *Dictee* critics imply that the formal change is sufficient or at least primary. As Cha writes in the introduction, she hopes that the anthology will be a "'plural

text' making active the participating viewer/reader, making visible his/
her position in the apparatus" (i.) Her own contribution to the anthology, "Commentaire," exemplifies faith in the power of disruptive
narrative to spark activity on the part of the viewer.

"Commentaire"

"Commentaire" is an "anti-symbolic," nonreferential text, in which the
processes of form are as crucial to its "comment" as its contents, as well
as a critical commentary on the processes of constituting meaning in art
(particularly film) and on the difficulty of making the critical comment
itself. The piece consists of sixty-five pages of primarily white words on
a solid black background or black words on a solid white background,
in either capitalized print or lowercase script. Interspersed with the text
are stills from Carl Dreyer's 1932 film *Vampyr* and photographs by
Reese Williams and Richard Barnes. The piece breaks down and
explores permutations of meaning, grammatical and reading conventions, the repression of difference and the illusion of wholeness ("projection mechanism"), framing, and time-as-frame.

From the beginning, the myriad significations possible from the simple plays on words and arrangement indicate the limits of criticism as
well as the ideological and critical issues tied to any creation of meaning. On the first two pages, the recto side is blank and solid white,
while on the verso side the first word of the piece, "COMMENTAIRE,"
appears in black letters on a solid white background (262–3).
Commentaire is here both a proper noun, as the title of the piece, and a
noun, the French for "comment." The commentary is the piece itself,
commenting on the rest of the anthology as well as its overall concerns:
commentary on the filmic apparatus and commentary on the possibilities for making commentary. The condensation of meaning in this first
word demonstrates how language works in the entire piece.

After a blank page, the word "COMMENT" appears on the recto side, at
the extreme right-hand edge of the page (265). The French adverb, *comment*, typically asks a question, such as *"Comment faire?"* ("What shall
we do?"). The term is also used to ask "what?" or "sorry?", and elicits as
the expected response a repetition and/or clarification of what was
previously missed or misunderstood. As an exclamation, the term also
expresses astonishment or indignation, such as *"Comment, c'est tout ce
que tu trouves à dire?"* ("What? Is that all that you can find to say?"). As
a question or exclamation ("how"), the word invokes an action as an
answer, a verb, and/or a description of that action, an adverb. In English,

"comment" can be a noun or a verb. The juxtaposition and play of *comment* and *commentaire* indicates not only the question (What is the comment? How will the comment be made?), but also that the comment (noun) will necessarily include the manner in which the comment is made (verb/adverb), or the "how." And this question, how to comment not only on film but also on film's "how," is the central question of the anthology.

On the following page (the verso side of two open pages), the word "TAIRE" appears on the edge of the left-hand margin. The French verb means "to conceal," to say nothing, to "hush up"; the English translation, "TO HUSH"—another word which, grammatically and connotatively, has several meanings (noun, verb, adjective, sound condition, reprimand/command, comfort, etc.)—is echoed later (266, 320). In addition, when read with the preceding page, we see that "*commentaire*," a noun, has been broken and split over the edge of the page leaf. The literal fracturing of the word, as well as its grammatical mutability, also suggests the breakdown of the definitiveness of "commentary." This commentary also encompasses the content-fixated film, literature, and art criticism that Deren and the psychoanalytic critics castigate so roundly, criticism blind to the filmic apparatus in particular, and therefore blind to the ideological process ("how") of not only film but its own mode of commentary as well.

That is, the "breaking up" of the word "*commentaire*" is a symbolic anti-symbol; it self-reflexively indicates the processes of, limits on, and problems with symbolic representation, and even suggests (by reference and by its own processes) what lies in and beyond the entire realm of interpretation and mimetic art. The juxtaposition of "*comment*" and "*taire*" suggests "how to conceal," the central modus operandi of all modern ideological apparatuses (hegemony, the commodity fetish, interpellation), concealment not only of a "thing" but more importantly of its own processes. This is also the formal imperative of the filmmaker, popular and traditional or experimental, because, as Baudry and Kuntzel demonstrate, the individual frames that constitute the film are repressed through the "projection mechanism." Furthermore, any comment on art conceals, leaves out, due to its ideological bases, lack of information, or the always-incomplete nature of signification. In addition, the juxtaposed words invoke the inability of interpretation to say/be/do either what the artwork is itself (the exposition must be at least one step removed from its object), and/or the "meaning," content, or experience to which the artwork refers, or from which it arises nonreferentially, or which it simply is.

The conspicuous arrangement of single words disrupts and therefore calls attention to Western conventions of reading (i.e., left-to-right, one page at a time). The piece conditions the reader, drawing on "old" and familiar ways of reading, to read in a "new" way. In other words, when a word flushed to the right-hand edge of a recto page is immediately followed by a left-flushed word on a verso page, the reader shifts from a "normal" reading practice to one that literally slips off the physical page (and over to the next) as well as the "page" constructed by our expectations as readers, inculcated by conventional reading practices. In this way, the form of the piece and the experience of reading it constitute part of the answer to the question/project posed by the opening pages. The question and its answer are thus intrinsic to the comment.

In similar ways, the piece manipulates terms, images, and permutations of synchronic framing and diachronic time-as-frame. Following the opening section, a sequence features black letters against a white background with a black border around the edges of the page (268–73). The word "COMME" ("like," "as") faces the word "COMMENT," and "COMMENT TAIRE" faces the word "TEAR." Then, "ECRAN" ("screen") faces a blank page. The frames, which vary in thickness and evenness, call attention to the "frame" in the sense of narrative, social, historical context, as well as the apparatus of film, in which the black frame around each individual shot becomes invisible in the projection. Furthermore, the "frame" of the movie camera and the screen, the "kino-eye," always leaves something out, concealing and excluding by default even as it shows. The play on the word "TAKES" likewise draws our attention to the framed-ness of film: the many "takes" necessary to get the shot right for a certain effect, the verb "to take," and "what it takes" (317). The viewer sees only the final "take," the product of hidden and discarded repetition; the cinema industry, particularly Hollywood, functions on and inculcates the "take"/profit logic; and "takes," or interpretations, can be mistaken, or multiple, or uncertain.

And again, the words draw our attention to the difficulty of commentary: to be like/as a comment is to be near a comment, but not the comment itself; or, to strive for a comment as transparent and direct as a white (*blanc*) screen, apparently hiding nothing, but which not only hides but has as its fundamental apparatus the "how" of concealing. All the possibilities and difficulties of the permutations of framing, meaning, ways of viewing/reading/interpreting are condensed: to get at "the meaning"; to "get" not only how the film means but also how it conceals in order to create meaning; to make a comment (which may be like/as experience); and, in understanding the how and the comment of the film and about the film, to make a commentary (non-interpretive art criticism) that is like/as the film (i.e., not the film, not a representation of it, not an "interpretation" of it). The mutability of the frames further reminds us that none of these elements remain fixed over time.

The simple words, with their surface opacity, seem endlessly overdetermined, indicating that despite the deceptive realism of the camera ("it just records reality"), film is actually an opaque art form—opaque not only in the sense that all art is opaque,[11] but because even if one were to "tear" through the "*écran*," to physically break through the surface of the image to dig deeper into its meanings (content and/or form), one would merely come out the other side of a relatively thin sheet of canvas, and the film would continue projecting on whatever lay in its path (including the clumsy interpreter's body protruding through the screen). In other words, to tear through the screen, which is merely any blank space, one has to understand the "how" of the filmic apparatus as well as the processes of meaning-production and viewing laid bare by semio-psychoanalysis and ideological analyses. It is never simply a matter of, as suggested on the following two pages, looking at what is "SUR" and "ECRAN," or on the screen ("SCREEN" and "ON SCREEN" are repeated later) (274–5, 290–2). At the same time, however, the images-on-the-screen and the words-on-the-page are all we have to go by. Again, the text calls our attention to the limitations and processes of viewing and reading that are usually repressed.

As the camera-eye provides/creates a synchronic frame, the manipulation of time itself provides another kind of frame, a diachronic one that guides our seeing. Later in the piece, the words "WENT / PAST / MINUTE / OR / MOMENT" appear in light grey down the middle of the verso side, followed by "ARILY" in the top left corner of the recto page (298–9). Two pages later, the words "MINUTE / BY / MINUTE / TO / MINUTE / OR" appear, again light grey and down the center of the page. And then, we are led over onto the next page, which reads, "TWO" (303–4). This expression is followed by variations of the word "hold": "HOLD" is followed by "TONGUE," which faces "HOLD" again (305–7). "Hold" is a film term, meaning to rest on an image (which by now we understand is not an ideologically innocent act); this word easily slips into the held tongue, the words kept in check by an internal and/or external authority. Then the term "noircir" (to blacken) faces "TO ONE MORE"; "noircissure" (black spot, smudge) faces "AND MORE," followed by "TIME" (308–12).

Once again we have the reference to the filmic apparatus that fuses the individual frames through the manipulation of time into a unity that is both artificial and real. The film is sped up, so the film goes past "minute by minute," and we miss the individual frames. Yet it is the relationship between the images, created through the "speeding up" of the reel, that makes the film a film. That is, the film reel is "sped up," but that is the "normal" speed—of the film, of perception, of life. And, to simply stop the movement of film (either a "hold," in the sense of freezing the film, or a shot that "holds" in the sequence of the film) does not necessarily reveal the apparatus of meaning-production. Yet to invoke an image that is part of a film (i.e., *Vampyr*) is to invoke the whole and the movements that make it "whole."

Two photographs included in the piece also highlight issues of framing. The first shows a drive-in, featuring a large movie screen, palm trees in the background, and time-lapsed car headlights transformed into lines of white light. On the facing page is an overhead shot of a small film theater in which "spectators" appear in various states of repose, leaning over and lying down in their seats, while the blank screen glows white (292–3). These images point to two important elements of the filmic apparatus: first, the processes of desire, (false) identification, and repression by the passive viewer; and second, the importance of time in producing the meaning-effect of cinema. With only the images onscreen (content), and with the spectators lulled into sleep, the prospects for understanding are grim. These photographs also indicate the deceptiveness of visuals or signs; lest we attribute some kind of "presence" to pictures as opposed to words, the text reminds us that pictures need the chain of significations as well as the mechanical process of film to mean anything. A visual is no less overdetermined than words on a page.

By laying bare the conventions of reading and viewing in a form that does not naturalize those processes, the piece embodies and engages the ideas of the anthology. The subject-viewer of film "sleeps," lulled into pseudo-conscious identification with the camera's false unity, which inculcates and reflects the false unity of the subject upon which hegemonic ideologies rely. In order to "wake" the subject/viewer/ reader, "Commentaire" disrupts the conventional processes of signification, reading, and viewing. In other words, here the intervention focuses on form in order to disrupt the processes of reading and viewing, in order to provoke the putatively passive subject into active, creative engagement. This project, as with work of Godard, the semio-psychoanalysts, and others, is not necessarily inherently problematic; what emerges as a potential danger is that this approach too often relies on an idealized, universalized viewing/reading process of subject formation that is inaccurate and increasingly detached from the world around it. An examination of a particular motif in "Commentaire" will provide insight into what I am identifying as a problematic in the anthology.

Black and White

Throughout the piece, terms and images of blankness, blackness, and whiteness haunt the "capitalized" terms of signification, framing, time, et cetera; they can mean anything or nothing, thus enacting nonrepressive/nonrepressing processes of signification, but their very indeterminacy points to the risk of excluding issues of content and context. An early sequence in the piece begins with, in white lettering on black, the two nouns "blancheur" ("whiteness," or "purity) and "COMMENTARY" facing one another, followed by "AS, LIKE" and "HOW" (278–9, 280–1). The "how" leads the reader onto the next page, where the tones are again reversed (black lettering on white), and the word "blanchir" (to whiten, to turn white) is in lowercase script (282). On the facing recto page, "HOW TO" is flushed right, leading the reader over to the next page, which reads "SILENCE," flushed left (283–4). On the following page, the word "blanchiment" (whitewashing, bleaching) appears. The capitalized directive-as-question of "HOW TO SILENCE" invokes, again, the imperative of apparatuses of power as well as (and not necessarily as insidiously) of film. Such sequences highlight terms referring to the "as, like" asymptotic approach to identity with a thing (either as mimesis, identification, or criticism), the implicit silencing, the opacity of film; the terms of whiteness seem organic parts of these projects, but they also draw attention to themselves as a distinct development in the text.

Other terms of whiteness and blackness are interspersed throughout the text. The words and backgrounds weave through the text, drawing attention to permutations of framing, meaning, ways of viewing/reading/interpreting. The words of whiteness include "blanc," "blancheur," "blanchir," "blanchiment," and "blanchissement" (the adverb form of "to launder" or "to whiten") (264, 289, 308, 310). The terms of blackness include "noir" ("black"), "noirceur" ("blackness," "black spot"), "noircir" ("to blacken"), and "noircissure" ("black spot" or "smudge"). Blank pages that are completely white or, more often, black also appear throughout the piece.[12]

What do these terms suggest? White space can be read generally as absence or silence, and has been associated more particularly with unwritten (or "unshot") women's writing. White space, particularly in images of the North Pole, also has been related to imperialist geographies and landscapes, also gendered.[13] Gilbert-Rolfe reads blank space in the contemporary world as a signifier in itself; instead of referring elsewhere in time or space (an act of signification to come, the inner workings of a machine), blankness itself is eloquent, mobile, active. Blankness is sublime loss, and, in particular, it is "the sign of an invisible and ubiquitous technological presence," in which we relate to surfaces purely by discourse (Gilbert-Rolfe 162). The blank film screen perfectly exemplifies such depthlessness; as we have seen, we cannot "break through" the physical screen in order to decode its significations, particularly its ideological work.

Furthermore, blackness and whiteness cannot but recall race, not only because Cha's best-known work, *Dictee*, foregrounds its concerns about immigration, nationalism, and translation, but also because Godard, the filmmaker invoked by Cha in the anthology, also incorporates a black, blank screen to refer to race. The *Groupe*'s 1970 film, *Vladimir et Rosa,* inserts Black Panther Bobby Seale into the Chicago Eight trial as "Bobby X." When X is taken from the courtroom bound and gagged, the screen goes blank (and black) in order, Godard's voice-over states, "to represent the absence/presence of the Black man at the trial" (qtd. in Monaco 238). This blankness becomes a quaintly earnest but fairly pointless gesture; a formal device signifying the "unrepresentable," it assumes the immutability of the "unrepresentable," or "ineffable." That is, the *Groupe* uses a formal device to signify that which cannot be represented, but they confuse the unrepresentable in the filmic apparatus with the socially suppressed. Not only that, they literally replace the "oppressed" with the "repressed." Filmic apparatuses and processes, which are ideologically neutral and can be broken down and examined and manipulated in different ways, are seen as inherently serving apparatuses of power. So, in order to disrupt these processes (and their effects on the passive subject-viewer), the filmmaker's resistance focuses on form.

Likewise, in "Commentaire," the terms and images of blackness and whiteness flicker in and out in total abstraction. Because the piece seeks to disrupt the passive reader/viewer by focusing on the processes of the text, signs lack any specific reference to the extratextual. The blank pages do not necessarily signal the racial absence toward which the blank screen in *Vladimir et Rosa* gestures, or the erasure of the human, or the modern subject's unconcern with how things work, or the whitewashing of inequality, exploitation, and oppression, or the revelation of the ideological processes of film. Arguably, these blanknesses, white or black, can mean anything or nothing at all.

"Commentaire" stages a sophisticated and, to a large extent, nonreductive exploration of both the processes of signification in the filmic apparatus, in criticism, and in art. The text "slows down" the processes of signification so that, in a sense, the pieces become visible. Moreover, the pieces themselves reveal further pieces, and all must be read together in order to understand the whole. On a very simple level, this approach requires a dialectical process of reading—which is always, arguably, worthwhile. At the same time, "Commentaire" replicates the issues plaguing the anthology: a focus on form/process; the turning-away from/rejection of content; the lack of historical context; only oblique suggestions of or references to the outside world; the subject-viewer assumed to be passively asleep (except, presumably, the implied sophisticated reader). The black, blank screen can be about "blackness," or blankness, or time, or nothing at all—the unfixity of its meaning is part of the point. While such a work can be useful (and beautiful), it is not, in itself, necessarily bad or good. Politically, it is simply ambiguous.

What "Commentaire" does point out, however, is the irony of the general reliance on the notion of a passive subject-viewer, which necessitates the focus on formal intervention. Like other avant-garde artists who want to shake viewer-subjects out of torpor, Cha relies on an implied, ideal, active viewer who nevertheless remains undertheorized. Who is this implied reader, and what makes possible his/her "process of intellection?" Although she does not say so explicitly, and although she obviously draws on the theories outlined in the anthology, Cha's reliance on this active reader complicates the bogey of the passive viewer.

Dictee and Otherness Postmodernism

Dictee, then, should be read against not only literary realism (Asian American or otherwise), but also modernism and other forms of postmodernism. Compared to her earlier, more abstract works, Cha's *Dictee* puts more emphasis on "content," or rather, contents. In particular, the novel deals with the Japanese colonization of Korea, contemporary antigovernment movements in South Korea, the history and processes of patriarchy, the Catholic church, the Homeric *Hymn to Demeter*, the films of Carl Dreyer, and the lives of various specific individual women. It draws on semio-psychoanalysis while also dealing with the ways that individuals (usually female, unnamed and abstract or specific historical figures) do not simply react passively, regardless of the various species of ideological apparatus. The "passive spectator" never truly exists—exposing, for example, the contradiction between the notion of the spectator as submissive and writing for a nonpassive audience. Subjects are neither unitary nor completely heterogeneous; different ideological interpellations and structural injunctions shape everyone in a number of ways. Furthermore, while the novel lays bare the ideological functions and underpinnings of "official" narratives like F.A. McKenzie's *The Tragedy of Korea*, it also attempts to lay out historical realities and alternative myths that, even though acknowledged to be ideologically complex in themselves, debunk the "official" ideologies. But these alternatives, particularly of women's lives, are not themselves "pure" or wholly separate from the dominant structures. One of the most valuable lessons of poststructuralism has been the understanding of power as multivalent and ubiquitous. So in *Dictee*, its central concerns suffuse the novel, emerging as themes not simply for organizational coherence but due to the ubiquity of the problems themselves. It explores, through different problems of representation, the effects of those processes on human subjects.

Dictee moves beyond the putative passive subject by emphasizing histories of resistance in a text that resists formally as well as in complex, dialectical relationships to the world around it. These include Korean resistance to Japanese colonization; immigrants' resistance to the interpellation of nationalisms; and the individual's resistance to dehumanizing military, political, and social institutions. Numerous active subjectivities populate the text and the process of reading it—the viewer, the author (evidenced by the many references to *Dictee* as a postmodern autobiography), Korean American immigrants, Yu Guan Soon, Catholic saints, and even the unidentified "Laura Claxton." Even before the advent of postmodernism, the text suggests, there is no such thing as a wholly passive viewer, but the form of the novel further works to scrutinize constructions of meaning, subjectivity, and history. Even if we can only know the history and reality through ideological texts, the novel suggests, there are better and truer histories, subjectivities, realities. At the same time, there is never any guarantee that those alternatives are going to be simple in themselves.

Because the novel has been written about so often and so thoroughly, my goal in this section is not to provide another thorough reading of the novel, but to engage with the ways that the novel's readings exemplify otherness postmodernism. For example, *Dictee* is read as denaturalizing and disrupting dominant narratives of history, ideology, citizenship, and the state—which it does—but the problem is that once again the poles of sameness and difference become oddly static in a ahistorical way. As apparent in the discussions in *Apparatus*, the disruption of realism can have various political meanings, so the extreme investment in form in *Dictee* criticism is puzzling. Since the actual interpretive practices used to theorize *Dictee*'s politics are not that different from that of Laclau and Mouffe's *Hegemony and Socialist Strategy* or of critics of "mainstream" postmodern literature, the difference in political value is often implicitly Cha's identity. This speaks to the ideological fantasy of otherness postmodernism that believes itself to have "uncovered" the workings of ideology but, due to social and structural pressures, continues along the same old path.[14]

In the 1990s, the claims of otherness postmodernism manifested largely in Asian American studies through readings of *Dictee*. For example, Shelley Wong points out that *Dictee* disrupts dominant historical narratives: "The spell that is to be broken is the naturalization of history promulgated by colonial and patriarchal discourses, a naturalization that involves a process of neutralizing or other rendering innocuous troublesome manifestations of political or cultural difference by insisting on a model of cultural identity and its corresponding narrative structure" (110). *Dictee*, according to Wong, "de-naturalizes received history and colonizing systems of representation," and in so doing "allows the suffering of history's losers, whose who are without, to be felt and seen again (111). While it is true that hegemonic historical narratives will "write out" the losers, what is important is not simply the disruption of "received history" that will allow historical injustices to come to light, but the *kinds* of challenges and revisions that are made to that history. Formal disruptions of a hegemonic historical narrative can have various kinds of political valences, so we cannot evaluate or understand those disruptions based on form alone. One example is the Holocaust deniers of the generally accepted narrative of the World War II genocide; another might be the Christian fundamentalists' narrative of the twentieth century as, rather than the "American century," one of deplorable moral decline. And since "brushing history against the grain" is not intrinsically good, the contending notions of history have to be evaluated or compared in some way. The historical narratives of the rulers has to be met with more than a plurality of competing stories, because some of those stories will not be interested in truth or justice, but rather in simply shifting power a different way. Because our received versions of history come from "colonial and patriarchal discourses," it may seem to us that any disruption of those discourses will be beneficial. But we live in a world of multiple contending "hegemonic" discourses, so while oppositional texts may seem to formally disrupt hegemonic discourses, increasingly we realize that in a world that the people who critique "hegemony" are not only the progressives but also reactionaries, fundamentalists, and neoconservatives. What matters is not only that we recognize multiple histories—just as important is *which* histories we recognize.

Again, part of the problem is that the paradigms of otherness postmodernism cast the issue in terms of specious and unnecessary dichotomies. If, as Hayden White and others have argued, history is written like a story and therefore cannot be the transparent record of facts and events, neither do we have to think of history as wholly discursive. In other words, history will and should be constituted out of competing discourses, some of which will have more basis in reality. While the hegemonic narrative will be as much a product of who is in power as the narrative's intrinsic merits, nevertheless, even the means for discerning the structures of power require reference to an external world in considering competing histories.

By the same token, the flaws of otherness postmodernism manifest in Lisa Lowe's discussion of *Dictee*'s complication of Althusserian interpellation. I agree with Lowe's reading that *Dictee* theorizes the dynamics of and possibilities in multiple, contradictory ideological interpellations and of different or "non-identical" positions in the social structure. Lowe writes,

> Cha episodically focused on sites of interpellation that are not only multiple but are also hybrid, unclosed, and uneven. This focus suggests that resistances to the hegemony produced by interpellating structures are not located simply or exclusively in the antagonisms produced by their demands for identity but that it may also be the non-identity of the irregularly multiple sites to those demands for uniformity which founds the condition of both inadequate interpellation and the subject's resistance to totalization. (146)

Lowe points out that contradicting or contending interpellations and social situations may enable resistance to one of those interpellations, such as in "the student's use of English to supplant the rules of French dictation or in the Korean American female narrator's critical stance with regard to the militaristic uniformity of South Korean nationalism" (147). Another example may be the contending ideological apparatuses of Japanese and U.S. imperialism; the "Clio History" chapter in *Dictee* includes excerpts from English-language American newspapers that critique the brutality of Japanese imperialism. She concludes, "Against the ideological subsumption of difference and particularity to imaginary equivalence, *Dictee* suggests that it is precisely at the junctures of proposed equivalence that ideology may be interrupted and challenged and that specularity, homology, and identification are each vulnerable from the standpoint of differentiated social and material relations" (151). Lowe is right in that, first, interpellations can be multiple and even contradictory, and second, the glaring contrasts between material and social conditions of the interpellated and the conditions of the subject he/she is supposed to be can produce resistance.

The problem lies in mistaking the descriptive accuracy of the contending interpellations for prescriptions about progressive politics. Lowe identifies sites of resistance as arising from the failure of interpellation when multiple hailings clash, but does interpellation necessarily have to be "totalized" in order to work? Althusser, as Lowe notes, relies on Lacanian notion of "splitting" and misidentification with the Other or capital-S "Subject" of the ideological state apparatus. If we take seriously Lowe and Cha's description of the contending interpellations that serve to constitute all subjects, then no one can actually be totally interpellated. In the complex political world we live in, *no one*—progressive or right-wing—is actually interpellated by only one ISA. In that case, if we are all multiply and often contradictorily interpellated, how can we determine which resistances and which interpellations are better or worse? By the same token, the resistances to hegemonic interpellations sparked by noncorresponding material conditions can take a variety of ideological forms. Again, it is not simply a question of whether multiple interpellations exist and clash, but what those interpellations are and how we understand them.

Take, for example, right-wing antigovernment extremists. Their interpellation as members of a putatively secular and united federal government (the U.S.) contradicts their interpellations as members of what is usually a strange mélange of white supremacy, libertarianism, survivalism, and Christianity. Often this may coincide with trade protectionism and anti-globalization, which the far Right, such as Pat Buchanan, are happy to exploit. The neglect of such everyday political issues can be largely attributed to the ideological fantasy of otherness postmodernism, or the belief that we sophisticated cultural critics have figured out ideology and power. If, as Rey Chow suggests, we let referentiality "erupt" into the discourses of poststructuralism and otherness postmodernism, what would we do with the phenomena of these right-wing extremists who, in seeing themselves as "oppressed"?

Lowe combines an insightful description of the struggle over floating articulations with a problematic valorization of alterity on a purely formal or structural level. Sameness, identification, and homology in ideological identification can be bad, but turning this equation into a law ironically ignores situations that pose more complexity. Lowe identifies the "fantasy" of ideological interpellation as the voluntary identification or dis-identification of the subject. Of dictation, she writes, "it 'captures' the subject precisely by means of its appeal to constructed imaginary equivalences or identifications" (150); this aids in constituting the fantasy of the subject, "whose pleasurable erotic forces derives from a fiction of identification (s)" (151). The assumption that ideology and hegemony work only or even primarily through totalization and identification seems strange in the age of postmodernism and late capitalism. How can one valorize difference and non-identity when difference, multiplicity, and flexibility are the key principles of late capitalism and neo-imperialism? *Dictee* calls for us to approach matters of form and ideology with more complexity than offered by the paradigms of otherness postmodernism.

For example, in *Dictee*, the chapter "Melpomene Tragedy" explores a complex interplay of multiple, simultaneous identifications and dis-identifications, none of which have simple valence. The chapter demonstrates how the typical ideological subject, rather than being passive or credulous under the spell of a hegemonic unitary and unifying ideological apparatus, constantly and actively struggles with the multiple ideological and structural demands on it. The chapter takes the form of a letter written in Korea to "Mother," "eighteen years" after both have left it, in which the speaker experiences an anti-government demonstration and reflects on its similarities to earlier demonstrations (*Dictee* 80). The text reads:

> We fight the same war. We are inside the same struggle seeking the same destination. We are severed in Two by an abstract enemy an invisible enemy under the title of liberators who have conveniently named the severance, Civil War. Cold War. Stalemate.
>
> I am in the same crowd, the same coup, the same revolt, nothing has changed. I am inside the demonstration I am locked inside the crowd and carried in its movement. The voices right shout one voice then many voices they are waves they echo I am moving in the direction the only one direction with the voices the only direction. The other movement

towards us it increases steadily their direction their only direction our mutual destination towards the other against the other. Move.

I feel the tightening of the crowd body to body now the voices rising thicker I hear the break the single motion tearing the break left of me right of me the silence of the other direction advance before...(*Dictee* 81–82)

The first sentences take the form of first-person plural, the "we" of the Korean people, and several other sections refer to Korea as "our country" and the Korean people as "us" (*Dictee* 28, 81). This claim on nation may seem to contradict the critique of patriarchal forms of cultural nationalism, which discouraged Yu Guan Soon's anticolonial efforts, but the two contending interpellations are not so much contradictory as qualitatively different—politically, ethically, and historically. In *Dictee*, the speaker's claim to "we" in "we fight the same war" is a ground-up claim based on commonalities and political realities, while the Other is an imposition from above to maintain certain forms of authority. Similarly, the notions of "the same struggle," "the same crowd," "the same coup," and "the same revolt" can only be understood through the interplay of sameness and difference. These struggles are historically different, but they are "the same" because the South Koreans find themselves again opposing an autocratic power. The failure of these historical moments to be different from this basic opposition testifies to the continuity of colonial and neoimperial powers.

In the following paragraph, the narrator's relationship to the crowd again draws attention to the complex dynamics of identification and differentiation. The point of view is simultaneously that of the narrator and that of the crowd: "I feel the tightening of the crowd body to body." That is, while the narrator herself can feel others pressing against her, here she speaks of the mutual and dispersed pressure everyone in the crowd experiences. While she is still the narrator, the point of view also becomes that of each person in the crowd, individual yet collective, experiencing a kind of Other-directed sameness and difference. The "I" is a specific and general individual—the narrator specifically as well as every other individual in the crowd experiences this—*and* part of several different collectives—the Korean people, the members of this particular crowd, individual human beings in any tense political demonstration. The mobility of point of view again appears in the final word of the second paragraph, "Move." This is what the individual and the crowd do, but it is also the command spoken by authority. So in this section, the points of identification are mobile. Here, communality is not only a kind of recuperation of consonant personal experiences but also an institutionally, ideologically imposed experience of common interpellation and alienation.

Ensuing sections also manipulate multiple points of view that seem to distinguish the narrator from others, but actually go on to push the boundaries of identification. For example, the police and soldiers are both differentiated and identified with. The narrator is distinguished from the police and soldiers quelling the demonstration when these official representatives "duplicate themselves, multiply in number invincible they execute their role. Further than their home further than their mother father their brother sister further than their children is the execution of their role given identity further than their own line of blood" (*Dictee* 84). But when the address shifts to second person, the police and authorities are paralleled with the narrator, the author, and even the reader. The text continues, "You are your post you are your vow in nomine patris you work your post you are your nation defending your country from subversive infiltration from your own countrymen" (*Dictee* 86). The "you" here serves a number of simultaneous functions. As in other sections of the novel, "you" may or may not refer to the narrator and reader because it could be generic (as in "don't you hate it when . . .?"); it also addresses the military representatives of state repression, while further suggesting that the kind of ideological interpellation these soldiers undergo can happen to anyone.

In *Dictee*, the narrator's identification with various points of view, and our identification of that narrator with the author, correlates to the complex of contradictions in multiple ideological "hailings." So, in the "you" passage above, while the police officer or soldier may be hailed as "you" by the state apparatus, thereby constructing a subject, the text shows us that that "you" is also multiple and contradictory. "You" as the reader, or the general "you" that includes the narrator—both of whom want to look on and judge from outside—can be implicated in this interpellation. Similarly, the various points of view in the "Melpomene Tragedy" chapter, put the speaker into multiple and even contradictory speaking positions. Such mobility of point of view and axes of identifications, cast in the present tense, suggest that our subjectivities are constantly in process, sometimes conflicting against one another. Furthermore, there is ostensibly no limit to the number of identifications. The "subject," whether according to army, nation, religion, or whatever ideological system, can be anybody, as the mobility of the narrator's identification demonstrates. That is, the blind police are not contrasted to crowd or the clear-eyed narrator; rather, we see how *all* ideological subject positions are constructed through multiple ideological hailings and structural pressures.

The One Who Is Diseuse

One recurring theme in readings of *Dictee*, like readings of texts of other minority and/or women writers, is that exclusion and oppression prompt marginal writers like Cha to produce texts that disrupt hegemonic narratives of history, nation and citizenship, gender roles and sexuality, and so on. But this often implicit argument has always disturbed me because it seems to discount the agency of that marginal writer. As Ralph Ellison writes in *Shadow and Act*, "The protest is there, not because I was helpless before my racial condition, but because I *put* it there" (137, emphasis in original). In other words, we need to more carefully and complexly scrutinize the relationship between the structural, social pressures on all writers and the aesthetic license and innovation all writers utilize. While it is true that different narrative and aesthetic forms have developed historically, I think we should be extremely wary about too quickly attributing a writer's aesthetic to any particular tradition or political situation.[15]

For example, to what extent or in what ways was Theresa Hak Kyung Cha marginal? Or, more to the point, to what extent does her work have to do with Asian American social movements? I do not mean that an author's work should or even can be judged by his/her life, but it is interesting to consider this question. At the conclusion of his critique of postmodernism, Andreas Huyssen distinguishes "otherness" forms of postmodernism because they are grounded in new social movements. Cha's general social location as an immigrant Korean American woman situated her in certain systems of patriarchy and racial formations, but Cha and her work, like that of any writer in relation to society and social movements, have a complicated relationship to what is generally known as the Asian American movement. For example, Cha attended Berkeley during the late 1960s and 1970s, but her interests lay more in film and performance art than the budding ethnic studies movement. Similarly, while Cha worked for Tanam Press in New York City in the 1970s, she was not affiliated with the New York-based Asian American Basement Workshop or the magazine *Bridge*. I am *not* saying that Cha's work is less politically insightful because she was not directly involved in the Asian American movement. My point is that when we make claims about minority texts being more grounded in community or social movements, we need to be careful about the extent to which this is actually true in particular cases.

In terms of marginality, Cha was in the middle of avant-garde art communities who generally felt themselves marginalized (and still do). That many of these intellectuals and artists who feel themselves marginalized by suburban brainwashed philistines were and are affiliated with rich, powerful educational institutions and certainly with cultural capital of the most rarefied sort is a consideration that often gets lost. I argue that this is certainly the case with otherness postmodernism. Again, I do mean that Cha necessarily thought this way; rather, once again my point is that the dynamics of marginalization and "otherness" are complex when a particular situation is examined in detail.

Furthermore, the critical bifurcation between Self and Other, or unity and heterogeneity, contrasts starkly with the novel's treatment of historical women who are "outside" and yet implicated in the structures of power. Critics tend to emphasize these women's outsiderness and the ideological processes that shape them, make their recovery difficult, and are disrupted by them. But another common element of these women, these "diseuse" who speak with great difficulty, is also their ideological ambiguity. In other words, while *Dictee* depicts the oppressive systems that cast these women as Other, the text also constantly shows the ideological flexibility of not only these women's legacies but also their lives. It is not simply that oppressive national, linguistic, educational, religious, sexual, and other systems demand a unity that these women disrupt. The consideration of their politics and social position is just as complicated as that of Cha's.

Take the text's use of the Homeric *Hymn to Demeter*, which, unlike that of Ovid and Catallus, specifically mentions Eleusis and the wait of nine days and nights. In Homer's *Hymn*, Persephone (or Kôre), while playing in a field with other women, is abducted by Hades to the underworld. The bulk of the story relates Demeter's search for her daughter and ends with the initiation of Eleusinian Mysteries, which were "the most important of the widespread Greek mystery cults of antiquity" (Foley 65), and the exclusively female rites for Demeter. Foley notes the ambivalence of the Mysteries. The *Hymn to Demeter* represents Demeter, despite her rebellion, ultimately submitting to the authority of Zeus and patriarchy; sexuality is a commodity under patriarchy, and martyrdom realizes the violence undergirding social institutions. Socially, the carnivalesque release of the rites enable the maintenance of order, particularly of women, the rest of the year. In other words, the celebration of female-female relationships in the women's rites for Demeter was underwritten by patriarchal sanction. Yet, they existed as a female celebration. In the same way, the text does not only treat the figures of Yu Guan Soon, the author's mother, Joan of Arc, and St. Thérèse as martyred women, but also depicts the ideological functions their "histories" serve in patriarchal, nationalist, religious, and other institutions. All of these women were martyrs, of a sort, for liberation; each claims her humanity through resistance to oppressive structures, and yet they are *of* those and other systems and institutions, which themselves change and can later claim them.

For example, the chapter "Clio History" juxtaposes the "official history" of McKenzie with the narrative of Yu Guan Soon. Helena Grice argues that doing so enables "the re-examination and re-evaluation of national history," which deemphasized her role in the anticolonial movement (Grice 45). But the chapter explores not only the patriarchy of nationalist narratives, but also neo-imperialist history; the multidimensionality, even if inadvertent, of McKenzie's study; the flexibility, or adaptability, of national discourse—which can and does easily incorporate Yu Guan Soon into its national myth when useful; and the ideological effects of juxtaposing two narratives. The original F.A. McKenzie's *The Tragedy of Korea* resigns Korea to Japan, blames the Koreans for their unwillingness to modernize, and recounts both the repression of and the resistance to Japanese imperialism. *Dictee* reproduces newspaper articles, many of them detailing Japanese ordinances in Korea, anticolonial efforts, and suppression, printed in McKenzie's book. But in the text is also included the heading "SUPPRESSION OF FOREIGN CRITICISM," which appears in the top margin of McKenzie's book (i.e., *not* part of the text itself). That is, the framing of the historical texts is brought directly into *Dictee*. The process of "getting to" these past lives necessitates awareness and critique of the ideological modus operandi of texts.

The reality being discovered, moreover, is just as complicated as the process of getting there. The newspaper articles cited in *Dictee* (via McKenzie) are taken from the first English-language newspapers in Korea, some of which were started by Western missionaries, who not only established educational institutions (including Ewha Women's University, Yu Guan Soon's school) and participated in anticolonial movements, but also paved the way for the recruitment of Korean labor and agreements between Japan (in the name of Korea) and the West, not to mention the later Cold War relations and division of Korea. In the same way, many of the early leaders of the Korean resistance, such as Syngman Rhee (whose letter to President Roosevelt appears in *Dictee*,

34–36) and Ahn Ch'ang-ho, were educated in the United States and were associated with Christian churches (Nahm 255, 226). Protestant churches became the main social institutions for expatriate Koreans, and in many instances this was due to the inroads made by missionaries in Korea (Choy 257–8). The critiques of religious indoctrination and patriarchy in other parts of *Dictee* serve to highlight the complexity of the anticolonial movement.

Furthermore, contemporary nationalism uses Yu Guan Soon's story as hagiography. Walter Lew's celebratory *Dikte for Dictee* includes passages from *Uri nara choun nara: Yu Kawn-sun we samil undong*, or "Our Country, Good Country: Big Sister Yu Guan Soon and the March First Movement" (54–69). The children's cartoon book shows Yu Guan Soon being told, "If you study hard, you will become someone who does well." At night, she prays tearfully, "Dear God, please give us courage and wisdom. Please bring our country together again soon" (Lew 59). In Korea today, the national independence museum shows a wax model of Yu Guan Soon's tortures. She is heroic (to us) because she was female and fought for colonial independence, but she was also Christian and a product of Ewha (founded by Western missionaries). Schools, churches, museums, and the mass market mobilize the image of Yu Guan Soon, as well as those of anticolonial fighters Ahn Ch'ang-ho and Rhee, for the triple inculcation of nationalism, patriarchy, and Christianity. These cannot simply be called deformations, as is the omission of her activities from the anticolonial histories; she *was* all these things.

The links to Christianity are problematic not only because it is itself an ideological harness, but also because it is the route through which many Koreans absorbed bourgeois individualist humanism (particularly ripe for exploitation under capitalism, whether on the sugar plantations of Hawaii in the early twentieth century or in the ever-expanding Korean multinationals of today), as well as Western hegemony. Christianity in Korea is inextricably tied to the narrow teleologies of modernization (newspapers, educational institutions) *and* actual assistance in anticolonial movements (which would later metamorphose into neocolonial relations with the United States), elements of the institution that the people themselves utilized in order to fuse in various incarnations (as nationalists and communists) against the Japanese and in other areas of life (women, structures of information dissemination), but with an institutional price.[16]

My intention here, as throughout this book, is not to reject wholly the insights of postmodernism or avant-garde art forms; a Godard film or a piece like "Commentaire" can be and is invaluable within a given sphere (modern art, film criticism, etc.). But I do want to question the notion that formal innovations and the particular strategies employed to read them necessarily constitute political resistance. While certain histories informing Cha's work (Japanese occupation of Korea, ensuing anticolonial movements, Korean diasporas, the life of St. Thérèse of Lisieux, etc.) have been examined, the text's formal disruptions still tend to be read ahistorically. Placing Cha's work in the histories of form indicated in *Apparatus* leads us, ironically, to the argument that the political intervention of *Dictee* stems less from its formal experimentation than from its emphasis on those suppressed histories. That is, the particular innovation of the novel comes from its coupling of the formal strategies, which always self-reflexively insist upon skepticism of signification, with the particular histories and contexts dealt with in the novel. In that sense, it responds not only to aesthetic realism or ideologies that depend on easy predication and identification, but also to postmodern and modernist aesthetics.

Seen in this way, we can say that Elaine Kim and others are right when they point out the importance of cultural context and even the author's identity. Rather than relying on old forms of identity politics (*Dictee* resists because of the identity of its author) or new (the aesthetic strategies of *Dictee* are more political than the often problematic Euro-American works that it may resemble because of the author's subject position), we see that the text achieves effects because it is in critical dialogue with other texts, writers, theories, and histories around it. To say that *Dictee* is not disruptive merely because of its form does not necessarily have to lead to a claim of "cultural ownership," but to a situation that developed out of debates on the politics of avant-garde art forms. In this case, if we do not think of identity as essential or determinate but as offering the possibility of cultural insight into social situations, then we can see where the difference may lie in texts by writers from marginalized groups.[17] But this is not always true, and such insight is not necessarily limited to members of marginalized groups.

Focusing on the formal innovations of a text for its political valence too often leads, oddly, to the attribution to a text of things that it alone cannot do. One critic suggests that *Dictee* resists "American exceptionalism" (Spahr 40), but the novel can and does become "exceptional" within literary critical institutions that value formal experimentation over literary realism. If, tomorrow, the tastes of American readers were somehow to turn to experimental novels by Korean American women writers, the publishing industry would not hesitate to make *Dictee* a book-of-the-month. The improbability of this scenario, in fact, has less to do with *Dictee*'s own formal innovations than with the social and political realities with which we all live. So I would suggest that it is a kind of wishful thinking to suggest that the text "returns us, as readers, to the material contradictions of lived political life" (Lowe 152). On the contrary, the notion of any form as some kind of uniform reflection of ideology risks leading artists, readers, critics, and subjects away from the material conditions that constantly interact with those forms.

This may be a subtle distinction, but I believe it is important to point out because it is often elided and leads to confusion. Criticism of Cha's work, particularly *Dictee*, exemplifies the celebration of otherness postmodernism. While the political valences of postmodernist art have been questioned, many critics in and outside Asian American studies attribute particular power to those contemporary experimental texts by minority and women writers, and especially women of color. A laudatory attitude toward avant-garde texts by minority writers only makes sense when such otherness postmodernism relate to political and social movements, seeking to retrieve lost histories and unseat hegemonic lies, freed of simplistic notions of identity, history, or epistemology. But such goals can and are shared with modes of aesthetic realism, and not all experimental texts (whoever the author) share these goals—which is why, as Brecht pointed out in his response to Lukács' dismissal of avant-garde art, we can never understand the politics of a text or identify "realism" by relying solely on formal criteria (Brecht, "Against" 109–10). In some ways, we have returned to the essential formulation of Vertov: form and politics function dialectically. But for us, this formulation has to be understood through the sieve of contemporary theory. The historical development, telescoped into *Apparatus*, demonstrates an aesthetic and—more importantly—critical and ideological trajectory that not only puzzles (depoliticized political criticism) but is also deeply problematic and unsettling. This tendency is not limited to criticism of *Dictee* but in fact permeates much of contemporary literary study, and as such it is important to be more critically aware of this tendency.

The critique of realist aesthetics hinges on the argument that its emphasis on sameness requires an exclusion of difference, and that therefore it not only mimics the logic of ideology, but also trains us to naturalize things like normative collective identities, subjecting subjectivities, exclusionary unitary histories, and the like. But such arguments betray their own tendency to homogenize. In discussing "difference," it would be inaccurate to equate all "differences." In fact, to reify difference—which is simply nonidentity—as inherently good and liberatory is to flatten all historical differences (differently historical) to formalist, idealistic sameness. This kind of empty sameness is untrue to the critics who, desiring a better world, value difference in its most liberatory forms.

CHAPTER THREE

Not Three Worlds But One: Thomas Pynchon and the Invisibility of Race

> If we replace the idea of the "nation" with that larger, less restrictive idea of "collectivity," and if we start thinking of the process of allegorization not in nationalistic terms but simply as a relation between private and public, personal and communal, then it also becomes possible to see that allegorization is by no means specific to the so-called Third World...For what else are, let us say, Pynchon's *Gravity's Rainbow* or Ellison's *The Invisible Man* but allegorizations of individual—and not so individual—experience?
>
> —Aijaz Ahmad

Whereas texts by women and minority writers, such as Theresa Hak Kyung Cha and Bessie Head, are almost always tied to the racial and gendered experiences of their authors—and therefore at least nominally of the structural situations rendering those particular aspects of their identities politically significant—the race and sex of the author of *Gravity's Rainbow* largely remain invisible.[1] I contend that this tendency demonstrates that, despite our ideological fantasy of postmodernism, our reading practices are still informed by identity politics and double standards. As Michael Bérubé notes, critics do not ask if Pynchon is "a legitimate voice of his people" or if the canonization of his work is "the work of guilty liberal academics who are bending over backwards to accommodate the writing of white male novelists" (297). Instead, critics feel licensed to declare *Gravity's Rainbow* "one of the great historical novels of our time" and "the most important literary work in English since *Ulysses*."[2] While I am indeed a fan of Pynchon's prose, my goal in this chapter is to examine and challenge the readings of Pynchon that reflect the differential approach to white and nonwhite, Western and non-Western, male and female writers.

Because Pynchon's writings are centrally concerned with issues of race and imperialism, the absence of discussions of race—whiteness or otherwise—in Pynchon criticism is striking. I argue that Pynchon's identity as a white man shapes the reception of his work as deleteriously as Cha's and Head's, *not* in the sense of unfairness or reverse discrimination, but in our critical inability to think beyond that identity as being without identity. The lack of discussion about race and imperialism in Pynchon criticism, *and* the apotheosis of it as the most brilliant work of postmodern genius *overall*, demonstrates this basic assumption about identity. Pynchon criticism exemplifies poststructuralist ethics' valorization of difference, which, by rendering racial, cultural, and epistemological difference incomprehensible and insurmountable, reinscribes it. Moreover, because Pynchon is a white man, he can be treated as an individual—a very idiosyncratic one at that—situated within Western literature overall, and not be expected to represent all white Euro-American straight men. Despite the insights of postmodernism that race, gender, sexuality, nationality, and so on, are constructs that shape everyone, these categories are still only applied to the Other.

Pynchon criticism, particularly of *Gravity's Rainbow*, exemplifies the tendency to emphasize the sublime and insuperable alterity; for postmodern critics, the inability of Western, logocentric knowledge to have contact with the Other and/or the past without imposing its ideological baggage renders those areas—the past, the Other—unknowable. This supports the power structures enabled by the ideological fantasy in that it allows for disciplinary divides between white, Western writers and nonwhite, non-Western writers to continue. In this chapter, I argue that while Pynchon's early works stop at the recognition of the Other and posit a self-flagellating white, male colonial self that only serves to recenter that colonial self, *Gravity's Rainbow* does try to move beyond that binary. First, I discuss some strands of Pynchon criticism, particularly in the treatment of the sublime and paranoia. Then I examine the genealogy of problematic treatments of racial others that emerge in Pynchon's early work, particularly as manifested by the Beats and modernists. Given this context, I argue that *Gravity's Rainbow* moves beyond treating the racial Other as the sublime limit of knowledge and embraces paranoia as a flawed but important pedagogical tool for all people. In fundamental ways, I will argue, *Gravity's Rainbow*, while acutely aware of systems of power that divide, reflects Aijaz Ahmad's critique of the Three Worlds theory that "we live not in three worlds but in one" (103).

The Limits of the Sublime

One of the defining characteristics of otherness postmodernism is the surrender to insurmountable alterity; the self and "that which cannot be known" are fixed into a set relationship, and dwelling within that impossibility of understanding, that tension between the desire for knowledge and the impossibility of knowing, is exalted into an ethical and political virtue. Whereas the Romantic and modernist sublime was marked by longing, nostalgia, and solace in the aesthetic form that gestures toward that which is terrible, awesome, and ungraspable, the postmodernist sublime embraces the impossibility of representation, and surrenders to its. Lyotard adopts the Kantian sublime's "incommensurability of reality to concept" from an aesthetics to an ethics and politics (79). Hayden White applies this notion to history; as Amy Elias writes, the "postmodern romance" is desire for "History as the receded, never-to-be-accessed sublime realm of Truth" (55). Demonstrating the political litmus test, postmodernists argue that "the only way out of the view of the Master for the Western, First world (particularly U.S.) consciousness may be a return to the premodern/postmodern recognition of the historical sublime" (Elias 197). By the same token, the ethics of the Other of Emmanuel Levinas and Drucilla Cornell posit the impossibility of understanding that Other as the basis for ethics. I argue, however, that the postmodern sublime and poststructuralist ethics, or the ethics of the Other, constitute, in Pynchon's terms, in an "approach and avoid" attitude to difficult issues of ethics, history, technology, race, and the structures and processes that create it. Instead, I concur with Joseph Tabbi's argument that postmodern *literature* starts to move beyond the crisis of the sublime, from postmodern theory into a "new realism."[3]

Pynchon criticism tends to be divided into two kinds.[4] The first consists of hunting down the endless references in Pynchon's works; I would characterize most of this work as politically harmless and often quite fascinating. The second trend in Pynchon criticism, however, calls into question the referentiality of the first sort of Pynchon criticism; this second kind also identifies itself with poststructuralism and postmodernism. The apotheosis of such postmodernist criticism was probably Alex McHoul's and David Willis' *Writing Pynchon: Strategies in Fictional Analysis* (1990). Targeting Pynchon criticism that fails to take into account contemporary literary theory, or "CLT," by which they mean poststructuralism in general and Derrida in particular, they complain that Pynchon criticism focuses too much on "exegetical drive" and on exhuming "realworld facts referred to in Pynchon's text"; uncritically assumes an "Author" as unified agent; and generally treats issues of authority, referentiality, meaning production, language, et cetera, unproblematically. This is a travesty because Pynchon's work is so "theoretically 'advanced'" (13). Reading "Pynchon as philosophy," they note that Pynchon and Derrida share bricolage (8–9), quotation (9), play (9–10), and a sense of "meaning itself only available via certain other texts" (7).

Along the same lines, reflecting the political litmus test of postmodernists, Ronald Cooley identifies the sublime end-limit of knowledge as necessary for any kind of critical of imperialism. Cooley argues that an anti-imperialist novel must not only be anti-imperialist in content, it must also "subvert two sets of novelistic conventions: the discursive conventions that make any attempt by an authorial I (however disguised) to tell the story of an other, a reductive, and potentially a totalitarian enterprise; and the narrative impulse towards closure—towards a re-estimation of order that is always in some sense political" (307–8). The second requirement (form) makes the first requirement (content) difficult, hence "the tension between radical politics and radical narrative form" (Cooley 322). Like many other literary critics, Cooley takes for granted the perfect alignment of form with politics, and his arguments suggest many assumptive rigidities; only non-Westerners can write experimentally formal critiques of imperialism, and *any* attempt to imaginatively represent the Other reenacts colonialism. Similarly, Stephen Weisenburger, in "Haunted History and *Gravity's Rainbow*," argues that against unitary official histories and resistant heterogeneities, argues that "murmurs," "wandering, ghostly, phantasmatic traces of the other that menaces hegemonic rationality," must "remain relatively disembodied in order to surprise" (18). William Spanos sums it up very nicely: "the invocation of content... is determined by a now delegitimated logocentrism that blindly privileges reference over representation, the signified over the sign, history over writing the politics of practice (action) over the politics of reading" (727).

The obsession with the sublime and the Other as limits of knowledge, to be approached but avoided, often manifests in Pynchon criticism as an oddly disconnected fascination with technology and/or an equally disconnected and odd dismissal of the possible truth-content of paranoia. Sometimes, technology becomes the sublime or end-limit of knowledge, particularly in relation to human actions. In doing so, Pynchon criticism resembles those strains of poststructuralist ethics that valorize without actually grappling with the real forms of difference in our world, and thereby reinscribe that difference. For example, Inger H. Dalsgaard's essay, "Terrifying Technology: Pynchon's Warning Myth of Today," after a sophisticated reading of how Pynchon undermines myths of technology, concludes with startling naïve questions:

> *Gravity's Rainbow* raises questions about our relation to the technologized society around us. Does technology run us, or we it? Did we set it in motion, and has it now become autonomous? Has technology created a postmodern predicament of powerlessness, isolation and loss of both identity and democracy? Or is it just a positivist, enclosed epistemological system, a metanarrative—a Rocket, say—which will have to come down or explode at some time? The rocket is a singularity but also, as Deleuze and Guattari suggest, a multitude of differences. It could be an untotalizable system or a transcending totalitarian system. (Dalsgaard 106)

The dialectical answer is that it is neither, or both. We are not powerless puppets, but we are certainly not free. We created technology not out of a vacuum, but through human and mechanical needs created by past generations, and technology dictates us (not *to* us as finished products prior to technology, but *creates* us) as we create more of it and react to it. The rocket may be one thing, one particular tangible object, but it is also a practical production that emerges from the past, directs future action and meaning, and yet is determined by human practice. As Ernest Mandel writes (in response to Adorno's critique of anti-bomb protests), military technology "cannot be applied independently of living people engaged into social activity" (Mandel 506). Even if one does not agree that class struggle is the final determinant of human history, one can still admit that technology cannot be or do anything apart from human activity.

Critics also read *Gravity's Rainbow* in particular as "debunking" paranoia, which is "a culturally produced and authorized narrative technology," preserving what Patrick O'Donnell characterizes as a "self-defeating," "familiar concept of subjectivity" (qtd. in Rosenfeld 340). Leo Bersani argues that paranoia preserves the polarity of Self and Other; therefore, the paranoid "We" loses out to "They" because the paranoid authorizes and enables a "They" "by a primary, founding faith in the unicity of the Real" (Bersani 108). Paranoia finds invisible connections in "orders" that differ from the visible and suspects there may be "a sinister, invisible design *in* the visible" (Bersani 102). Paranoid logic is simply a reflection of instrumental logic, the desire to totalize and organize, a naïve belief in referentiality, and is therefore simply a part of the problem.[5] Therefore, Slothrop's disintegration frees him from paranoia and "the targetlike singleness of a rich and unique self-hood" (Bersani 116). Marc Redfield concurs that "a postmodern sub-lime would imply a double gesture of illusion and demystification," or "the inevitability of both totalizing pattern and its failure" (159). Ungraspability is the best resistance to, as Osbie Feel puts it, "their rational systems" (639).

But as Slavoj Žižek writes, "The dismissal of the 'paranoiac,' ideolog-ical dimension of conspiracy theories should alert us to *actual* conspira-cies going on all the time. Today, the ultimate ideology would be the self-complacent critico-ideological dismissal of conspiracies as mere fantasies" ("Ongoing" 319–20). Žižek points out examples of actual conspiracies, such as car companies, road construction companies, and public agencies collaborating to destroy a public transportation system for L.A. ("Ongoing" 319). So the lack of a single unified historical con-spiracy does not thereby render all plots and conspiracies nonexistent. Žižek argues that the "pluralist dynamics of sociopolitical deterritorial-ization"/schizophrenia/"the multitude" and the "paranoiac logic of the One" are "two sides of the same coin" ("Ongoing" 316). Like the notion of ideological fantasy, the false dichotomy between sameness and differ-ence leads to a privileging of difference that actually licenses the contin-uation of power systems. As Knight argues, the problem today is not too much paranoia but *not enough*.

Likewise, I would argue that, in *Gravity's Rainbow*, paranoia's narra-tive purpose is to enable a movement toward "grasping." Three central characters in the novel—Tyrone Slothrop, Oberst Enzian, and Vaslav Tchitcherine—experience an increase in awareness as a *result* of para-noia, or the sensation of unseen structures, plots, and groups as they affect the individual.[6] While none of them find a singular answer or key, nevertheless their experiences reveal levels of conditioning and self-deception in the individual, as well as the reality of outside systems. A "They" exists, but it is not clear what the exact relation of the self to "Them" is, and it is not clear how the self is part of Them and/or obeys Them, and how to extract oneself. What is clear is that one has to break away from Them in some way, at least cognitively, and the process of realizing any of this in the novel often begins with paranoia.[7] And these terms—in the novel as in life—do not have to be *either* an empiricist, positivist totality *or* a schizophrenic chaos. As Nadine Attewell has pointed out, mediations between "good" and "bad," such as a nonde-bilitating understanding of complicity and, I would add, situatedness, are necessary not only for good politics but for a more *true* understand-ing of how the text—and the world—work.

"White Fantasy" and the Baedeker Trick

Pynchon's early work, influenced by the Modernists and the Beats, ventures closer to engagement with the Other than his literary influences, but until *V.*, it only *approaches* the Sublime, or the postmodernist limits of knowledge. As Pynchon recalls in the introduction to *Slow Learner*, the 1984 collection of his early short stories, the 1950s and early 1960s, he writes, were "a strange post-Beat passage of cultural time," a "transition time" in which "our loyalties [were] divided" (9). On one hand, the liberation of the Beats and new American writers thrilled young writers. "Against the undeniable power of tradition," he continues, "we were attracted by such centrifugal lures as Norman Mailer's essay, 'The White Negro,' the wide availability of recorded jazz, and a book I still believe is one of the great American novels, *On the Road*, by Jack Kerouac" (7). At the same time, he describes them as experiencing Beat counterculture second-hand: "the parade had gone by and we were already getting everything secondhand, consumers of what the media of the time were supplying us" (8, 9). Furthermore, they had inherited a troubling set of cultural attitudes from these forebears: Pynchon apologizes for the "unacceptable level of racist, sexist and proto-Fascist talk" in his short story "Low-Lands" (11). Although he would like to be able to attribute those attitudes to his recurrent character, the lovably dissolute Pig Bodine, Pynchon writes, "sad to say, it was also my own [voice] at the time," that of "a smart-assed jerk who didn't know any better" (11, 12). He shared in "a set of assumptions and distinctions, unvoiced and unquestioned, best captured years later in the '70's television character Archie Bunker" (11).

The political, aesthetic, and countercultural legacy with which Pynchon starts out includes both crude Archie Bunker-isms as well as the white hipster's fascination with and appropriation of African American people and culture, as epitomized in such seminal works as *On the Road* and "The White Negro."[8] While there may have been potential in white bohemians fleeing the suburbs to congregate in Greenwich Village and embrace African American cultural forms, in practice it more often dehumanized black people and decontextualized black art forms, ignoring and thereby covering up the social and economic disparities between ethnic groups. The white bohemian's attitude of adoration and worship vis-à-vis the "Negro" was akin to the abjection of male Renaissance poet toward his lady muse; it was a false valorization that objectified the Other in order to erect the author's own literary and cultural reputation. Depictions without history, self-reflexivity, or attention to actual material conditions were politically meaningless and even reactionary.[9] The Beats, despite innovations in style and content in reaction to the erudite stylistic constructions of the high modernists and literary institutions, were nevertheless continuous with an older tradition of American literature in their depictions of racial others.[10] Most importantly, white writers like Kerouac ignored the anger, and the experiences and structures causing that anger, which helped give shape to the cultural forms and the artists they admired. It was a way to be "different" without being political and/or recognizing their own faults.[11] Mailer, on the other hand, wanted to tap into black anger and marginalization to give birth to the white hipster. Despite some dim awareness of exploitation and anger, Mailer quickly passed into appropriation. In "White Negro," Mailer writes how he wanted (to be) a white antiestablishment, anticultural-mentor in the "hipster," or the "white Negro," who would serve as a kind of cultural mentor. The hipster is an "American existentialist" (*Advertisements* 339), "the bohemian and the juvenile delinquent" crossed with the Negro: "The hipster had absorbed the existentialist synapses of the Negro, and for practical purposes could be considered a white Negro" (*Advertisements* 340, 341).

Similarly, Pynchon's early short stories reflect a kind of glibly colonial imagination, in which one's stories can be transplanted to exotic environ based on travel guides and encyclopedias. He calls this a "strategy of transfer," which he describes as "displacing my personal experience off into other environments" (21); he believes he can do this because he ignores his own situatedness in the world. In his early stories, Pynchon uses what he refers to "the old Baedeker trick," which involves plundering books of history and information to provide "all the details of a time and space I had never been to" (*Slow Learner* 17). The 1899 Baedeker guide to Egypt provided information for the early short story, "Under the Rose" (1961), while "the regional guide to the Berkshires put out in the 1930's by the Federal Writers Project of the WPA" was a background source for "The Secret Integration" (1964) (*Slow Learner* 17, 21). The Baedeker served, as Douglas Ivison notes, "to define Egypt for its European readers" (135). "Under the Rose," Pynchon adds, is also influenced by spy novels, particularly those of John Buchan (*Slow Learner* 18), and overall "operates mostly within the imperial naming of the world" (Ivison 134). Pynchon notes that this approach is "ass backwards," since what is necessary is "some grounding in human reality" (18). He writes that early on, "Somewhere I had come up with the notion that one's personal life had nothing to do with fiction, when the truth, as everyone knows, is nearly the direct opposite" (21). But he comes to realize that fiction is in fact extracted from one's own personal life, from its deeper layers as well as the world that constitutes and is constituted by it: "The fiction both published and unpublished that moved and pleased me then as now was precisely that which had been made luminous, undeniably authentic by having been found and taken up, always at a cost, from deeper, more shared levels of the life we all really live" (21). This situatedness, in which the self is not just implicated but can also *be the Other*, is what I argue will differentiate *Gravity's Rainbow* from Pynchon's earlier works.

We can see the development of a more complex understanding, in which the self is situated and the Other cannot be simply cast as irrevocably unknowable, in Pynchon's works before *Gravity's Rainbow*, particularly his first novel *V.* (1963) and a 1966 article on Watts published in the *New York Times Magazine*. *V.* evinces a change in emphasis and approach to knowledge. In "Under the Rose," the Baedeker provides context unproblematically, as if such catalogs of exotic lands could constitute a reality. In contrast, when the short story is reworked into the third chapter of *V.*, the novel makes it explicit that Maxwell Rowley-Bugge, a British tourist in Alexandria, "exists, though unwillingly, entirely within the Baedeker world" (70). In other words, Pynchon starts to deal with fact that individuals can and are trapped by the limits of their knowledge. Ultimately, however, in *V.*, the limits of racial and cultural otherness fail to constitute more than the unknowable sublime.

V. follows Herbert Stencil's search for "V.," a mysterious woman referred to in his father's journals. The ninth chapter of the novel, "Mondaugen's Story," takes up the question of imperialism in greater detail, with primary emphasis on the destructive effects of imperialism on the imperialist. In 1922, Kurt Mondaugen, a young engineering student, is sent from Munich to the Warmbad district, near Windhoek, in South West Africa (now Namibia), administered then by South Africa. His assignment is to study "atmospheric radio disturbances," or "'sferics" (230). At the threat of a Bondelswaartz (blacks of the Bondel) uprising—the message goes out that "Abraham Morris [a leader of the anticolonial resistance] has crossed the Orange" (231)—Mondaugen is warned to leave his station and take refuge. Although a self-professed coward, Mondaugen cannot leave his antennas required to detect the 'sferics. He goes instead to the fortress/mansion/farm of Foppl, bringing the message "the days of von Trotha are back again" (233).[12]

Mondaugen arrives to "a party in progress" reminiscent of that in Poe's "Masque of Red Death" (234). The theme of the party is 1904, with guests instructed to dress up as movie stars and soldiers of the time. Mondaugen notes that Foppl not only wants to "yarn about the past" but "seemed under compulsion somehow to recreate the Deutsch-Südwestafrika of nearly twenty years ago, in word and perhaps in deed. 'Perhaps' because as the siege party progressed it became more and more difficult to make the distinction" (240–1), particularly in the torture and murder of Bondels. The madly desperate guests *become*—in both narrative content and form—the repetition of the traumas of 1904.

General von Trotha is the spectral figure of Red Death who arrives at the party and brings disease, with his visage "besprinkled with the scarlet horror" of imperial slaughter (Poe 259). Foppl says, "I am von Trotha's arm, and the agent of his will" (240). Von Trotha is the real historical person who led the German slaughter of Hereros and Hottentots in South-West Africa in 1904. Mondaugen's discovery of a hanged Bondel sparks this explanation:

> It had been a popular form of killing during the Great Rebellion of 1904–07, when the Hereros and Hottentots, who usually fought one another, staged a simultaneous but uncoordinated rising against an incompetent German administration. General Lothar von Trotha, having demonstrated to Berlin during his Chinese and East African campaigns a certain expertise at suppressing pigmented populations, was brought in to deal with the Hereros. In August 1904, von Trotha issued his "Vernichtungs Befehl," whereby the German forces were ordered to exterminate systematically every Herero man, woman and child they could find. He was about 80 per cent successful. Out of the estimated 80,000 Hereros living in the territory in 1904, an official German census taken seven years later set the Herero population at only 15,130, this being a decrease of 64,870. Similarly the Hottentots were reduced in the same period by about 10,000, the Berg-Damaras by 17,000. Allowing for natural causes during those unnatural years, von Trotha, who stayed for only one of them, is reckoned to have done away with about 60,000 people. This is only 1 per cent of six million, but still pretty good. (245)

The text explores the consequences of genocide and imperialism, but is ultimately limited in its treatment of the Other. Mondaugen asks, "What was 1904 to these people?" (237), he soon discovers the reasons for their nostalgia. Mondaugen sees Foppl, "dressed in his old private-soldier's uniform," kiss a portrait of von Trotha (252–3). Foppl says, "I loved the man ... He taught us not to fear. It's impossible to describe the sudden release; the comfort, the luxury; when you knew you could safely forget all the rote-lessons you'd had to learn about the value and dignity of human life" (253). The text is not very subtle about the colonies as the unleashing of the darkest desires, festering under repression, of the European colonists and imperialists. Furthermore, the ironic last line of the passage above links 1904 to the Holocaust, emblematic of a wider tendency in Europe toward genocide and self-destruction.

Although I disagree with Cooley about the requirements for an anti-imperialist novel, I concur with his argument that Pynchon's *V.* only *appears* to fit the requirements for a Western anti-imperialist novel. The novels' critique of imperialism is made through the presentation of the history of Empire as "the steady advance of an 'empire of the inanimate,' as a pathological degeneration from life into death, and as self-parody, repetition with a difference (where difference is conceived only as debasement and decadence)" (Cooley 315). But the critical aspect of *V.* hides its "mystificatory" or reactionary aspects:

> In rewriting *Heart of Darkness*, along with a host of other modernist texts and a vast body of popular adventure literature, Pynchon repeats and perpetuates the reactionary discourse of his "originals." In *V.*, as in *Heart of Darkness*, the horror buried within the civilized self is revealed through the encounter with a primitive Other, where the horror is much closer to the surface. Similarly, in repeating the cliché of imperialist fiction, even while reversing their targets, Pynchon authorizes the process of reducing the other to a stereotype. (Cooley 320)

In *V.*, the "horror buried within the civilized self" is revealed not only through the encounter but also by what the "civilized" have *done* to the "primitive other"; but all the while, the "other" remains a stereotypical cipher. The narrative's explicit sympathies are with the Bondels for what has been done to them, and the results of genocidal imperialism and colonialism are depicted as a Red Death for the Europeans, but the Bondels in *V.* are victims or doomed martyrs, remaining as flat and indistinguishable as the Denver Negroes in *On the Road*. At the end of the chapter, Mondaugen rides off with a Bondel who "had lost his right arm," and who tells him, "My woman, younkers dead" (279). The victim remains opaque. At the end of the chapter, the unnamed Bondel lets Mondaugen ride behind him on his cart, and dozes under the hot sun, "his cheek against the Bondel's scarred back," and "they seemed the only three animate objects on the yellow road" (279). The Bondel sings a song, which is "in Hottentot dialect, and Mondaugen couldn't understand it" (279). Mondaugen's inability to understand reflects the novel's inability to go beyond a Modernist version of the primitive Other. Mondaugen's incomprehension may imply something beyond "the

Baedeker world," but what that may be is not specified. The text focuses primarily on the colonizer's point-of-view and soul-rot, but there is little exploration of *reasons* or connections between, say, American racism and European imperialism, other than speculative but vague psychology. For instance, the only reference in this chapter to American racism is jazz playing on a gramophone where there is no one to hear it (243).[13]

Similarly, Pynchon's 1966 article, "A Journey Into the Mind of Watts," demonstrates a naïve an attitude toward race and "reality," but at the same time it also demonstrates a rising tension. In terms of race relations and construction, Pynchon pits "white fantasy" against "black reality," but through manipulating perspectives and focalizations, particularly of the second-person "you," the essay demonstrates a latent ambivalence to its white fantasy/black reality model. Critics have noted that the development of such themes and formal strategies will be important to Pynchon's later fiction.[14] In terms sadly applicable to the present day, the article addresses a white audience (willfully) ignorant of not only the conditions in Watts but also the fundamental relationship between the "reality" of Watts and the "white fantasy" of the rest of Los Angeles. If the general question is "Will there be a repeat of last August's riot?," white people in particular are wondering, "Why is everybody worrying about another riot—haven't things in Watts improved any since the last one?" (35). The article goes about showing that "the answer is no" (35). Despite "social workers, data collectors, VISTA volunteers, and other assorted members of the humanitarian establishment, all of whose intentions are the best in the world," in fact "nothing has changed" (35). For example, the article begins with an all-too-familiar story: Leonard Deadwyler, a young black man, is shot by two white Los Angeles police officers, who are then cleared of all charges. Since the riots, there has been "little building here, little buying," and buildings that were burned are "still waiting vacant and littered with garbage" (80). Given this stasis, "there is little reason to believe that now will be any different, any better than last time" (81). So, "as far as Watts is concerned, it's still very much open" (34).

Pynchon argues that the primary problem is differing cultures as different *realities*: "lying much closer to the heart of L.A.'s racial sickness is the coexistence of two very different cultures: one white and one black" (35). The "L.A. Scene," the product of the mass media, "is basically a white Scene, and illusion is everywhere in it" (78). Hollywood white kids opt for hallucinogens like LSD because "he is conditioned to believe so much in escape," and "the white L.A. Scene makes accessible to him so many different forms of it" (80). While the white culture is "concerned with various forms of systematized folly—the economy of the area in fact depending on it" (35), the "black culture" must face "basic realities, like disease, like failure, violence, and death" (78). The white culture has "mostly chosen—and can afford—to ignore" the black (78), and "the two cultures do not understand each other, though white values are displayed without let-up on black people's TV screens, and though the panoramic sense of black impoverishment is hard to miss from atop the Harbor Freeway, which so many whites must drive at least twice every working day" (78).

Despite its good intentions and many insightful observations, overall the article shares the colonial imagination of the early short stories in that the narrator believes that Watts can be "read" easily. In the light of day, there is no "mystery" to Watts; "all of it real, no plastic faces, no transistors, no hidden Muzak, or Disneyfied landscaping" (78). In Watts, "no one can afford the luxury of illusion," and "the kids are so tough you can pull slivers out of them and never get a whimper" (78). In "the heart of this white fantasy" of L.A., "in a pocket of reality such as Watts, violence is never far from you" (78, 82). So, toward the end of the essay, he asks "what, from the realistic viewpoint of Watts, was so abnormal?" (84). He quotes a participant in the riots, "Man's got his foot on your neck... sooner or later you going to stop *asking* him to take it off" (84). Thus, "the violence it took to get that foot to ease up even the little it did was no surprise" (84). The difference in the understanding of violence as a reaction to a situation of naturalized violence exposes the basic unreality of white culture in contrast to the reality of black culture. At the same time, the assumption that black culture is not constructed assumes a kind of primitivism or instinctiveness that places them on a separate sphere from whites.

Because black residents of Watts know "more of what goes on inside white heads than possibly whites do themselves" because the white culture "surrounds" and "besieges" Watts (80, 78), Pynchon attempts to force the white reader into some awareness of the Other's experience. To make the white readership understand, the second-person "you" is used to describe what it is like for denizens of Watts; this "draws the reader imaginatively into the dramatic predicament of the blacks," exploiting "perspective to *force* some kind of awareness of Watts on to the reader" (Seed, "Watts" 55):

> Like after you have driven, say, down to Torrance or Long Beach or wherever it is they're hiring because they don't seem to be in Watts, not even in the miles of heavy industry that sprawl along Alameda Street...

> If you do get to where you were going without encountering a cop,
> you may spend your day looking at the white faces of personnel men,
> their uniform glaze of suspicion, their automatic smiles, and listening to
> polite putdowns. (80)

The use of the second-person pronoun is a vehicle for not only the reader
but also the author to attempt to empathize with unfamiliar experiences; its use evinces Pynchon's attempt to cognitively put himself in
someone else's place. But the fantasy/reality binary are inadequate
terms. Although the primary difference seems to be between the "reality" of Watts and the "fantasy" of white L.A., the article is conflicted.
As Seed and Plater ask, how does Pynchon manage to escape the "white
fantasy"—or does he (Plater 109; Seed, "Watts" 59)? It is true, as Seed
argues, that Pynchon builds up his narrative authority through the
plausibility of various rhetorical strategies, but he also draws on previous cultural valorizations of black culture as a critique of white corporate culture, such as that of Mailer and Kerouac. Foremost is its critique
of white illusions via a sometimes simplistic attitude about Watts and
black culture. He assumes there is no "mystery" to Watts, as if it were
an open book to be read easily, or as if a journey into the mind of Watts
were a simple matter.

But if the article draws on this tendency, the article also departs from
it by going further and deeper into historical and social detail. In doing
so, Pynchon's picture of reality versus unreality—despite itself—serves
to paint a picture of a larger reality in which everybody is caught.
Although black and white are opposed, several times it becomes clear
that this racial topography is also a class geography, in which Watts
locals complain about "Negroes living in better neighborhoods like to
come in under the freeway to a red-light district" (80).

In painting this wider picture, the second-person pronoun "you" is
used not only, as Seed points out, to "force" an awareness on white readers, but also to explore the ways individuals in different situational positions are enmeshed:

> The killing of Leonard Deadwyler has once again brought it all into
> sharp focus; brought back longstanding pain, reminded everybody of
> how very often the cop does approach you with his revolver ready, so that
> nothing he does with it can then really be accidental; of how, especially
> at night, everything can suddenly reduce to a matter of reflexes: your life
> trembling in the crook of a cop's finger because it is dark, and Watts, and
> the history of this place and these times makes it impossible for the cop
> to come on any different, or for you to hate him any less. Both of you are
> caught in something neither of you wants, and yet night after night, with

casualties or without, these traditional scenes continue to be played out all over the south-central part of this city. (35)

The "you" in this passage is at first the young black man of Watts and the (probably white) reader. But "these times make it impossible for the cop to come on any different, or for you to hate him any less," so both the cop ("he") and "you" are caught within a system, frame, and/or history that creates both of "you" and from which neither can escape. So then the "you" becomes both the reader, black Watts resident, and white cop, and "both of you" are caught, and "neither of you"—or, it is implied, none of you—want this situation. And yet this situation repeats itself with a mechanical inexorability that is, ironically, enacted by all its participants (and actively desired by some).

The tension in the reality/unreality opposition becomes clear at the end of the article, which ends with Watts' own "drift away from reality" toward mythmaking in several different veins. Residents remember the riots not as "chaos" but like a dance, "a coordinate and graceful drawing of cops away from the center of action, a scattering of The Man's power" (84). Others compare it to music, and Pynchon ends the essay by describing an art festival at a junior high school in the heart of Watts. This description of the "mythmaking" of the participants, despite the tensions in the essay, speaks to an awareness that race cannot be easily bifurcated into fantasy and reality, both of which are readily apparent to the "neutral" observer. The community art pieces Pynchon describes at the close of the essay gestures toward understanding the dialectical relationship between reality and fantasy for *everyone*.

If Pynchon's early novel *V.* and article aim toward a white readership, at times romanticizing black culture, they also demonstrate increased concern for cultural and political realities, particularly group structures and the reality of the individuals constituting them. Pynchon deals increasingly complexly with issues of differing realities and point-of-view, and of the relationship of "mythmaking" and "illusions" to "reality." In other words, we see Pynchon grappling with the limits of knowledge and empathy. *Gravity's Rainbow*, published seven years after "Journey Into the Mind of Watts," delves much deeper into questions raised by the article and *V.* by connecting all of them together.

One World Theory

Pynchon is famous for the vast amounts of information he incorporates, not only to provide the proper setting and props for his stories but also to delve deeper into the histories solidified in those things. *Gravity's*

Rainbow pays excruciatingly painstaking attention to dates, place-names, brand names of large assortment of products (from candy and gum to bomb parts), as well as mythologies ranging from astrology and numerology to Kabalistic and Teutonic. Weisenburger notes that some of Pynchon's main sources include Hendrik Gerhardus Luttig's *The Religious System and Social Organization of the Herero: A Study in Bantu Culture* (1933); Richard Sasuly's *IG Farben*; and Thomas G. Winner's *Oral Art and Literature of the Kazakhs of Russian Central Asia* (1958) ("Pynchon's Hereros" 37, 44). These are "well-reasoned" and "political" choices; as Weisenburger notes, "In each case we see Pynchon selecting the text which provides the most acute angle of attack on the vices of imperialism" ("Pynchon's Hereros" 44). Furthermore, in using these and other sources, he is "preternaturally alert for moments of personal testimony," often "buried in footnotes or beneath heaps of technical data and objective detail" (Weisenburger, *Companion* 8). All this information is woven into the novel's complex, multileveled narrative and historical/fictional universe. Qazi writes, "Pynchon's imaginative universe is continuous with the real historical world and this only becomes evident after the reader sees how Pynchon uses the historical version of reality to fabricate the world of his fictions" (15).

Within the inundation of information of the novel (which reflects the world), the experiences of three central characters prove parallel: Tyrone Slothrop, whose American hipster personality is satirized in his code name, "Schwarzknabe," which means "black child" (286; Madsen 285); Oberst Enzian, leader of the Zone-Hereros; and Enzian's half-brother, the Soviet agent Vaslav Tchitcherine.[15] These three are doppel-gangers from the "three worlds," each occupying and discovering the structures of which he is the intersection, facing the dispersal and partial knowledge of paranoia. Tchitcherine's girlfriend Geli Tripping initially mistakes Slothrop for the Russian (290). Slothrop wears Tchitcherine's shoes (295), and rides the same horse Tchitcherine once rode, Snake (342). Tchitcherine is obsessed with his half-brother Enzian, compiling a dossier on him (352). Like Slothrop and Enzian, Tchitcherine is paranoid about "They" (349), presumably the ones who place a copy of Tchitcherine's file on Enzian in the official dossier on Tchitcherine himself (352). All three search for The Rocket, itself a text that has to be unraveled in reading the novel. Each starts out with an ostensible mission, their subjectivity comfortably, if not happily, interpellated in ideological-political systems. But then they are bombarded with information; Pynchon uses voluminous research both to attack capitalist, imperialist, psycho-sexual, and other exploitative, repressive systems, *and* to demonstrate, inhabit, and build into the text the problem of knowledge, viewpoint, interpretation, erasure—the problems of knowing reality. This produces, for characters, readers, and perhaps even author, paranoia. Contrary to some Pynchon critics, who argue that the novel exposes paranoia about "Them" as an ideological fantasy that sustains subjectivity, I argue that paranoia, while perhaps the inevitable condition of knowledge in a world where no one can know everything, nevertheless serves as almost a pedagogical tool for these characters. That is, each starts to understand that the world as they knew it is probably not how it really works, and this starts to break down their subject roles. Technology plays a central role in their quandary: What is technology? Is it driving the bad guys, or vice versa? Who is the real culprit? Beyond the information they can gather and the connections they can make, they are not *sure* and therefore may be paranoid, but like us, at any given moment they have to act on the best knowledge that they have. Perhaps they cannot identify a *singular* They or Other, but they can recognize complex systems of power and counter-struggle. Nevertheless—this is the predicament of the characters as well as us—one has to do *something*. And if we must act, then we have to get more and better information, with no promise of resolution, and we have to be willing to leave behind the illusions, securities, and privileges to launch into the unknown. Existential freedom in such a complex, overdetermined world is frightening, but it is also where each of the characters finds themselves at the end of the novel.

The breakthrough of *Gravity's Rainbow*, in relation to the Beats, Moderns, and Pynchon's earlier works, is that *these* characters—First-, Second-, and Third-World—experience parallel unmoorings. It is not the colonized Other that makes the colonial Self realize his depravity. These previous notions are alluded to earlier in the text, but the ultimate fates of these characters, bombarded by mysterious forces and too much information, recognize their complex, flawed subjectivities in a way that the earlier works—and much postmodern theory—do not. These characters are not realist representations so much as, to invoke Ahmad, allegories for experience, or, as the text puts it, "pretexts": A "spokesman for the Counterforce" tells the *Wall Street Journal*, "We were never concerned with Slothrop *qua* Slothrop." "You mean," the interviewer asks, "that he was more a rallying-point." "No," answers the Spokesman, "not even that...Some called him a 'pretext.' Others felt that he was a genuine, point-for-point microcosm" (738). Slothrop is a pretext for the project of the novel, as all characters are, and he is also a "genuine, point-for-point microcosm" embodying all the traits

(American racism, appropriation, male libido, liberal, developmentalist, hipster, consumer, etc., on their own as well as within larger structures) that are attacked in the novel, and whose saving grace is his paranoia. If paranoia does not provide a single, unitary answer, for all three characters paranoia proves a vital tool toward something like freedom.

Tyrone Slothrop

In London 1944, Lt. Tyrone Slothrop—whose name, Salman Rushdie points out, is an anagram for "sloth or entropy" (Rushdie 356)—starts life in *Gravity's Rainbow* as *the* "Yank," the stereotypical American, a well-meaning, slovenly ne'er-do-well.[16] He works for ACHTUNG (Allied Clearing House, Technical Units, Northern Germany) inspecting bomb sites (17–18). Drawn from Pynchon's own ancestors, Slothrop's antecedents are traced to the Puritan William Slothrop, the "very first" in America, and "shit, money, and the Word, the three American truths, powering the American mobility, claimed the Slothrops, clasping them for good to the country's fate" (28). His desk is littered with the historically accurate detritus of American consumer culture, and his sexuality mysteriously corresponds to the V-2 rockets peppering London; Slothrop keeps a map of conquests, the location of each star also happens to match the location of German bombs—*before* they strike. Despite himself, Slothrop personifies the destructive tendencies of Western, masculine sexuality and colonialism; Slothrop's erection "hums from a certain distance, like an instrument installed, wired by Them into his body as a colonial outpost here in our raw and clamorous world, another office representing Their white Metropolis far away" (285).[17]

We get an empathetic picture of Slothrop who, although he really means well, fails to go beyond racist fears and appropriations of the Other. Slothrop undergoes a Sodium Amytal session to "help illuminate the racial problems in his own country" (75). Told to talk "about the Negroes, in Roxbury" (62), "upstairs in the men's room at the Roseland Ballroom" in Boston circa 1939, Slothrop drops his harmonica, his "jive accessory," into the toilet and plunges in after it (63). Stuck halfway, hearing the music downstairs, he "remembers" New York, suggesting a Beat/hipster past:

> . . . on 7th Ave., between 139th and 140th, tonight, "Yardbird" Parker is finding out how he can use the notes at the higher ends of these very chords to break up the melody into *have* mercy what is it a fucking machine gun or something man he must be out of his *mind* 32nd notes

demisemiquavers say it very (demisemiquavers) fast in a Munchkin voice if you can dig *that* coming out of Dan Wall's Chili House and down the street...(63)

The narration takes on Slothrop's point-of-view and tone, echoing the voice and attitude of Kerouacian hipsters. Slothrop's ecstasy is ironic because he is, as soon becomes apparent, an antihero.

He plunges into the toilet and away from Malcolm X/Detroit Red, "the very tall, skinny, extravagantly conked redhead Negro shoeshine boy" (64).[18] We're told:

> If Slothrop follows that harp down the toilet it'll have to be headfirst, which is not so good, cause it leaves his ass up in the air helpless, and with Negroes around that's just what a fella doesn't want, his face down in some fetid unknown darkness and brown fingers, strong and sure, all at once undoing his belt, unbuttoning his fly, strong hands holding his legs apart—and he feels the cold Lysol air on his thighs as down comes the boxer shorts too, now, with the colorful brass lures and trout flies on them. He struggles to work himself farther into the toilet hole as dimly, up through the smelly water, comes the sound of a whole dark gang of awful Negroes come yelling happily into the white men's room, converging on poor wriggling Slothrop, jiving around the way they do singing, "Slip the talcum to me, Malcolm!" And the voice that replies is who but that Red, the shoeshine boy who's slicked up Slothrop's black patents a dozen times down on his knees jes poppin' dat rag to beat the band....—this Negro whose true name now halfway down the toilet comes at last to Slothrop's hearing—as a thick finger with a gob of very slippery jelly or cream comes sliding down the crack now toward his asshole, chevroning the hairs along like topo lines up a river valley—*the true name is Malcolm*, and all the black cocks know him, Malcolm, have known him all along...(64)

Here, the "white men's room" means both the white bathroom and the room of the white man. Slothrop's racial and sexual anxiety for the Other, the "black cocks," is comically literalized into flight into excrement. The "fetid unknown darkness" of the toilet into which he is fleeing is the "dark gang of awful Negroes" that he flees. Slothrop is more than happy to be a hipster grooving on Charlie Parker, but when he is vulnerable—whether through desire or not-desiring—it becomes "*they*" are "jiving around the way they do." The exposure of appropriative hipster hypocrisy reduces Slothrop to, ironically, a moment of understanding. Slothrop has only known "the shoeshine boy" as "Red," "jes poppin' dat rag to beat the band." The description of Red echoes the caricatured language of the "blackface" minstrelsy, which is a mimicry of the clownish language that blacks have used to fool and defend themselves against whites, who have expected blacks to stay safely in their places by acting according their (whites') own stereotype of them. Slothrop finally learns by listening to the others that Red's "true name" is Malcolm—but that is, of course, *not* his real name, at least according to Malcolm X himself, because American blacks "could never know" their "true African family name" (Haley 203). The "X" replaces "the white slavemaster name of 'Little' which some blue-eyed devil named Little had imposed upon my paternal forebears" (Haley 203). The "true name" indicates both Red's real name as well as the history that makes any "real" or accurate family name impossible. While Slothrop is exposed, the invocation of the romanticized Malcolm X recalls the history creating them both.

Inside the toilet, he comes across an array of excrement identifiable by type, color, consistency, food origin, and class. Learning to read these characteristics, Slothrop becomes "shit-sensitized" (65). His descent into the defiled, besides making him a part of it, reveals it is not just monolithic but varied and characterizable. That is, perhaps the hysterical fear of transgression takes different forms. For example, identifying the shit of John F. Kennedy triggers a nostalgic romanticization: "If anybody could've saved that harp, betcha Jack could . . . for the sake of tunes to be played, millions of possible blues lines, notes to be bent from the official frequencies, bends Slothrop hasn't really the breath to do . . . not yet but someday" (65–66). The romanticization of the blues is yoked to a liberal nostalgia for Kennedy as an individual savior, the ultimate hipster, and both idealizations are mocked.[19]

Later in the novel, after taking on a number of different incarnations, including Ian Scuffling, an "English war correspondent" (256), the comic-book hero Rocketman (366), and Plechazunga, the mythological pig-hero (567), Slothrop forgets his search for the rocket and (a possibly nonexistent) Jamf, and is being "broken down and scattered" (738). The last we hear of him, literally, is his harmonica, recovered (although the Sodium Amytal session was supposedly a hallucination); he can now play the blues because he has stopped trying. The fate of Slothrop, embodying hip American individualist liberalism, is to disintegrate. Jeffrey Baker reads Slothrop's disintegration as reducing him to a counterproductive "mindlessness": "Slothrop reflects too much of the 'glozing neuter' mentality of the hippies whose brains have been 'ravaged by antisocial and mindless pleasures'" (Baker 106). In this reading, the deconstructed Slothrop's amnesiac blues harmonica-playing in the mountains recalls Leary's "tune in, turn on, drop out."

But Baker misses the sarcasm of the phrase "antisocial and mindless pleasure," which comes from the section titled "The Low-Frequency Listener," in Episode Six of Part Four. In the formally heterogeneous section of various narrative styles and discourses, including comic books, letters, travel handbooks, and scientific writing, a disintegrating Slothrop desperately attempts to reach via radio an Argentine anarchist, the revolutionary Squalidozzi he had met earlier in Part Two, Episode Seven, although "the reason why is no longer clear to him...All he knows is that finding Squalidozzi, right now, is his overriding need" (681). In control of the airwaves is Rohr, a Jehovah's witness who had been in the Ravensbrück camp, where 92,000 of its 132,000 prisoners were executed (Weisenburger, *Companion* 285–6). Slothrop hears "rumors of a War Crimes Tribunal under way in Nürnberg" (681), although "undenazified Nazis" are still running loose in "unaccounted-for submarines holding their own secret shipboards tribunals" (681). In this context, "no one Slothrop has listened to is clear who's trying whom for what, but remember that these are mostly brains ravaged by antisocial and mindless pleasures" (681).

As the bundling-together of desires for death (his own and others'), Slothrop's decomposition is presented as positive. The passage implicitly critiques postwar moral posturing while many Nazis remained free, "undenazified," both as overt racists and xenophobes *and* as members of larger multinational and governmental institutions with convenient memory lapses of their own complicities. The novel juxtaposes dissolute heterogeneity with the "society" and the "mind" of the underlying structures and connections between the "G5" and the Nazis. Slothrop's disintegration is the dissection of the various drives, interests, and narrative myths that constituted him as the "Yank," but *his* disintegration does not mean that every subject and concept must disintegrate. Moreover, the fact that everyone does not have to disintegrate does not mean that therefore everyone and -thing must be a unitary, easily explicable, and/or fixed. His uncertainty and ignorance does not mean that knowledge is not out there. And the "enemy," or governments and corporations, are both heterogeneous and structured, with connections as well as disparities.

Slothrop's disintegration takes places amidst comparisons, connections and the much-discussed notion of "correspondences" made, as well as undermined, by the text and its characters. An article by Kirkpatrick Sale, Pynchon's college friend, describes the "shadowy world of Nixon's bedfellows" (14), "the economic sovereigns of America's Southern rim" (9), a good number of whom hold high political positions (9–10), provide financial backing for Nixon (10–11), and constitute his inner circle (11–14). They are "almost a second government, an unofficial but very important nexus of power behind the acknowledged civics-textbook institution" (14), and Sale documents how the "energy crisis" was "created not so much by diminishing supplies as by the oil interests, both those with international ties who wanted to increase shipments from abroad and domestic producers along the Southern rim" (15). In the same way, *Gravity's Rainbow* makes links for World War II, but mixes historically documented phenomena with fictional, or paranoid, ones. The fictional links are of two kinds: First, some are surmised connections between historical figures and entities, constituting charges of collusion, corruption, et cetera. Second, are conjured products, companies, events, et cetera, that link the corporations into the narrative(s) of the novel, particularly the sexual, psychoanalytic threads.

An example of the first kind is found when the paranoid Slothrop realizes that the Nazis used "Royal Dutch Shell headquarters *building*, at the Josef Israelplain [a city street].... for a radio *guidance* transmitter" (241; Weisenburger, *Companion* 127). That is, a German radar-guidance tower was located above the Royal Dutch Shell building in The Hague (240; Weisenburger, *Companion* 134). Slothrop asks an employee of Shell, "doesn't it strike you as just a bit odd, you Shell chaps working on *your* liquid engine *your* side of the Channel you know, and *their* chaps firing *their* bloody things at you with your own... blasted... Shell trans*mit*ter tower" (241). Captain Bounce, "a 110% company man" (240), is unfazed: "No, I can't see that it makes—what are you getting at?" (241). He reassures Slothrop, "It's only a 'wild coincidence'" (241). Shell Oil, an entity "with no real country, no side in any war, no specific face or heritage" (243), is indicted not for being a "traitor" to one side or another, but for being part of the larger, indiscriminating systems that profit from the war. Slothrop, after various misadventures on the trail of the V-2, realizes that "all the rocket intelligence is being *gathered*—into the office of who but Mr. Duncan Sandys, Churchill's own son-in-law, who works out of the Ministry of Supply located where but at Shell Mex *House, for Christ sake*..." (251). Sandys, husband of Winston Churchill's daughter, was parliamentary secretary to the Ministry of Supply and headed Britain's intelligence-gathering work on German V-weapons program, and he did work out of the Shell Mex House (Weisenburger, *Companion* 121). As Weisenburger points out, all this information is accurate, but the implication of cooperation with Germans is Pynchon's invention.

An example of the second kind of paranoid link is found in the novel's use of the actual chemical company IG Farben, the novel's biggest corporate culprit, coming to stand, in both the novel and subsequent criticism, for impersonal corporate greed and corruption. IG Farben was "Germany's largest industrial cartel during the thirties and, with the Krupp firm, a kingpin of the German rearmament program," with well-documented ties to the OKW (German Army High Command) as well as Shell Oil and DuPont (Weisenburger, *Companion* 48). IG Farben manufactured Zyclone-B, the gas that was used to murder millions in the concentration camps. In the novel, IG Farben is the producer of the fictional plastic Imopolex G, a "new plastic" that combines "good strength with a low power-loss factor" (249), and the rocket with which it is made, the Rocket 00000. The text recounts IG Farben's close ties to DuPont, including IG Farben's subsidiaries American IG Company and Winthrop Chemicals (249; Weisenburger, *Companion* 133), as well as its role in the operation of the German, Hugo Stinnes, who managed "to put the horizontal electrical trust of Siemens-Schuchert together with the coal and iron supplies of the Rheinelbe Union into a super-cartel that was both horizontal and vertical, and to buy into just about everything else—shipyards, steamship lines, hotels, restaurants, forests, pulp mills, newspapers," while also "speculating in currency, buying foreign money with marks borrowed from the Reichsbank, driving the mark down and then paying off the loans at a fraction of the original figure" (284). Stinnes "more than any one financier...was blamed for the Inflation" of 1921–25, which he supposedly engineered to negate stiff reparation payments decreed by Treaty of Versailles (284–5; Weisenburger, *Companion* 151). Stinnes' "foreign connections went all over the world—Brazil, the East Indies, the United States" (285), and Dr. Jamf negotiates contracts "for supplying tons of private currency known as Notgeld to Stinnes and colleagues" (285); Jamf is fictional, but the Stinnes' actions were real. The *Notgeld* was the secret currency Horace Greeley Hjalmar Schacht, the head of the Reichsbank known as "Hitler's banker," provided to German manufacturers for transactions among themselves (Weisenburger, *Companion* 151–2). Weisenburger also notes that Schacht "arranged massive donations of cash that sealed Nazi party victories in the crucial elections of 1933" (*Companion* 152). Slothrop discovers that some of the banknotes were contracted to "a certain Massachusetts paper mill" named "the Slothrop Paper Company" (285). In discovering these connections, Slothrop also discovers that he was the experiment in the "Schwarzknabe project" run by IG Farben and

Dr. Jamf, in which "T.S." was sold out by his father (for, among other things, tuition for Harvard).

So although Slothrop realizes he cannot necessarily finally understand what is driving Them—technology, sexual desire, money, power—he does start to understand the flexibility of power; the possibilities and realities of connections, conspiracies, and complicities; and the necessity of some kind of resistance. Slothrop's paranoia is both trustworthy, revealing vital information, as well as destabilized—meaning that it is fallible. Also, he acts despite partial knowledge; "glozing neuter" is not an answer. The last significant act of Slothrop is to warn the Schwarzkommando that Major Marvy is going to raid them (562). This last gesture suggests the beginning of translation of new knowledge—produced in part by paranoia and in part by more accurate understandings of the world—into meaningful action.

Oberst Enzian

As with the Beats and moderns, in *Gravity's Rainbow* the Zone-Hereros are not real initially. The first mention of the Zone-Hereros suggests they are not real and/or are peripheral to the main action. The Schwarzkommando are the subject of a film shot at the White Visitation, featuring various operatives in "plausible blackface," "all playing the rocketeers of the fictional Schwarzkommando" (112–3). When Slothrop first hears of this, he reacts, *"Black rocket troops? What bizarre shit?"* (288). By the same token, in the first two parts of the novel, the character Enzian himself appears only in the thoughts of Lt. Weissman, in a flashback about his "Herero aide," the phrase "...mba rara m'eroto ondyoze...mbe mu munine m'oruroto ayo u n'omuinyo..." left untranslated in the text (152). Most readers experience, at least provisionally, Mondaugen's experience riding behind the Bondel in the final scene of *V.*; most readers will not understand this "song."[20]

But at the beginning of Part Three, "In the Zone," we learn that they are not *somewhere else*, they are *here*, literally and figuratively. On a train, Slothrop runs into the racist Major Marvy, who explains the Herero presence in Europe: "the black cadres had no more future in Africa, stayed on in Germany as governments-in-exile without even official recognition, drifted somehow into the ordnance branch of the German Army, and pretty soon learned how to be rocket technicians...if they're getting' together now, oh dat's *bi-i-i-g* trouble!...A-and they're *headin'* for *Nordhausen*, pal!" (287–8). Marvy is then thrown off the train by Oberst Enzian, "a tall African with a full imperial beard" (288). Enzian introduces himself as a member of the Schwarzkommando and tells Slothrop, "There's no story. We're DPs, like everybody else" (288). After "sixty percent of the Herero people had been exterminated" by von Trotha, as described in *V.* (323), some had been brought by early missionaries and soldiers as "specimens of a possibly doomed race," converts, and servants, while others are brought as part of a Nazi scheme to set up black juntas to take over British and French colonies, and "they are people now, Zone-Hereros, in exile for two generations from South-West Africa" (315). They "grew up into a white-occupied world. Captivity, sudden death, one-way departures were the ordinary things of every day" (323), and now they too search for the Rocket 00000, reportedly at Nordhausen. While Africans were once kept in line— "often with death"—and safely at a distance, a generation has gone by and "now the Herero lives in his stepfather's house" (74).[21]

If the Zone-Hereros are a people, then Enzian is their leader, and they are on a mission to find the Rocket. Enzian shares with other characters the fascination with the Rocket, the violence of Western sexuality, and Weissman/Blicero, the white patriarch of this violence, who decoded the 'sferics message in *V.* and "not only coordinated the S-Gerät [V-2] project at Nordhausen, but also commanded the battery that fired Rocket 00000" (563). Weissman, of all the characters, sums up the colonizer's corruption in far-away lands as depicted in *V.* Like Katje, Enzian was Weissman's former aide/lover of Weissman/Blicero, who "gave his African boy the name 'Enzian,' after Rilke's mountainside gentian of Nordic colors" (101). He used to call Weissman "Omuhona," or "lord, master" (101; Seed, "Herero" 37). If von Trotha was Red Death, Weissman is White Death, the colonial stepfather desiring and inculcating desire in the destructive power of the bomb.

But divisions, differences, and the impossibility of homogeneity within this group arise instantly and abundantly. Enzian is known as "Otyikondo, the Half-breed" because his father is European, a Russian; Tchitcherine is his half-brother (316). He is not unique in this; among the Zone-Hereros, "there's German, Slavic and Gypsy blood mixed in by now too" (316).[22] Furthermore, a faction of the Zone-Hereros has embarked on race-suicide, opting "for sterility and death" as "a political struggle" (316). This struggle takes place within the group and within and between each individual, the "public" political struggle shaping "private" sexualities.

> They call themselves Otukungurua. Yes, old Africa hands, it *ought* to be "Omakungurua," but they are always careful—perhaps it's less healthy

than care—to point out that *oma-* applies only to the living and human. *Otu-* is for the inanimate and the rising, and this is how they imagine themselves. Revolutionaries of the Zero, they mean to carry on what began among the old Hereros after the 1904 rebellion failed. They want a negative birth rate. The program is racial suicide. They would finish the extermination the Germans began in 1904. (316–7)

"Kungurua" means "emptied out" (Seed, "Herero" 38), so "otukungu-rua" means inanimate, nonliving "Empty Ones," as they are known. As living beings, they *should* use the oma- suffix, but they choose the inanimate. This indicates that, trying to return to the "origins" of the 1904 Hereros, they choose to be inanimate, nonhuman human beings carrying out the colonizer's process of literal and cultural genocide: "It was a simple choice for the Hereros, between two kinds of death: tribal death, or Christian death. Tribal death made sense. Christian death made none at all" (318).

The Europeans do not recognize their own violence returning to them as the *rejection* of their form of death, in favor of a self-appointed, "freely" chosen form of death. This idea of race suicide comes from W.P. Steenkamp's 1935 pamphlet, *Is the South-West African Herero Committing Race Suicide?* Steenkamp is one of the "rational men of medicine" (317), who, as Pynchon writes in his 1969 letter to Hirsch,

> ...attempts to explain the declining birth-rate among the Hereros with numbers like overpopulation and Vitamin E deficiency, and to discount the notion, apparently widely-held at the time, that the Hereros were deliberately trying to exterminate themselves. But I find that perfectly plausible, maybe not as a conscious conspiracy, but in terms of how a perhaps not completely Westernized people might respond. They had no concept of property in the European sense before the missionaries came, they felt themselves integrated into everything, like mystics in deep trances or people up on acid; their cattle had souls, the same souls as their own and possible part of a universal soul, though you'd better check that out. But they had no hangups sacrificing cattle, it was part of a universal scheme, and so it's doubtful if they'd have any hangups sacrificing themselves either, given a unified concept of creation, which shows up in religions all around the world, Christianity being a glaring exception. And German Christianity being perhaps the most perfect expression of the whole Western/analytic/"linear"/alienated shtick. (qtd. in Seed, *Fictional Labyrinths* 242)

The imperialists, such as Steenkamp, see only mystery, "natural forces," and raw data, when they are actually seeing the results of their own actions on others. In the letter, reflecting his earlier form of multicul-turalism relativism, Pynchon casts racial suicide as simply a morally neutral, radically different conception of the world. In other words, here the Other is simply Other.

In *Gravity's Rainbow*, however, the Zone-Herero are shown at war with one another over the notion of race-suicide. Enzian, the focalizer with whom we are encouraged to identify, believes that it is a result of *adopting*, rather than rejecting, the colonizers' logic. Pynchon attempts to imagine the struggle of the real ex-colonized in the fictional-yet-literalized struggle among the Zone-Hereros. Enzian and his faction try to prevent the Otukungurua, who "visit" Herero couples who plan to keep their children, coercing abortions. They "have learned their vulturehood from the Christian missionaries" (519). The Empty Ones believe they will find "the Center again, the Center without time, the journey without hysteresis, where every departure is a return to the same place, the only place" (319).[23] The Empty Ones participate in the *process* begun by the colonists, while Enzian and the other Zone Hereros try to react against this antihuman process. The racial suicide program of the Empty Ones is a nihilistic resistance because, in the Zone, searching for the Rocket, Enzian feels that "the mythical return" is impossible, fleeing them as circumstances and possibilities change (519).

And this struggle does not take place only on the "public" plane: it takes place "mostly in silence, in the night, in the nauseas and cramp-ings of pregnancies or miscarriages" (316). Instead of "political strug-gle" (316), "there is no outright struggle for power. It is all seduction and counterseduction, advertising and pornography, and the history of the Zone-Hereros is being decided in bed" (318). Although the lack of open political struggle troubles Enzian (316), it is not in fact all "adver-tising and pornography." Violence undergirds the Empty Ones cam-paign, both immediate violence and the continually resurrected violence of the colonial past. The sister of one of Enzian's lieutenants, ironically named Christian, is pregnant and plans to have the child. When Enzian and the Zone-Hereros break into the basement room of Maria and her husband, Pavel, they find only "the brown ellipse her blood made on the torn ticking" and "washing-blue in grainy splashes in the corners, under the bed" (518-9). "Washing-blue" further connects the struggle to the history within and beyond the novel; it is one of the dyestuffs manufac-tured by IG Farben and a toxin that Steenkamp records was used by Herero women as an abortifacient after the arrival of Europeans (Weisenburger, *Companion* 227).

In these ways, rather than a inscrutable, homogenous, one-dimensional, faraway Other, the Zone-Herero are depicted as variously complex, conflicted, complicit, and confused. This, I contend, is a much more "respectful" approach to the Other than the "Africanism" alluded to earlier. As Žižek writes, "one sign of respect is that you can insult the Other" ("One Measure"). If not precisely insulting, such complex realism militates against the sublime racial Other of Pynchon's modernist and Beat predecessors. But the text does not stop at depicting the Zone-Herero as a discrete, separate group from everyone else. Like Slothrop, Enzian starts to question his mission, his role, his interpellation, and this manifests as paranoia.

During their search for Maria (part of their conflict with the Empty Ones) as well as the Rocket, Enzian and company ride through the Jamf Ölfabriken Werke AG factory, which is supposed to be shut down. They find it not in ruins but "*in perfect working order*" (520). The IG Farben subsidiary factory is a sign of what Weisenburger calls "transnational economic interests (cartels) just waiting to leap back into operation" (*Companion* 227). Seeing this, Enzian is flooded with "an extraordinary understanding" that undermines his sense of certainty and fills him with paranoia (520). They had assumed they were to be "the scholar-magicians of the Zone," "with somewhere in it a Text, to be picked to pieces, annotated, explicated, and masturbated till it's all squeezed limp of its last drop...well we assumed—natürlich!—that this holy Text had to be the Rocket" (520). Instead, he realizes that "the real Text" may be "somewhere else" (520). Enzian sees the factory and thinks, "if I'm riding through it, the Real Text, right now," or if he passed it "somewhere in the devastation of Hamburg" (520),

> ...if what the IG built on this site were not at *all* the final shape of it, but only an arrangement of fetishes, come-ons to call down special tools in the form of 8th AF bombers *yes* the "Allied" planes all would have been, ultimately, IG-bombing, by way of Director Krupp, through his English interlocks—the bombing was the exact industrial process of conversion, each release of energy placed exactly in space and time, each shockwave plotted in advance to bring *precisely tonight's wreck* into being thus decoding the Text, thus coding, recoding, redecoding the holy Text...If it is in working order, what is it meant to do? (520–1)

He realizes, "It means the War was never political at all, the politics was all theatre, all just to keep the people distracted" (521).

Here, his paranoia takes the form of "blaming" Technology, or wondering if it is the driving force, a tendency that some Pynchon critics have shared. He wonders if the war was "being dictated instead by the needs of technology...by a conspiracy between human beings and techniques, by something that needed the energy-burst of war" (521). The war cry was "Money be damned, the very life of [insert name of Nation] is at stake," but that meant "*dawn is nearly here, I need by night's blood, my funding, funding, ahh more, more*" (521). The "real crises," then, "were crises of allocation and priority, not among firms—it was only staged to look that way—but among the different Technologies, Plastics, Electronics, Aircraft, and their needs which are understood only by the ruling elite" (521). Enzian realizes that the "real Text" may not even be the multinational corporations but the demands of technologies. But again, the internal and external conflict problematizes any easy answer: the argument arises in his head, often repeated—albeit dogmatically—by "the younger Schwarzkommando," that there would be no Rocket unless "some specific somebody with a name and a penis hadn't *wanted* to chuck a ton of Amatol 300 miles and blow up a block full of civilians" (521). This internal voice argues, "Capitalize the T on technology, deify it if it'll make you feel less responsible—but it puts you with the neutered, brother" (521). Enzian is reminded, through the voice of the younger Herero, that a "ruling elite," a "somebody with a name and a penis" puts the responsibility and agency ultimately back in human hands.

Instead, Enzian realizes, "we have to look for power sources here, and distribution networks we were never taught, routes of power our teachers never imagined, or were encouraged to avoid" (521). It will be necessary "to find meters whose scales are unknown in the world, draw our own schematics, getting feedback, making connections, reducing the error, trying to learn the real function.... zeroing in on what incalculable plot?" (521). The Jamf Ölfabriken Werke waits "for its Kabbalists and new alchemists to discover the Key, teach the mysteries to others," but Enzian realizes that the "key" could easily be one of many other "ruins" in other cities or countries (521), waiting to spring invisibly back into dehumanizing action. The sheer multitude puts him right over the edge: "YAAAGGGGHHHHH!" (521).

Certainty about the passage is undercut by the revelation that this is "stimulant talk," because Enzian has been "stuffing down Nazi surplus Pervitins these days like popcorn" (521–2). He moves on "into some other paranoid terror, talking, talking, though each man's wind and motor cuts him off from conversation" (522). But we hear some of this "paranoid terror":

> Enzian can project himself back in the Erdschweinhöhle starting a new file on the IG—see it getting fatter and fatter as the interlocks develop, the books are audited, the witnesses come—not forward but sideways at least, always in shadows...And if it should prove not to be the Rocket, not the IG? Why then he'll have to go on won't he, on to something else—the Volkswagen factory, the pharmaceutical companies...and if it isn't even Germany then he'll have to start in America, or in Russia, and if he dies before they find the True Text to study, then there'll have to be machinery for others to carry it on...Say, that's a swell idea—call the whole Erschweinhöhle together, get up there say, *My people, I have had a vision*...no no but there *will* need to be more staff, if it's to be that big a search, quiet shifting of resources away from the Rocket, diversifying while making it look like an organic growth....if the Schwarzkommando mission in the Zone has been truly revealed just now, then there'll have to be something down about Ombindi, the Empty Ones, doctrine of the Final Zero. More staff will mean more Zone-Hereros, not fewer—more information coming in about the enemy, more connections made will mean a greater threat to the people, will mean the tribal numbers will have to increase. Is there an alternative? no...he would rather ignore Ombindi but the needs of this new Search will not allow him that comfort now...the search will rule...(525)

The line "I have had a vision" plays on Martin Luther King, Jr.'s, famous words, but "vision" also refers to Enzian's drug trip. He rejects both liberal, individualist leadership and drugged-out neuter, deciding that the future course will require *more* people to research the "True Text" of the structures of power, and therefore he will have to deal with the Empty Ones. The emphasis is placed on the search but without certainty about the object of that search, in large part because those objects and texts, while identifiable, never remain fixed in the constant flow of human activity.

Vaslav Tchitcherine

In the first episode of Part Three, we meet Vaslav Tchitcherine, a Soviet intelligence officer, "another rocket maniac" (290). Like Slothrop and Enzian, when we first meet him, he is a somewhat willing cog in corporate, cultural, and psychic systems of which he is only dimly away. He has professional and personal missions. A member of the Soviet army,

he has been assigned to a branch of the Soviet army engaged in imposing languages across the Soviet empire. He has been given this unpopu-
lar job—journeying to the farthest-flung outposts of the Soviet
empire—because of his personal obsession with finding his half-brother,
Enzian; the "Weird Letter Assignments" are given only to "ne'er-do-
wells like himself" (352). He thus becomes an agent of the "New Turkish
Alphabet" (339), although "there is strong native resistance in Central
Asia these days to anything suggesting Russification, and that goes even
for the look of a printed language" (354).

Imperialism, here, takes place on an axis apart from the First World
or the West of Europe and the United States. In "the early Stalin days,"
Tchitcherine is stationed in Russian Kirghizistan, "to give the tribes-
men out here, this far out, an alphabet: it was purely speech, gesture,
touch among them, not even an Arabic script to replace" (338). By 1881,
Russia controlled Central Asia by means of the abolition of conquered
national cultures and a systematic policy of Russification; Russian colonists settled among local populations; traditional forms of government,
such as tribal sultans, were replaced with Russian military and civilian
administrators; and Kazakh courts were replaced with Russian courts
(Winner xiii, xiv). Furthermore, the very nations themselves were rear-
ranged, and "the political and national unity of the conquered peoples
was disorientated by a new arrangement of the border lines and political
zoning which cut through the old national lines" (Winner xiv).
Tchitcherine, the colonial bureaucrat, hates the place, as foreign to him
as South-West Africa is to Foppl. He curses "Army, Party, History—
whatever has put him here" (339). He is assisted by a "traveling 'native'
schoolteacher Dzaqyp Qulan" (339–40), "an Educated Native Speaker"
whose father was killed during the 1916 massacres of Kirghiz by Russian
settlers (340). The uprising is attributed by the Soviets to "Western
paranoia," "the doing of foreigners, an international conspiracy" perpe-
trated by German and Turkish agents. After all, "How could there be
Kazakh, Kirghiz—Eastern—reasons? Hadn't the nationalities been
happy? Hadn't fifty years of Russian rule brought progress? enrich-
ment?" (340).[24]

Tchitcherine shares not only a "search" with Enzian and Slothrop,
but he also experiences paranoia about Them. Seeing Slothrop disguised
as a Soviet agent talking to Major Marvy, he thinks "who's the mysterious Soviet intelligence agent...? Paranoia for you here, Tchitcherine.
Maybe Moscow's been tipped to your vendetta" (564). This paranoia
turns out to be justified, because later we learn Tchitcherine's vendetta
is indeed noted by the Soviet bureaucracy.

Listening to Major Marvy blather on about I.G. Farben, Tchitcherine, like Enzian, has a moment of paranoia-induced clarity. He sees a "very large white Finger, addressing him," "calling Tchitcherine's attention to—"

> *A Rocket-cartel.* A structure cutting across every agency human and paper that ever touched it. Even to Russia . . . Russia bought from Krupp, didn't she, from Siemens, the IG . . .
>
> Are there arrangements Stalin won't admit . . . doesn't even *know about*? Oh, a State begins to take form in the stateless German night, a State that spans oceans and surface politics, sovereign as the International or the Church of Rome, and the Rocket is its soul. IG Raketen. Circus-bright, poster reds and yellows, rings beyond counting, all going at once . . . Tchitcherine is certain. Not so much on outward evidence he has found moving through the Zone as out of a personal doom he carries with him—always to be held at the edges of revelations . . . He will never get further than the edge of this meta-cartel which has made itself known tonight, this Rocket-state whose borders he cannot cross . . .
>
> Sadly, most sadly, everyone else seems to be in on it. Every scavenger out here is in IG Raketen's employ. All except for himself, and Enzian. His brother, Enzian. No wonder They're after the Schwarzkommando . . . And when They find out I'm not what They think . . . (566)

Tchitcherine realizes that he is not simply a Soviet bureaucrat or a Marxist revolutionary, but a bureaucratic cog in multiple explicit and unacknowledged systems. Then he too begins to panic.

In a flashback, Tchitcherine remembers shooting up with his colleague Wimpe, and a conversation about "political narcotics. Opiates of the people" (701). Wimpe replies, "Marxist dialectics? That's *not* an opiate, eh?" (701). "It's the antidote," replies Tchitcherine, whereas Wimpe replies that it "can go either way" (701). If "the basic problem . . . has always been getting other people to die for you," religion worked for a while, but "even since it became impossible to die for death, we have had a secular version—yours. Die to help History grow to its predestined shape. Die knowing your act will bring a good end a bit closer" (701). This conversation recalls Simone de Beauvoir's observation that ossified forms of Marxism and psychoanalysis have become religions just as much as Christianity (34). Tchitcherine and Wimpe shoot up "theophosphate"—not "*thio*phosphate," meaning "*indicating the presence of sulfur*," but "*theo*phosphate," which, Wimpe tells him, means "*indicating the Presence of God*" (702). The dream of an all-powerful or singular key to being and history is seductive but ultimately illusory and hallucinatory. Tchitcherine realizes that *"everything is connected"* (703)—that there are patterns—but that a singular explanation for everything may not exist. Paranoia is what leads Tchitcherine to relinquish unicity (of the Party, of his single-minded search for Enzian) and become receptive to other possible connections and patterns.

Chasing Enzian in the Zone, paranoid by his growing awareness, Tchitcherine is reassigned to Central Asia again, and he realizes that this is, "operationally, to die" (706). Therefore Tchitcherine, too, goes AWOL, and his final meeting with Enzian is anticlimactic but significant. Geli, whom Slothrop calls a witch, puts a spell on Tchitcherine so that when he finally meets Enzian, they do not recognize one another: "Enzian on his motorcycle stops for a moment, mba-kayere, to talk to the scarred unshaven white . . . They talk broken German. Tchitcherine manages to hustle half a pack of American cigarettes and three raw potatoes. The two men nod, not quite formally, not quite smiling. Enzian puts his bike in gear and returns to his journey. Tchitcherine lights a cigarette, watching them down the road, shivering in the dusk" (734–5). "Mba-kayere" means "I am passed over" (Seed, "Herero" 39). We are told, "This is magic. Sure—but not necessarily fantasy. Certainly not the first time a man has passed his brother by, at the edge of the evening, often forever, without knowing it" (735). This act of human reciprocity is able to happen because, for the time being, they are both "preterite," or "passed over." Paranoia leads Enzian and Tchitcherine to question how their social fields are defined by a hegemonic discourse, and they become involved in and create other networks and projects that may constitute more hopeful alternatives. What neither of them does is disappear off into the sunset as opaque signifiers of otherness.

Paul Bové writes, "Pynchon's creation of the Zone Commandos perfectly dramatizes a profound analytic and imaginative sympathy for human beings entangled in the midst of human history" (673). I agree with his readings not only of the Zone-Herero but also of Slothrop and Tchitcherine—indeed, most of the hundreds of characters in *Gravity's Rainbow*. Pynchon's treatment of these three particular characters in what we think of as "three worlds" resonate with Aijaz Ahmad's argument *against* such divisions. As Ahmad says, the axes of struggle cannot be contained along nationalist lines or the Three World Theory; rather, power and resistance are ubiquitous and cut across all the various kinds of groups that we understand. To this end, *Gravity's Rainbow*, like *Dictee*, explores both differences and parallels of particular situations, rather than privilege an abstract logic.

If the "sublime" of postmodern literature invokes both closure and the impossibility of closure (of narrative, of signification, of the subject, of groups), then while critics have emphasized the latter (nonclosure), I want to draw our attention equally to not necessarily "closure" but the processes and structures that *Gravity's Rainbow* demonstrates at work in the world, in different ways yet still united and connected. So, for example, the Other can be imagined as complex, just like any other person; the subject-in-process can be paranoid and unsure, yet still have some knowledge and agency. In fact, I think that is what most of our lives are like. Furthermore, *Gravity's Rainbow*, certainly compared to Pynchon's earlier work and that of his literary influences, engages and respects "the Other" enough to take such an ambivalent and problematic notion as "race-suicide" seriously. He presents a debate *among* the community. Not that this should be any kind of final word; rather, the literary imagination can try to move beyond the romanticization, appropriation, and simplification of the Other that Pynchon inherited from the Beats and the Moderns. Also, we may note, this moves beyond the postmodernist stopping at the limit, giving in to the unknowability of the "sublime" and thereby allowing liberal multiculturalism and its problematic bases to continue.

Gravity's Rainbow cannot adequately represent the three worlds; my point is that no one can. It is Enzian's *nonrepresentativeness* that breaks through previous depictions of the Other in Pynchon's antecedents and in his own earlier work. The novel's renderings of the multiple experiences of otherness and paranoia are more sophisticated, complex, and realistic than postmodernists' awed surrender to the sublime. As Masao Miyoshi writes, "The border between beings must remain passable at least in the imagining" (46). That readers may expect and/or look for representativeness—or *not* expect it—speaks more to our reading practices and our problematic understandings of race, culture, and literature.

CHAPTER FOUR

Analyzing the Real: Bessie Head's Literary Psychosis

And I was later, much later, to discover with the poets and the novelists that the dialectic was not just a tool but a felt sensibility.

—A. Sivanandan

South African/Botswanan writer Bessie Head's 1974 novel *A Question of Power* has challenged literary critics in all kinds of ways. Readings of the novel tend to focus on either the realistic sections of the novel, which deal with self-sufficiency, economic development, community and inter-/intra-ethnic conflict endemic to the postindependence, neoimperial condition of late-twentieth-century decolonized nations; *or* the modernist/postmodernist nonrealist hallucinatory and "fantastic" sections, with particular emphasis on psychoanalytic readings. My reading joins the "real" and the "unreal" strata of the novel to argue that they are in fact inextricably interwoven and mutually determinate in the novel's complex analysis and argument of the condition of the subject in and of the modern world. The novel's principle specters—Sello, Dan, and Medusa—are not merely manifestations of the narrator's individual psychosis or her helpless responses to the ideologies oppressing her. Rather, the novel constitutes a complex exploration of the processes of power (economic, political, cultural, social, sexual) that help form both the subject and the social field in intimate and overdetermined ways. Reading the novel as *both* a political-cultural social analysis as well as a journey into the phantasms of the unconscious of the subject—both "real" processes—provides wider insight toward less Euro-centric, more globally informed psychoanalysis (understanding of the subject in general) in postcolonial, late capitalist postmodernity.

As in *Dictee* and *Gravity's Rainbow*, in *A Question of Power,* power does not simply manifest in one hegemonic interpellation or narrative, such as a singular Western, patriarchal, linear power structure. Rather, contending structural pressures war over the interpretation of particular moments. In other words, ideological struggle does not simply take the form of a proliferation of differences against an ideological unity, but rather takes place through contending historical formations, structures, and discourses that are flexible, overdetermined, and yet to some extent identifiable. Interpellation—or rather, interpellations—can be partial, conflicting, and inconsistent, yet to some extent their origins in or service to a particular historical structure or system can be delineated. As in *Gravity's Rainbow*, the Other or the sublime do not actually remain unknown, but in *Question of Power*, rather than the paralleling of apparently disparate situations, there is a dissection of the multiple forces at work in one particular situation, particularly the overdetermined historical process of modernization and its concomitant demands on subjectivity, desire, and culture. Such processes can never be simple or static, so *A Question of Power* stages itself in terms so overdetermined and complex that readers have tended to approach the novel as the manifestation of the sublime, or the overwhelming unknown, of madness, gender, race, or general Otherness. Part of my argument is that the novel has also been chronically underread due to latent racism and sexism.

Head's difficult novel has resisted readings, particularly political analyses, not only due to its extreme experimental style but also, I would add, due to the very complexity of its subject matter. Craig MacKenzie concludes that the disconnection between "reality" and "Elizabeth's nightmares" must arise from authorial "confusion" (31, 33). Because she achieved fame for being "almost solely responsible for the inward turning of the African novel" (Garrett 122), some critics assume that Head must be "generally hostile to politics" (Nkosi 102). Others point out that this definition of "politics" is too narrow. Political readings of the novel have examined the novel's unblinking depiction of "the postnationalistic stage" of the splintering of groups formerly united by anticolonial struggles (Matsikidze); the parallel between the cultural oppression of the individual and the political oppression of the state (Lorenz); and the ability to overcome alienation and social contradictions through the processes of politicization and work (see Guerts, Johnson, Ogungbesan, and Ogwude).

Some critics interested in political readings have chosen instead to focus on Head's early and later novels, seeing the realism in content and form as more engaged with social issues. Garrett argues that *Maru* uses pastoral and Utopian elements alongside realism to resolve symbolically "the real underlying contradiction between fundamentally different social and political organizations" (131). Eilersen reads *Bewitched Crossroad* as Head's "most political" novel, and Clayton adds *BC* is the "fullest statement of her critique of South African history and society" (55). Her early novels and later works, including *The Cardinals* (1960–62), *When Rain Clouds Gather* (1969), *Maru* (1971), *The Collector of Treasures* (1977), *Serowe: Village of the Rain Wind* (1981), and *A Bewitched Crossroad* (1984), utilize "realism" in different senses: the early novels use literary realism, while the later works are a combination of historical and sociological research, interviews with local people, and literary realism.

The Cardinals, *When Rain Clouds Gather*, and *Maru*, try to resolve the clash between modernization and traditional cultural patterns by developing a type of character whose superior ability and morality is so evident that everyone gives way to him/her. Obstacles, whether people or things, literally drop down before this moral figure, and a small ideal community is forged in a pastoral setting. This moral sovereign takes many shapes and forms and is surrounded by two different types of characters. Some characters are good but are weaker, due to some deficiency, and simply become followers of the central character. Meanwhile, other characters are morally reprehensible never have a chance, simply fading away. The morally superior protagonist is almost always of an extremely "lowly" background and has surmounted great odds to survive. In these early works, Head's breathless writing style is evident, but the narratives for the most part follow conventions of realism. These novels fulfill a writerly and readerly desire to have clearly defined oppositions between good and evil through definite points of view and characters whose role, if complex on the social plane, are inwardly simplistic.

The later, outward-looking or more overtly political novels tend to focus on the moral exemplars in the form of "great men," and again "evil" is clearly demarcated. While Head emphasizes interviews with villagers in *Serowe* and focuses on the oppression of women in the short stories in *Collector*, these tales of the "common people" are the landscape of the social body beset by problems that call out for a "great leader." Three leaders determine the fate of the people of Serowe in three phases of political-economic-social development: 1) Khama the Great, 2) Tshekedi Khama, and 3) Patrick van Rensburg (Clayton 60; Eilersen, *Bessie Head* 162). They represent "the three stages of the development of education in village history: the missionaries' education of a few children sitting out under a tree; the establishment of village schools making primary education available to all; the introduction of secondary and vocational education" (Eilersen, *Bessie Head* 158). The short stories in *Collector* are the most pointed in their critique of the situation of women, although "she does recognise the fact that the three stages through which rural African society has passed during the last hundred years have in part been responsible for the shaping of most male attitudes" (Eilersen, *Bessie Head* 168). *Bewitched Crossroads*, although apparently romanticizing the past, shows the history of Botswana to be anything but "pure" or simple. As Head notes, Botswana is a mix of many things, and her work shows that Khama was simply savvy enough to manipulate existing institutions in favor of his people. The critiques she makes and the information and beauty she captures in these three latter works are valuable, but, again, her emphasis on "great man" or even "great soul" ideology cripples the analytical power of these novels. I believe, therefore, that the insights of *A Question of Power*, although more abstract, are also more dialectical and deep.

A Question of Power poses particular difficulties because it exceeds the paradigms of otherness postmodernism. Particularly in reading the nonrealistic parts of the novel, many critics have deployed strategies I identify with otherness postmodernism. Rose, Hogan, and Coundouriotis argue, variously, that the novel rejects universalizing and totalizing claims about the subject, truth, and power. Pearse reads Elizabeth, Dan, and Sello as, respectively, the conscious self, the subconscious, and the unconscious, but concludes that the novel's ending is "escapist" because these various polarities remain unresolved (81, 92). In "Bessie Head's Syncretic Fiction," Linda Susan Beard synthesizes all these elements into what she identifies as three "dominant voices" in Head's work that emphasize paradox, simultaneity, and heterogeneity as the best means of achieving genuine comprehensiveness and wholeness. Likewise, Kapstein characterizes Head's use of madness in the novel as "disruptions of reality, perception, and orientation," a kind of transgressive "radical rhetorical strategy" (96, 72). But rather than adhere to any single axis of oppression or identification, the novel attempts to take the full complexity of existence into account at once. Roger Berger notes the relevance of Fanon's insight into the colonial encounter for *A Question of Power* (32), but Elizabeth's anxieties are not only racial, but also gendered, sexual, moral, religious, economic, et cetera. Coreen Brown warns against reductive readings by only race or gender (91–92). Balseiro writes, "like the emergent South African nation,

Bessie Head offers a tempting terrain crossed by races, by languages, and by opposing ideologies" (21), but as Cancel points out, Head is also writing about her adopted country of Botswana and the village in which she lived (194).

Likewise, critics have wanted to focus on Elizabeth's/Head's madness as a form of autobiography. The issue of autobiography has been a vexed one. Head herself wrote that her 1974 novel *A Question of Power* was "a completely autobiographical novel taking a slice of my life, my experience, and transcribing it verbatim into novel form. It was maybe the way in which I interpreted experience... It was the type of experience that needed interpretation and analysis" (Beard, "Bessie Head" 45). But as she suggests, even simply "transcribing" what happens involves a process of analysis and interpretation. Furthermore, my contention is that the complexity of Head's work arises from artistry, not neurosis. The essays in *Emerging Perspectives on Bessie Head*, edited by Ibrahim Huma, deal with this issue in productive ways. As Elder cautions, even though Head drew on autobiographical information for her works, her novels should not be characterized as autobiography (9), and *A Question of Power* is not "a case study of its author's mental illness" (9, 11). As Elder puts it succinctly, "Elizabeth is not Bessie" (11). In this chapter, while I draw on information from Head's life to indicate concrete links to the historical moment in which she is writing—links that can then be interpreted and inflected in many ways—I agree that that we should not read the text as pure autobiography or that her life should determine the meaning of the text.

Furthermore, sometimes as a direct result of autobiographical readings, *A Question of Power* has been treated as a bit of "culture," in David Treuer's sense of a cultural artifact desired by the outsider. First, there is the matter of the culture being represented. Bessie Head is often referred to as South African, although she spent most of her life and wrote most of her corpus in Botswana. At the same time, she initially felt uneasy in the country and never learned Setswana, the language of the Motswana people. Much of her later nonfiction (oral stories and a history of Botswana) suggests her process of coming to terms with her adopted homeland. Nevertheless, to read Head's work as representative of either South Africa or Botswana would vastly simplify that situation—as would reading any minority text as "the" authority on a community or situation. Head herself registered great anger at the suggestion that any one text could be enough to understand a country or a people. By the same token, neither is her text a helpless expression of the conflicting ideologies and structural pressures on her. Sometimes some otherness postmodernist readings seem to suggest that authors write a certain way because they are forced to by gender, race, ethnicity, sexuality, or some other factor. *A Question of Power* is neither simply a direct transcription of experience (as Head herself suggested, because even a transcription of experience implies interpretation), nor a nonlinear, nonrealist, psychological text because she is a third-world woman. These are all constitutive elements, but, as Ralph Ellison wrote, "The protest is there, not because I was helpless before my racial [or gendered or sexed or national, etc.] condition, but because I *put* it there" (137).

Despite her claim that "I have always just been me, with no frame of reference to anything beyond myself" ("Notes from a Quiet Backwater" 33), Head's actions and thoughts occurred in complex interconnections to the social and political parameters of the time. For example, both her individualism and her communalism were conditioned by her relations to the historical moment(s). On one hand, her tendency toward individualism is explicable as a reaction to the group movements of the 1960s and 1970s. Her individualism also took shape and borrowed from modernism, Cold War anticommunist ideology, and capitalist subject formation. She was a great admirer of D.H. Lawrence and Pasternak, influenced by them in not only style but also content. In *The Cardinals*, the protagonist (modeled on Head) stops reading the communist party literature foisted on her by her foster father once she stumbles upon Darwin's *Origin of the Species*, the "precise and logical arguments" and "quiet, ecstatic beauty" of which "never failed to awaken a delirious response in her" (11). Furthermore, she was such a fan of Ayn Rand that she named her son Howard after the protagonist of *The Fountainhead* (Eilersen, *Bessie Head* 54). She had also turned to this individualism before to protect herself from the social hierarchy of the Cape Town colored community, declaring, "I detest snobbery but I'm a mental snob.... I search avidly for anyone really intelligent... Heavens! I will not ape anybody. I am an individual. No one shall make me ashamed of what I am!" (Eilersen, *Bessie Head* 40–41). In an early essay titled "A Personal View of the Survival of the Unfittest," she similarly states that "There is not a single church I care to enter" and that she is a "private person, with an intense, private obsession, consumed with curiosity at the riddle of my own life" (qtd. in Eilersen *Bessie Head* 79). And her particular brand of individualism was overlaid with and informed by her admiration for anticolonial leaders and figures, or "great men." She wrote the foreword to the 1982 reprinting of Sol Plaatje's *Native Life in South Africa*. Plaatje was a model of walking a political fine line; his book, like *Uncle Tom's Cabin*, appealed to British morality to try to turn it against its own legacies. Head also spent a great deal of time later in life researching and writing about Khama the Great and his son Tshekedi Khama, "two of the greatest black leaders the continent may ever know...men distinguished for their personal integrity and the power with which they articulated the hopes of their people" ("Social and Political Pressures" 24).

On the other hand, her focus on individuals, herself or others, mingled with admiration for the individual and sometimes hatred for the mass, also came mixed with a desire to work with and for others, to be part of a group and to situate herself in it. In this vein, she later drew on orature and professed a great admiration for the "middle phase" Brecht, "after he had read *Das Kapital* and became the great convert to Marxism" ("Writing Out of Southern Africa" 23). She claimed Brecht gave her the courage to write about the time when "the people would experiment with anything new—new ideas for educational progress, new agricultural techniques, new anything...I recorded everything, counting tables and chairs in great detail" (23). In one of her last interviews, she described herself as "highly individualistic person" who was also sensitive to environment: "On the one hand, there's this strong individualist apparently above environment and everything. And then, on the other hand, I feel comfortable blending in with my surroundings" (Beard, "Bessie Head" 47). My point here is that Bessie Head cannot be read in only *one* context; like Theresa Hak Kyung Cha and Thomas Pynchon, she was a writer open to many intellectual and ideological influences *and* subject to various structural pressures. To read her work as representative of South Africa or Botswana or as some manifestation of the "Other" is to starkly underread it, yet the reason we continue to do so is because the contours of otherness postmodernism do not take us beyond a world defined by identity politics, imperialism, and patriarchy. Rather, we can try to approach her text with the open-mindedness and variety of contexts it demands of us.

Questions of Power

Head's novel explores how morality is actually ideological interpellation, not simply on the level of ideology of "what you think," but also on the level of "reality." The neglect of struggles over meanings cedes ground to power, but at the same time it is not enough simply to replace one fantasy with another. The "morality" enjoined by various interpellations is also tied to ontologies, or understandings of the nature of reality, and power structures, and the text demonstrates that while "reality" is multileveled and overdetermined, it also suggests ways to understand it.

Head's novel makes an important intervention in psychoanalysis, comparable to that of Fanon's. Although Freudian and Lacanian psychoanalysis recognize "morality" as a battleground for the subject, these forms of Eurocentric analysis often ignore the ideological and historical contexts of such processes. The *bildungsroman* exemplifies in literary form the assumption that individual and linear subject-development is universal. In contrast, Head's novel posits an alternative picture of subjectivity in form and content. Head's novel situates a partially free, partially determined subject in a world of psychically and ideologically overdetermined moral injunctions. Various colonialist, patriarchal, racist, and bourgeois ideologies lay claim to morality in contradictory ways that place the subject in an impossible bind and drive him/her mad. Furthermore, although Head does not discount the reality of mental illness, she situates psychic phenomena in history. As Hershini Bhana points out, because "madness is not a culturally neutral concept," any kind of psychological analysis has to be "read against the grain of its universalizing claims that mask its racist underpinnings, in order to re-situate mental illness within a politicized and historical framework" (34–35). In other words, as Carol Anne Taylor observes, *A Question of Power* itself is a form of theory.[1] We could see this as a "return of the repressed" that invigorates the insights of psychoanalysis without, as Fanon suggests, the "guilt" of white liberalism that fetishizes otherness.

A Question of Power presents various models or modes of morality (including amorality) and subject development, scrutinizing them in excruciating detail to reveal the ideological underpinnings of these various ideas of moral subjectivity. We are presented with an acute portrait of the clash of different, overdetermined, and even contradictory ideologies and orders of being in southern Africa in the late 1960s and early 1970s, the context in which Head is writing. In the novel, the protagonist Elizabeth, while living and working in a village in Botswana, undergoes a series of hallucinatory episodes featuring the figures of Sello, Dan, and Medusa, and she suffers two mental breakdowns. Processes of subject formation, morality, and encounters with the real occur in several ways, often simultaneously, because ideological interpellation and the complex articulations of the subject do not happen along any one axis. In the novel, many of these axes can be grouped into three categories, which correspond to the progressive stages in the novel: the moral clarities and feudal systems of the distant past (Sello the monk) and the bourgeois humanism and nationalist ideologies of the present (Sello of the brown suit), and the postmodern schizophrenia of the near future (Dan). The first two modes preoccupy the first part of the novel, titled "Sello," and the third mode takes up most of part two, named for "Dan." In all three categories, notions of morality and subjectivity are closely tied to constructions of the body. These modes are distinguished formally by subtle shifts in motif and style, as well as by correlation with hallucinatory and "real" characters.

While I am reluctant to strictly correlate these modes directly to the stages of premodernity/precolonialism, modernity/nationalism, and postmodernity/globalization, because these correlations can be problematic and because the text stretches, crosses, and exceeds those categories, the novel does repeatedly refer to people, ideas, and symbols associated with these periods. All these different economic, political, and ideological modes do coexist in the context in and of which Head writes. So while I recognize the risk of applying an arbitrary sociohistorical-theoretical progression to the novel, I would argue that they are relevant because they are evidenced both in the novel and the historical context in and of which Head is writing. Although these are principally Western historical modes (i.e., the premodern, modern, and postmodern eras), they are global in the sense of analytical categories as well as historical periods. For example, the "postmodern" era is characterized by transnationalism, globalization, and cosmopolitanism. The epistemological imperialism with which some people have charged postmodernism indicates the kind of looming authority *A Question of Power* depicts. That is, even if we are not really all subsumed under postmodernism (and I do not think we are), that specter exists as a global category. Similarly, the West's "modern" period, as many scholars have shown, depends on both figurative and literal colonizations of the East and South. Bessie Head, although she lived most of her life in South Africa and Botswana, was influenced by the increasingly globalized political world as well as the remaining and continuing British colonial and missionary educational systems.

Destabilizing these problematic ideological constructions of the premodern/modern/postmodern modes is a multileveled irony in the text, through which a repressed "real" asserts itself repeatedly, although never in simple or direct ways.[2] Even when Elizabeth, the character, is not fully conscious of the ideological frameworks of events, the text subtly reveals, connects, and critiques these discourses and relations of power. The language and structure of the text prods at the manifest meanings of events and words in order to force reconsideration of both the text and the world, and the processes at this level of the text overlap with, but are distinguishable from, the omniscient narrator or Elizabeth. This process "debunks" the rhetoric of the three modes, implicitly suggesting ways to think beyond and outside of these dominant ideologies. So, for example, the notion of morality in both the first and second modes involves suppression of the body, while the third mode, drawing on resentment against the pitfalls of the first two modes, rejects the entire concept of morality as corrupt. The novel demonstrates that this total rejection of the entire notion of morality—one might call it "post-ideological"—can be as problematic and destructive as previous moralities. The undercutting process of novel ultimately reveals heteronormativity as an unspoken system of morality that undergirds the sexualized, racialized demarcations throughout the three modes, thereby destabilizing the supposed distinctions between them. As I will discuss, although Elizabeth wants to be identified with the bourgeois white man to constitute herself as a moral subject, homosexuality's interruption of heteronormativity masquerading as morality shows that identifying as a white man cannot suppress the body, and subsequently forces recognition of her own body. Thus Elizabeth is unable to repress the body—any body. At the same time, the text demonstrates that Dan's apparent rejection of morality is yet another tool of domination. So Elizabeth must redefine concepts such as morality, and while the end of the novel does not present any easy solutions, the conclusion of the novel resonates with hope.

To demonstrate these processes, I will first outline the three "modes," making the case that such stages exist and that the language of the novel undercuts them as it progresses. Then I will examine how this continuing challenge of the novel—the return of the real—stages a subtle war between the modern and postmodern modes in the second part of the novel, particularly in terms of morality and the body. Then I will show that rather than choosing between a previous version of morality or rejecting any notion of morality, the novel manages to show that each choice can be ideologically problematic. Ultimately, the novel implies that, despite the reality of the oppressive and repressive power of these different orders or modes, the repressed can become conscious knowledge of the situation. For example, all the various ideologies cast as "immoral" the outsider or Other—particularly black, mixed-race, and/or female—so Elizabeth must either go mad, caught in ideological systems that cast subjectivity in opposition to *her*, or pose countering models of morality and subjectivity. The novel thus presents the reality of overdetermined ideological interpellation, the possibility of agency, and productive ethical choices, although not in any easy or predetermined way.

Sello the Monk: Worship

Although the modes function synchronously at the time of the novel's events, the first mode, embodied in Sello "the white-robed monk" (23),[3] corresponds to the distant past and premodernity and the direct exploitation of early capitalism and colonialism. Early on, the text establishes the first mode's associations with a "set pattern" (27) and hierarchy; repressive desublimation; "the Father" and authority; the Oedipal complex and Fanon's "closed society"[4]; questions with written answers from the past and/or messages from God (rather than two-way communication) or a Socratic dialogue ("question and answer"); and the silent conveyance of meaning without the symbolic order of language. With clear-cut morality, evil is sin and "the people" are "one." This section also refers to a number of Gods and prophets, including the Judeo-Christian God, Jesus Christ, Krishna, Osiris, Buddha, and David, as well as other myths, folklore, and theologies. Interestingly, the novel also tends to place Marx and socialism in this mode, not necessarily Marx the dialectician but more the totalitarianism of Stalin or vulgar Marxism, because here the moral or "good" subject is constituted as obedient to a central divinity. In this mode, the moral self should be debased, self-flagellating, and asexual. For example, to Elizabeth the vagina is "not such a pleasant area of the body to concentrate on, possibly only now and then if necessary" (44). The "real world" embodiments of this mode include Mrs. Jones, Kenosi, and the English farm manager. Kenosi, whose presence is "one of the miracles or accidents that saved [Elizabeth's] life" (89), is Roman Catholic and lives on a cyclical schedule; at one point she describes her annual Christmas routine: she goes to midnight mass at church, attends a feast on Christmas Day when "there is always someone slaughtering a cow" (90).

The moral subject is supposed to be an obedient student, but this unquestioned obedience proves to be problematic, as enacted by Elizabeth's relationship to Sello the monk. Sello embodies "goodness" and its ideal manifestations, an abstraction beyond the impurities of the material world. As the "prophet of mankind," Sello appears as a "monk-robed" man, meditative, paternal, and patronizing. He "eternally sits" in his chair in his "billion cycles" (93, 34). Despite (or due to) his self-abasement—"I thought too much of myself. I am the root cause of human suffering" (36)—Elizabeth mindlessly adores and worships him. She is all too willing to relinquish agency, consciousness, critical analysis, and responsibility: "her face was always turned towards Sello, whom she adored... She seemed to have been only a side attachment to Sello" (25). In fact, she has "no distinct personality apart from Sello" and "was entirely dependent on Sello for direction and equally helpless" (32, 35). Although he warns her, "You have an analytical mind. You must analyse everything you see," "she too rapidly accepts Sello as a comfortable prop against which to lean" (29). Failing to heed his warning, Elizabeth sees "the poor" turn their backs to Sello, and they tell Elizabeth, "There is an evil in your relationship with Sello... He is controlling your life in the wrong way" (32). Here, "the poor" speak the real; this mode, although attractive, is fairly easy to demonstrate as problematic, because such relations are not the dominant currency in the mid- to late-twentieth century. Even Sello himself explains the problem with Elizabeth's relationship to him: "the title God, in its absolute all-powerful form, is a disaster to its holder, the all-seeing eye is the greatest temptation. It turns a man into a wild debaucher, a maddened and wilful persecutor of his fellow men" (36–37). In uncritical worship without analysis and critique, the self relinquishes the responsibility of self-scrutiny, leaving no guard against the fallibility of human "saviors." But, ironically, Sello's very warnings, administered as lessons, contribute to her worship of his goodness.

While Elizabeth's conscious reconsideration of her relationship to Sello the monk is a more complicated process, the novel undermines his authority even as it depicts it. In the midst of her rapturous abjection to Sello the monk, he remains elusive. On one level, Sello invokes the inability to speak the divine name and the non-necessity of verbalizing "eternal" truths, and his sermons on the fallibility of all people ironically serve to strengthen his status as the truth-giver. At the same time, the language also implies vagueness and uncertainty:

> There was no warning. There was no explicit statement—here I am, with a height of goodness you cannot name; there I was, at some dim time in mankind's history, with a depth of evil you cannot name. Here I am, about to strip myself of my spectacular array of vesture garments as they said I ought to, and to show you my own abyss. There are so many terrible lessons you have to learn this time; that the title God, in its absolute all-powerful form, is a disaster to its holder, the all-seeing eye is the greatest temptation. It turns a man into a wild debaucher, a maddened and wilful persecutor of his fellow men. He said none of this. Only at times when a wild terror overcame her mind did he step in with the kinds of statements that restored her mental balance. (36–37)

On one level, this passage simply relates what Sello teaches. At the same time, he makes "no explicit statement," and he "cannot name" the heights of goodness or the depths of evil. He speaks of "some dim time" that is unspecific, uncertain. He is only "about to" strip off his "spectacular array of vesture garments," and all he has are "kinds of statements." This can mean both the statements themselves as well as something that only approaches them. The unspoken suggests some kind of holy ineffability as well as doubt, prescription, and instability. In this passage, as Sello articulates how absolute power corrupts, Elizabeth the character continues to worship him, but the text undermines Sello's words even as he speaks them. The manifest content of the words adhere to the ideological program of control through obedience, while the latent content of the undercutting, double-voiced language betrays the reality—in the nonpresence or unreality of Sello's holiness—of the situation.

The conflict between and transition from the first to the second and third modes are portrayed as a result of the subject's disillusionment with the first mode's cosmology. Sello's teachings are cast as performances, with the double valence of enactment and charade; Sello's "initial *presentation* of constructive goodness in *images* and *pictures* had been a *put-together* whole of observations and tentative feelers he had put out towards the souls of others. He had *presented* it to Elizabeth as a *form of* teaching" (62, my emphasis). Elizabeth comes to reject Sello as an actor, a charlatan, who is "deliberately manipulating the words and gestures of the people who approached her" (62). Monks are "delicately-buffered" and full of "principles and platitudes" (65), and Elizabeth sees through such platitudes by uncovering the "half-concealed" portion of history, such as "the peculiar Al Capone-like murder of Uriah" by David (65). The emergence of the real in the very human lives of its "gods" thereby motivates her movement into the humanistic but still moralistic second mode. This disillusionment is complex; it is both real, as a disappointment in an expectation, and also available for manipulation by other people, ideologies, and forces in ways that may be quite independent of its initial cause and validity.

Sello of the Brown Suit/Medusa: Modernity and Its Repressed

The second mode, embodied in Sello of the Brown Suit, deals with the most pressing issues of Head's time, particularly bourgeois humanism, economic development, and nationalisms. Sello the monk evolves into "Sello of the brown suit," with his discussion of "evolution" (62), "liberation" from the confines of religion (41), and modernization, as evidenced by his new attire. Exploring the tensions between humanism and nationalism, this section emphasizes individualism and political organizations of *individuals* as well as group purity. This mode also refers to anticolonialism, decolonization, and Cold War Manicheanism. It stresses economic development through tropes of accumulation, modernization, and organization, and the universalist rhetoric of bourgeois humanism is interrogated through depictions of a forced naïveté/innocence (don't want to know because there is nothing to know) and false hail-fellow-well-met's masking structural inequalities. The various aspects of this mode have in common an emphasis on structures, patterns, planning, and an increasing focus of humans on one another (development of bureaucracy), with authority not in the hand of "God" or gods as "Father" but human figures. This mode also includes education in English; Elizabeth thinks, "Someone had set the pattern, and it remained the furthest reach of the children's imaginations" (67).

The bourgeois humanist planning and modernization of this second mode reflects the "present" of the novel, the 1960s and 1970s, a time of rapid economic development in Botswana. Foreign investment flowed into the relatively stable, newly independent nation (Botswana gained independence from English in 1966) in the form of "expatriate personnel"—such as the characters Eugene and Tom in the novel—as well capital for numerous diamond mines, around which the nation's economy was organized (Parsons). Largely due to such economic programs, Botswana's economy grew thirty-fold between the 1960s and 1980s, the gross domestic product going from less than $80 per capita to $1,000 per capita during that time (Parsons). But as several scholars have noted, this economic growth has not been accompanied by social and infrastructural development, and in fact has hindered growth in other areas. As Maipose writes, "Botswana is widely known for its remarkable economic growth and prudent macro-economic management," but the "quality of life for most Africans has either not risen or has done so only marginally since the 1970s." Overdependency on one export economy "sometimes prevent[s] balanced, equitable forms of growth and development," shifting resources away from other sectors, like agriculture, and resulting in an undiversified economy, vulnerable to external demands (Mhone and Bond 237). Despite the country's economic success, Mhone and Bond note in 2002, unemployment is still very high and rising (235), and the nation has "one of the highest rates of HIV/AIDS infection in the world" (Maipose). Every development plan by the Botswana government has articulated the need to "diversify the economy" and generate employment, but these plans have failed, primarily due to "market forces," or the interests of foreign capital, and diamond exports still constitute one-third of the country's gross domestic product (Mhone and Bond 234, 237–8). So despite the push for modernization in terms of economic development, the rhetoric did not fit the reality of poverty, disease, and unchanging circumstances. Mhone and Bond conclude, "the benefits of globalization for Botswana are not evident" (245).[5]

In this era of rapid modernization, Sello of the brown suit embodies the rhetoric of bourgeois humanism, which proclaims that:

> ...a heaven had been planned directly around the hearts of men and as, bit by bit, its plan unfolded they called it so many names: democracy, freedom of thought, social consciousness, protest, human rights, exploration, moral orders, principles and a thousand and one additions for the continual expansion and evolution of the human soul. (54)

The "worship," student-teacher hierarchical model of the first mode is replaced by a vision of horizontal relations between human beings. As Sello of the brown suit says,

> ...a part of my present evolution is African, and I hear the beginnings of a great symphony, a complete statement for the future about the dignity of man, where none is high and none is low but all are equal. The difficulty here is that it hasn't yet swelled up to a loud and conscious declaration of the African civilization. We are a rising civilization. (62–63)

This mode claims a kind of "African realism" with "the strange logic of deliberate planning," a "present face-to-face view of evil" and "courteous respect" in which "Christianity and God were courteous formalities people had learned to enjoy with mental and emotional detachment," because "the real battlefront was living people" (66). Religion becomes an intellectual, "detached" endeavor, because real investment is in human beings, so God is redefined: "God was the totality of all great souls and their achievements; the achievements are not that of one single, individual soul, but of many souls who all worked to make up the soul of God, and this might be called God, or the Gods" (54). Feeling "liberated" from "the ghastly deathbed of black-magic rituals, miracle-performing, cloistered halls, the insane, raving power-maniac world of the Pharaohs" (41), brown-suited Sello feels as if given "the essential secrets, the essential clues to the evolution of the soul" (41). The past mistake had been to pray for an abstract love to descend from God, in whatever form, into the hearts of humans. Now, heaven, or a utopian society, can be created out of the multiplicity of human actions.

"Evil" is anything that impinges on the autonomy and separateness of each individual, including the racist genocide of Nazi Germany, apartheid South Africa, and the sweeping generalization of Elizabeth during her first breakdown, when she yells at the sales clerk "Oh, you bloody bastard Batswana!!" (46–47, 51). These episodes are cast as bad, or antithetical to the morality of this mode. At the same time, "evil" is failure to fit into the group. Medusa taunts Elizabeth, "You're not linked up to the people. You don't know any African languages" (44). In other words, this mode expresses the Cold War Manichean logic of We Individuals versus They the Collective, but "We Individuals" just as powerfully forces conformity with the group. The modern era makes the apparently contradictory demand that the moral subject be an autonomous individual within the group; what Elizabeth encounters in this phase is the group ideology of individualism, and this repressed contradiction enacts the forced naïveté also characteristic of this mode.

Clearly, a number of specific ideologies are operative in this mode, but the strongest vein, during this time of economic development and social modernization, is the bourgeois humanism with which Elizabeth identifies. And although humanism does not have to—because there are many different kinds of humanism—this particular brand of colonialist, patriarchal, bourgeois morality relies upon suppression of the body. This works along several axes. As Fanon observes, the immorality of the black person is projected onto the entire body; drawing on Sartre's study of anti-Semitism, he argues that whereas with Jews one thinks of money, with blacks, "one thinks of sex" (*Black Skin, White Masks* 160), and "it is in his corporeality that the Negro is attacked" (163). Therefore, "to suffer from a phobia of Negroes is to be afraid of the biological" (165). Similarly, in *The Critique of Dialectical Reason*, Sartre argues that the bourgeois attitude of "everything in moderation" (food, sex, alcohol, exercise, etc.) distances the self from the biological and its appetites, which is the "human" element that the bourgeoisie have in common with the dissipated aristocracy and the animal-like working classes. Therefore, bourgeois "morality" is a separation from the lower classes (770–2). Similarly, in Western traditions, women have been associated with the body in opposition to the male intellect.[6] Elizabeth distances herself from the body to be "moral," but "morality" here means not only white but also male, while the body is associated with the black and female, the impure and dirty. So Elizabeth distances herself from the body, her body or anyone else's, and anything associated with the body, in order to be constituted as moral and human. Despite her rejection of the body, blackness, and femaleness, however, the "real" forces a level of awareness.

The text demonstrates how the rhetoric of certain kinds of humanism begins to ring hollow when the categories of human and moral—which are identical in this mode—are limited, and when the still existing inequalities are denied under that rhetoric. Sello of the brown suit embodies the shining surface of bourgeois humanism that exalts human beings (members of the group), while Medusa is the repressed of modernity, or that which falls outside the category of human being. Furthermore, this mode ignores the reality of communal ways of being, particularly as represented in the novel by Kenosi, Elizabeth's only village friend. Sello of the brown suit may proclaim, "let people be free to evolve, let everything alone and re-create a new world of soft textures and undertones, full of wild flowers and birds and children's playtime and women baking bread" (64), but he also declares, "Ah, I'm gaining control of the God show again" (41). Even as the second mode debunks and substitutes itself for the first, we see that even this new human-centered ideology can be manipulated for control and power. The real, or the *way things are* in contrast to the prescriptions of ideological morality, disrupts Elizabeth's identification with this humanist morality in two principle ways. First, the very language in which the second mode is conveyed suggests its willful blind denials. Second, the figure of Medusa arises as the overdetermined embodiment of all that is repressed and denied by modernity; she does not appear in sympathetic form, but with all the terror and prohibition demanded by the dominant ideology.

The language of the novel undercuts this second mode even while portraying it in the depiction of the "real-world" character Eugene. Modeled closely on Head's associate Patrick van Rensburg, a politically progressive Afrikaner who also sought refuge in Botswana, Eugene is the founder and principal of "Motabeng Secondary School," as well as the various "Brigades" for teaching and developing local trades. Eugene "totally blurred the dividing line between the elite who had the means for education and the illiterate who had none. Education was for all" (72). But this utopian ideal cannot overcome structural inequalities and often refuses to acknowledge it. When Elizabeth tries to tell him of her tortures, he turns away: "he did not want to hear any details about the country or anything else," preferring to believe her nervous breakdowns came "out of the blue" (52). Eugene reflects the guilty repression of bourgeois humanism, or not wanting to know because there is nothing to know. He believes vaguely that South Africans "usually suffered from some form of mental aberration" (58), rather than considering that Elizabeth's neuroses may have something to do with the situation, or "the details about the country," whether South Africa or Botswana. Although his writings repeat phrases like "skill, work, fullest development of personality and intellect" (57), he is still the patriarchal head of the household; his wife, "a quiet pretty woman," types out "his enormous correspondence and endless pamphlets on educational programmes for developing countries" (56). Likewise, the economy and society of Motabeng are undergoing an uneven process of modernization, through the efforts of the Secondary School, the Brigades, and the Peace Corps, in ways that Eugene had not foreseen. The village women begin to work as "housekeepers and nursemaids for the children of the teaching staff" (55–56). The school attempts to establish a local trade economy, but the members of the cooperative trades face difficulty due to the larger economic realities. The villagers exchange their "meanly hoarded coins" to buy not only necessities but also Western products like "Fanta" (154). Wrapped in his own rhetoric, he ignores the existing structural inequalities in his world.

This "repressed" reality cannot stay repressed, particularly for the subject who inhabits the space characterized as nonhuman by colonialist morality. But, again, the real does not reemerge in any simple or direct way; rather, Medusa erupts in angry, hysterical episodes. Medusa embodies the eruption of psychic, political, and social repressions that often accompany an insistence on sameness, whether in Enlightenment humanism or anticolonial nationalist movements. As Taylor notes, "Head's Medusa exerts the power of oppressive constructions of race, sexuality, and other modern 'demands' for difference-as-perversity"; for Elizabeth, desiring to identify with Sello of the brown suit, Medusa is the "internalized—or already produced—construction of oneself as horrific" (105). The repressed of bourgeois humanism emerges with angry force. Medusa preys on Elizabeth's sense of exclusion; upon first arriving in Motabeng, Elizabeth feels deeply alienated from the villagers. Her inability to speak Setswana past "the first five lines" of a greeting and inability to offer "delicious tidbits of gossip" distances her from the social network of the village (20). Medusa "simply wanted to be the manager of the African continent with everyone she found disagreeable—OUT" (64). "You don't know any African languages," Medusa taunts Elizabeth, "We don't want you here. This is my land.

These are my people. We keep our things to ourselves" (44, 37). "The wild-eyed Medusa," we are told, "was expressing the surface reality of African society. It was shut in and exclusive" (38). The specter of Medusa excludes Elizabeth from the group, casting her into the nether regions occupied by those who are designated as nonhumans by colonialist, bourgeois humanism. That is, Medusa turns the tables on Elizabeth, excluding her along a different axis, but this situation also indicates how reactionary nationalisms can appropriate and reinflect the selective humanism of racist bourgeois humanism. Medusa also initiates the sexual attacks that Dan develops later, assaulting the politely disembodied bourgeois morality of Sello. Smiling, Medusa imparts "top secret information" to Elizabeth: "Without any bother for decencies she sprawled her long black legs in the air, and the most exquisite sensation travelled out of her towards Elizabeth" (44).

Medusa, the dark, female, sexual, wicked underbelly that must be repressed by the smiling, shining evolution of Sello of the brown suit, symbolizes the "internal darkness" that humans must face after the death of God(s) (40). We are told that "a man is overwhelmed by his own internal darkness," and "when he finds himself in the embrace of the Medusa she really is the direct and intangible form of his own evils" (40). Elizabeth tries to deny these attacks, identifying with the dominant model of the moral (white, male) subject, and not as black, female, and sexual: "it was not maddening to her to be told she hadn't a vagina. She might have had but it was not such a pleasant area of the body to concentrate on, possibly only now and then if necessary" (44). But even as Elizabeth struggles with the dominant ideological interpellation, the novel lays bare the underpinnings and the "repressed" of those ideologies.

Dan: Postmodernism and Schizophrenia

The second half of the novel, titled "Dan," deals with phenomena and ideas resonant with postmodernity. Characterized by confusion, contradictory interpellations, and incoherence, Dan appears after Elizabeth's disillusionment with Sello of the brown suit, and Dan's sole purpose is to acquire and maintain power. To do so, he first woos Elizabeth romantically, politically, and intellectually, and then, once he has "flung a hook right into her pain- and feeling-centre" (117), he terrorizes Elizabeth with a program of "shows" in a *Clockwork Orange*-like conditioning, in ways reminiscent of Medusa. Throughout this half, the text demonstrates the workings of Dan's nonsystematic or post-ideological strategies or "mechanics of power" (13), while also exposing and undercutting them. For Dan, nothing has intrinsic meaning, and everything can be used for his purposes. To achieve his ends, he says, "I don't care what I do" (114), and to win "total control of the situation" (144), Dan uses and does "whatever happened to be the issue of the moment" (127). He takes a number of shapes or roles, including a "Casanova" and various dictators, trying to assimilate and subjugate Elizabeth through the use of various interpellations, or discourses that permeate not only the social sphere but also "hard-wire" the individual's consciousness (13). Whereas Sello the monk wanted her as a student and servant, and Sello of the brown suit wanted her as a worker and humanist, Dan wants only to use her for his own ends, and he will use anything to meet those ends. In fact, "there wasn't any filth he couldn't cook up as long as he was sure of dominating the nightmare" (144). In this sense, Dan is a cipher, because he does not have a fixed content; rather, like power structures in our own time, he manipulates relations of power, crossing and transgressing preexisting delineations of race, gender, nation, sexuality, morality, and whatever else happens to be available, with no goal other than his own will to power.

Dan first appeals to Elizabeth's disillusionment with the Sellos, and this basis in disillusionment resonates with much of postmodern thought. Just as skepticism of humanism, modernity, rationality, nationalism, morality, et cetera, have found expression in varieties of postmodernisms (aesthetic, political, social, epistemological, economic), Dan invokes the cynicism possible once it becomes clear that "the prophecies aren't coming true," that philosophies of love and totalizing systems do not immediately heal the world (25). Dan appeals to Elizabeth because she is disillusioned with Sello; part one ends with Elizabeth rejecting the hierarchizing and systematizing dreams of both Sello's: "Oh God... May I never contribute to creating dead worlds, only new worlds" (100). Having witnessed the "performance" of the "Medusa triangle" (107), as well as Sello "stripped of his garments," or the death of the Father (God, colonizers, Marx), now "every inch of [Dan] spelled outrage at Sello's evil" (144). Dan uses Elizabeth's confusion and her rage against both incarnations of Sello for his own purposes. In one scene, Dan's interaction with "The Father" recalls failures of some "saviors," or the former rebel heroes turned national leaders that Fanon describes in *Wretched of the Earth*. Dan and "the Father" appear to harmonize, but Dan claims otherwise: "He and I," says Dan, "have performed the same roles in your destiny. How often has he heard that cry for help? But how much more often have I?" (106). Dan's strategy here is twofold. He wants to expose the rhetoric of saviorhood as a fraud while at the same time employing it. In other words, Dan out-Fathers "the Father," or manipulates the rhetoric and pose of saviorhood for political ends, and at the same time points out that "the Father" originated this façade. Furthermore, if we read "the Father" as Marx, Dan's criticism echoes George Padmore's critique of the Soviet Union/Third International for abandoning or subordinating interest in anticolonial movements.[7] Dan's words reinvoke "the Father" for a variety of reasons, but Elizabeth realizes that Dan only claims identification with "the Father" "to create a hero-image of himself in her mind, to claim a greater achievement or status with her, without having to prove anything" (107).

Dan also woos Elizabeth using the discourse of romantic love:

> When he talked of love to her ... His love was exclusive, between her and him alone. They ought to be silently wrapped up in it, with no intruders. The pathetic appeal had a corresponding appeal in her. He'd flung a hook right into her pain- and feeling-centre. This he was to use as he pleased: "Now cry, now laugh, now feel jealous." And he adjusted the button to suit his needs. (117)

This process is complicated. Dan's work here is part of the flexible "hard-wiring" he uses for control; that is, he will use anything, particularly notions of romantic love, for his purposes. At the same time, because Dan's tactics will change so drastically later, his appeals to romantic love are exposed as yet another ideological tool of domination. Furthermore, as I will discuss in the next section, Elizabeth does not really wish to identify as a woman because she desires to identify as a white man, or a moral being according to bourgeois humanism. That is, while Dan's assaults do terrorize her on one level, on another level they also serve to fulfill Elizabeth's wishes.

Dan thus "conditions" Elizabeth for two weeks by appealing to her disillusionment and notions of romantic love, and he is quite satisfied, "as though he had triumphantly acquired Pavlov's dog" (106):

> He did not want to upset Elizabeth and the phenomena of heaven he'd staged for her. Besides, he had to fix up his electrical wiring system (her whole body was a network, a complicated communication centre); everything depended on the efficiency of it. He couldn't get the wires in the right place if she was nervy or jumpy. As soon as the stage was set, he let loose. (126)

Then he launches his assault on Elizabeth via internalized processes of control that the novel puts in terms of modern media technologies. For example, some of his assaults are referred to as "records": "the records went round and round in her head the whole day. He turned on a record of whatever happened to be the issue of the moment...he turned these records on so violently that they reached pitches of high, screaming hysteria in her mind" (127). Sometimes the records taunt her for not being African enough because she is mixed-race, sometimes they attack her for not being properly feminine and sexually desirable. Similarly, Dan's images play "on the cinema screen of [Elizabeth's] mind" (127), and we are told that "Dan was a great one for the right atmosphere and lighting-effects" (108). Dan's media blitz on Elizabeth calls to mind the jump cuts and short attention spans of today's media: "He was in such a hurry. He had so much to accomplish that he threw scene after scene at her" (115). Life with Dan is characterized by such "incoherence" (176), and Elizabeth finds questions and a "sane, reasonable reply" impossible in the face of the "power of assertion" and the simply "shocking" (47).

He continues Medusa's assault on Elizabeth's femininity. Long series of pornographic acts are performed and flaunted in front of Elizabeth by Dan and a series of women with names such as Miss Glamour, Miss Beauty Queen, Miss Buttocks, and Miss Legs. Extending and echoing Medusa's earlier tortures, he tells her,

> "You are supposed to feel jealous.
> You are inferior as a Coloured.
> You haven't got what that girl has got." (127)

Through the cacophony, and on the basis of disillusionment, with previous concepts such as "justice," "morality," and "love" exposed as ideologically problematic, Dan proceeds to creates "a world where no one loved anyone" (168). In this sense, Dan further correlates to what we might think of generally as postmodernity, particularly postmodernism's critique of authenticity, subjectivity, and agency. For Dan, meanings are flexible and relative, contingent upon image and power; Dan does not have a preset "ideology" but a flexible strategy of assault. Dan, then, is purely performative. His "shows" do not constitute reproductions of an original or falsifications of an authentic truth; rather, they indicate a norm while also constantly destabilizing those norms. For example, when he makes a show of indignation at Sello, Dan is neither faking nor telling the truth; rather, he is interested in using Elizabeth's sense of "justice" and integrity against her by demonstrating that both Sellos with their ideological-moral systems are fallible. In demonstrating each Sello's "crimes," Dan utilizes an all-or-nothing logic—a line of reason that he certainly does not use consistently—to argue that because Sello has been inconsistent and hypocritical, he and his ideas must be rejected altogether.

Similarly, the conception of an autonomous, individual subject dissolves. In its place, Dan constitutes Elizabeth as the nexus of various contradictory discourses and injunctions. Elizabeth's "personality" becomes a "loosely-knit, shuffling ambiguous mass," and "private thought" is "entirely disrupted" (62, 148). Elizabeth is "not supposed to sort out one thing from another" (148); she is not supposed to make distinctions, differentiations, but passively observe "hell" or the heterogeneity of Dan's "shows." We are told that Elizabeth "wasn't thinking coherently at all, or sorting anything out. She was just the receiver of horror, her whole life was suspended. She was losing track of the personality pattern she'd lived with since birth. It was being thrust aside by one monstrous event after another" (131). With a general inability to communicate, language and images do not express; instead, they create reality. For example, Elizabeth begins "to believe her own nightmare" (140), and Dan's "training" and "shows" eventually result in an identical "model" of Elizabeth (193).

But Dan tortures not only Elizabeth; we are told that "he was applying the hawk's eye to Africa" (137), suggesting that this disillusionment, skepticism, and cynicism will spread in the postcolonial era. The text captures and presages the logics of what Matsikidze identifies as "the postnationalistic stage" of the splintering of groups formerly united by anticolonial struggles, as well as that of neoimperialism and of the vicissitudes of formerly colonized nations.[8] Along the same lines, Dan resonates with many of the economic, existential, and political phenomena associated with postmodernism. Whereas Eugene and Sello of the brown suit emphasized development and planning, Dan utilizes flexibility, mobility, heterogeneity, and the compression of time and space. Whereas the Sellos preached suppression of desires, Dan not only pressures Elizabeth to fulfill her desires, he wants to create the desires that she will be driven by the need to fulfill, thereby defining her. In Dan's world, alienation is the normal condition of existence within structures one is helpless to change; or rather, alienation is the norm because there is nothing to be alienated from. And particularly as reflected in the "real world" parts of the novel, the *appearance* of horizontal equality and cultural relativism belies the strengthening of exploitative, dehumanizing structures and processes that people recognize and only barely suppress, if at all.

In order to identify and subvert this slippery but ubiquitous mode, the novel embodies it not only in Dan but also in the "real" parts of the novel. For example, Camilla, one of the Danish instructors at the Motabeng school, embodies this third mode in the "real world" of the novel. She is a "half-mad" woman of "jarring interruption[s]," "speeding" around and "creating a turmoil of distraction, shattering the sleepy murmuring peace of the garden" (74–75). Her voice is a "scatter-brained assertion of self-importance," always insisting all attention be focused on her (75). She never simply speaks; she shouts, exclaims, races, shrills, calls, chatters, associates, pants (74–78). Her superior social position enables her to change Elizabeth's reality: "All of a sudden, the vegetable garden was the most miserable place on earth. The students had simply become humiliated little boys shoved around by a hysterical white woman who never saw black people as people but as objects of permanent idiocy" (76). For Camilla, time and space are compressed; when Elizabeth lists all the errands she must complete, Camilla offers to use her Landrover to "do all that for you in half an hour" (77). And in Camilla's world, "houses were loved, not people" (78). At the same time, Elizabeth also sees Camilla as "crazily, pathetically human" when she unintentionally blurts out her difficulties with "so many children" and her husband (79). Again, the text undermines the antihumanism of the third mode by suggesting the humanity within even a person like Camilla.

The third mode is also explored and interrogated in a scene in which Elizabeth argues against the liberal relativism of her friend Tom, an American Peace Corps volunteer who first appears in Part Two, by exploiting his own logic and by manipulating her words and images (131–7). Tom, upset upon hearing that the United States has entered Cambodia, declares, "I don't know why they bother to involve themselves in world affairs," he says, "Wherever America goes she only hands the poor Coca-Cola and chewing-gum" (132). Tom is particularly angry because U.S. policies abroad may hit a little too close to home, his own reason for being in Botswana being primarily "rapid economic development," his "pet subject" (132). Development falls into the second mode, and Tom argues on the basis of a humanist morality characteristic of that mode:

> He'd earnestly tried to impress upon Elizabeth that she ought to support, morally, Mao Tse-tung, Castro and Nyerere because they stood for

rapid economic development. He'd included Nkrumah, who had already disappeared in a coup. When Elizabeth protested he said, quite calmly: "Nkrumah made a few errors, that's all. But he stood for rapid economic development." (132)

But the argument begins to take on the strategies and logic characteristic of Dan. It becomes ridiculously performative and "foolish" (132): Tom claims that the only supporters of "rapid economic development" in the United States are "the Black Power people," whereupon he jumps to his feet, "thrust[s] one fist high into the air and said: 'Black Power!'" (132). Taken aback, Elizabeth asks, "Do they really go around sticking their fists in the air like that?" (132), prodding at the validity and seriousness of Tom's performance. Elizabeth counters him by making provisional use of his own humanist rhetoric, saying "I don't want exclusive brotherhoods for black people only" (132). Tom replies by falling back on the relativism of the third mode, saying, "it's not the same thing... They're right. You don't know America" (132), and a little later he concedes that she may be "right about Africa" but "wrong about America" (133). Tom submits to Elizabeth only after she herself uses some performative tricks that play on guilt and relativism. She becomes "a great orator" captivating "her audience of one," although her son Shorty has gotten used to her "high drama" and ignores her (134), reminding us that this is a performance, perhaps just one of many. She says, "if you saw the soul of the black man the way I saw it, you'd feel afraid. Pretty mental analysis is nothing compared to the real thing" (134), and she "assumed the deeply scarred expression of the poor who had addressed her some time ago" (134). This pushes Tom into acceptance and obedience—a condition characteristic of the first mode—out of liberal guilt: "He turned towards her a face flaming with light," saying "Yes, that's right" (135). Elizabeth uses Dan's logic and strategic performances to maneuver Tom into the role of obedient student, but in doing so, the text shows us that the fundamental problems—with the ideologies of the modes and in this particular conversation—have been elided, not resolved.

Morality and the Body

The clashes between these orders of being reveal that, like those of Medusa, Dan's taunts that Elizabeth is insufficiently feminine and sexual do not really bother Elizabeth, because her identification as a moral, bodiless white male subject takes precedence over her identification as a inferior, mixed-race, female object. That does not mean that Dan's messages are not operative, interpellating Elizabeth and everyone else, and that does not mean that Elizabeth can voluntarily escape those ideological pressures. Rather, Elizabeth is subject to multiple and even contradictory directives that have different degrees of importance, and in that particular historical moment, in that place, such bourgeois humanistic morality is predominant. But this imposed, desired identification proves impossible; the reality of the body even for white male subjects appears for Elizabeth in the form of homosexuality. In the novel, Elizabeth's actual neurotic breaks occur *not* when Dan assails her femininity, but when he mentions gay men. Elizabeth, then unable to take refuge in her disembodied moral subject, must recognize her own body in sudden outbursts that seem to come out of nowhere.

One of the most notable aspects of *A Question of Power* is its graphic sexuality, particularly in contrast to Elizabeth's aversion to sex and to the absence of such grotesque depictions in Head's other works. Although the figure of Dan seems to terrorize Elizabeth, Dan and his "nice-time girls" do not really "tempt" or denigrate Elizabeth. Instead, they reify the "moral," disembodied subjectivity of the second mode that Elizabeth desires. To be this moral subject, she must reject being female and black, and identify as a white man. But even identifying as a white man fails to suppress the body; the fact of homosexuality and the ideological work of heteronormativity as an interdiction force Elizabeth to recognize the reality of the body and, thereby, her reality as black and female. In other words, the real will not stay repressed.

Dan's women are repeatedly revealed as flawed and "dirty" in contrast to Elizabeth's cleanliness and superiority, and the language of these sections constantly undermines Dan's pronouncements. As Dan tells Elizabeth, "My darling, if you call me I'll come to you. I don't like women like that, they're too cheap" (129), and he deems most of his girls "dirty" or flawed in some way (164). Even though Dan's messages are inconsistent and contradictory, Elizabeth's disdain for "women like that" increases (164). The women of his harem are a "motley crew," either professionals/goddesses with defects or local girls who need polishing. Elizabeth may not have "got what these girls has got," but her "personal possessions" possess "the property of cleaning up 'dirt'" (128). And although Head usually uses the indicative mood and active verbs (no matter how strange or "unreal" the events of the narrative), many descriptions of Dan's girls take the form of hypotheticals and conditionals. The women are "presented as" something and are "supposed" to become something; the fulfillment of their roles is uncertain.

We are presented with an array of anxiety-inducing female figures that actually affirm Elizabeth's superior status. "Miss Body Beautiful" causes Dan to "panic" because "there was something fearfully wrong" with her (146). "Madame Squelch Squelch," whose pelvis is made of "molten lava" and whose symbol is "darkness," is "despised" by Dan, who throws up "after the job" of making her "impotent" (164–5). "The Womb," a local woman whose purpose is to protect Elizabeth from direct contact with Dan by remaining in between them (115, 146–7), is made "classy" by wearing one of Elizabeth's dresses, and she fears Elizabeth (165–6). "Madame Loose-Bottom" vanishes when she faces Elizabeth (164). The "upperclass" "Sugar-Plum Fairy" resembles "a true-romance story from a woman's magazine," and although "delicate" is "always ready to 'go' " (165):

> Sugar-Plum seemed to revel in tortured love affairs; this seemed to have been the pattern of their relationship in their past lives. Dan was always the hopeless outsider given crumbs by the lady, and it seemed a sweet anguish to the lady to tear herself between the grand Lord she usually married and Dan whom she loved, then didn't loved, then loved. Presumably this kind of anguish heightened their love, made it terribly sacred, holy and beautiful. (165)

Sugar-Plum is "slumming" with Dan, but Dan has to give her up for Elizabeth. Dan plans to marry "Miss Pink Sugar-Icing" for her money, but she is "very boring" (166–7). As a cosmopolitan woman with jazz records, "April in Paris, Autumn in New York" (166), time and place are nothing to her. "Miss Pelican-Beak" is good only as long as her various "coloured panties" last, and then Dan deems her "too pushy for the new world" and breaks her legs, elbows, and pelvis (!), decorating her with "tiny, pretty, pink roses for a new image of tender love" (167–8). She has to wear one of Elizabeth's bras to absorb her "harmless qualities" (168), and he "redesigns her pelvis" like Elizabeth's, "which was extraordinarily passive and caused no trouble in the world" (168). The nymphomaniacal "Miss Sewing-Machine" is ordered "to go and wash in Elizabeth's bath-tub. Apparently, this would stop her promiscuity" (128). "Miss Wriggly-Bottom" is an appealing child-like girl who "looked Chinese," but she dies because "she couldn't go with a man the whole night" (129); her sex is "outside," while inside there is only a "vacuum" (129).

These women have it drilled into *them* that "any possession of Elizabeth's they could get hold of would give them some kind of holy immunity or make them doubly attractive" (128). But the description also suggests uncertainty: Elizabeth's possessions "would"—not "will"—make them holier and more attractive. Furthermore, the women do not naturally feel that Elizabeth is superior to them, they have it "drilled" into them, suggesting that discourse of power creates their "reality" as well. If these displays are genuinely meant to make Elizabeth want to submit, they make a poor case. The women are "cheap," and even Dan's "goddesses," whom he treats with "holy awe," are less clean than Elizabeth and instructed to bathe in her tub. Nothing about these women's sexuality really appeals to Elizabeth, so these displays are not really terrorizing. They are wish fulfillments, albeit in nightmare form, that justify remaining exactly as she is.

Dan loathes Elizabeth and does not want to touch her, but ironically this loathing serves to support Elizabeth's desire to be a certain kind of subject. Dan has "a leprosy-like fear of Coloureds or half-breeds" (127), and is "afraid he might have to touch the half-breed at some time and contaminate his pure black skin" (127). He does not want to touch her; *his* desire for racial/bodily purity makes him not want her, so it is not really *her* fault that she is undesirable. In other words, he desires blackness and he does not want her, so she must not be black. At the same time, Dan's obsession with sexual and moral purity leads him to treat Elizabeth, in opposition to his "nice-time girls," as morally and sexually pure, a Virgin Mary figure.

This morality is connected to attempts to reject the body in order to reject being female and black. Several early passages in *A Question of Power* demonstrate how Elizabeth identifies herself as a man among men, concerned with masculine things, and denies identification with blacks and the Batswana. Tom tells Elizabeth that she is "a strange woman" who draws men to speak to her of "deep metaphysical profundities" rarely shared with women. Sello says "Yes, that's right," and "off went the chair with a loud 'ting.'" Tom says, "Did you hear something... I distinctly heard someone say 'Yes, that's right'" (24). Tom leaves, certain he heard something, but what stays with Elizabeth is that "their deepest feelings they reserve for other men" (24). Sello's "unreal" words approving Tom's characterization of Elizabeth as like-a-man become "real" when Tom hears them; in other words, Tom and Sello make Elizabeth a man. She wants to disassociate herself from the corporeal and become pure intellect or spirit, like men, particularly holy men like Sello the monk. She thinks, "Why yes... that was the only reasonable explanation of the relationship between Sello and her. The base of it was masculine" (24). Her early "journey" with Sello is described as "dark heaving turmoil," not for "women with children" but for men (50). Nevertheless, she is the chosen one, the "prophet" of God, who is "Man" (206), whom Sello sent in to face Dan because she "still topple[s] giants with a stone sling" (199). Here she identifies with David, although earlier in her struggle with Dan she describes herself as a weak David "with no sling" and "helplessly feminine" (119).

Likewise, a "persistent theme" in Dan's "drama" is that Elizabeth "was not genuinely African; *he* had to give her the real African insight," and "in almost every way she had to be aware of Africans as a special holy entity and deep mystery he alone understood" (159). But Elizabeth does not identify with Medusa, the repressed African-woman-as-Other, but with Eugene, the white male moral subject. After her second breakdown, she rejects being an African in the mental hospital, shouting at the Batswana nurses, "I'm not an African? Don't you see? I never want to be an African. You bloody well, damn well leave me alone!" (181). The attendants seem to believe her and, although all patients must work in the hospital, they do not require Elizabeth to do so. When the white psychologist, the only one in the country (181), whom she calls "a semi-literate quack doctor from Europe" (182), identifies with her as "a comrade racialist" (184), she is "abruptly restored [to] a portion of her sanity" (184). Elizabeth's encounter with the European doctor is not a version of the colonial encounter; he affirms her identification as not-black. She feels consciously guilty, but her neurotic symptoms are eased.

But although she rejects the body to reject blackness and femaleness, this rejection proves untenable. The "real" forces a level of awareness on those who cannot repress the situation due to historical, social, and economic privilege. Nevertheless, the *self,* itself prescribed by context, emphasizes and insists on its "mental oneness" in reaction to the constant, consciously recognized disruption of the image of self. The ego overcompensates by insisting on its own unity. The conscious conflict between the self-identified-as-white/male/"moral" (non-body) and the self-identified-as-black/female/vulgar manifests itself in a hysterical insistence on an image of the "mental oneness" of a unified self without a body (without gender, race, class, etc.).[9] This insistence takes place because the self's desired wholeness is constantly undermined as reality conflicts with various ideologies of moral subjectivity: theological ideologies of the spirit; bourgeois humanism and liberal views of the social body as constituted by atomistic Cartesian individuals; and sexism, racism, and other oppressive and exploitative systems.

Elizabeth's greatest neuroses arise when her identifications as not-black and not-female, by virtue of not having a body, fail. Several times in the latter part of the novel, Dan raises the specter of homosexuality as a seeming non sequitur or random attack, and each episode provokes a crisis in Elizabeth. She reacts this way because the specter of queerness makes male-male relations corporeal and sexual, thereby rendering impossible Elizabeth's rejection of the body by identifying as male. It debunks the mind-body split, and as with "the primal scene"—Freudian or Fanonian—the repressed cannot really stay repressed. Confronted with the specter of homosexuality, Elizabeth claims, "It's surely quite all right. I haven't any fixed opinions on this subject" (139), but the more she protests, "the more a revulsion, an overpowering horror of men, arose in her" (139). Her failure to reject being female and make herself a male turns into revulsion of the men who have power over her in patriarchal systems.

As we have seen, Dan's sex shows do not really or do not only terrorize Elizabeth. This proves to be the wrong tactic because, "sex had never counted in the strenuous turmoil of destiny" (63). Although he takes her hand "to show her what linked them together, eternally"—that is, romantic love—Elizabeth is "ungrateful" (148), picking up a book to escape into the life of the mind. Dan then attacks her "life other than this" by undermining its assumptions. Dan says, "He's a homosexual, he also sleeps with cows and anything on earth" (148). Elizabeth then reacts very oddly to this declaration; Dan and Sello "become merged as horrors in her mind," and her "private thought" shatters (148). She bursts out suddenly, "I'm sorry I kissed Woody, who was married . . . And even then he could not kiss nicely at all" (149). This is the first mention of "Woody" and such events in the novel. In other words, despite Elizabeth's insistence to the contrary, she is a woman with a body. Furthermore, if Dan has her saying "the opposite of what she was feeling," perhaps she did not find the kiss unpleasant. In any case, the body and sexuality have arisen not as distanced doppelgangers, like Dan's women, but in Elizabeth's own experience, and her identification as a man has failed to banish the body.

In another scene, Elizabeth picks up a two-volume account of the Oscar Wilde trial and a biography; she adopts the attitude, "It doesn't matter where a man evacuates" (137–8). Despite this lofty sentiment, however, the body becomes an immediate reality: "it was one thing to adopt generous attitudes, at a distance. It was another to have a supreme pervert thrust his soul into your living body" (138). Then, once again the focus shifts from homosexuality to being an embodied woman in a world in which woman can be treated as sexual objects: "it [is] like living in the hot, feverish world of the pissing pervert of the public toilet—the sort of man who, in buses and cinema queues, pressed himself against a woman" (138), and when the woman turns around and rebukes him, he smirks and says, "You're like that too. You're just pretending" (138). Again, the scene invokes not merely heterosexual sex but the power relations between men and women imprinted onto, enacted by, and constituted in the body and mind. Elizabeth cannot really be immune to such attacks. We can read this as a kind of primal "sexual encounter" for women, parallel to the "colonial encounter" for the colonized.

When Elizabeth faces the specter of homosexuality, the body returns, both male and female. The ego's insistent identification with the specular moral figure (white male) fails, and Elizabeth reacts to all this with horror. Becoming a "man" fails to protect her from being a "woman," or a body and a sexual being in overdetermined and multiple political-sexual systems. According to Elizabeth, while gays are accepted at the margins of society and consciousness, "normal" people "do not think about it at all" (117). But this statement is not true, or only partially true; the repression of queerness merely masks the punitive policing of heteronormativity. Elizabeth's question "What was she to do with this record inside her head?" questions "the normal" ideological-moral assumptions conflicting in the novel. The answer to that rhetorical question may be that sexuality (the body and its associations that place you in the world) and the socioeconomic conditions of your past (the world that made you) cannot be repressed; or rather, they may be repressed for a while but they never go away. Those "records" rely upon repression, but those "repressed" histories return in altered forms. Unlike Eugene, Elizabeth cannot repress the reality of herself—her body, her gender, her ethnicity—and of her situation.

So, on one hand, the return of the real explodes the morality of colonialist bourgeois humanism, exposing it as racialized and gendered. On the other, the struggle between the second and third modes reveals that the relativism of Dan is also ideologically laden; the absence of meaning allows concepts, subjects, and social structure to be determined by power. In other words, when it suits him, heteronormativity operates as an ideological tool for Dan just as much as it did for Sello. The ideology of modernity may be predominant in the era of rapid economic development and nascent independent states, but the novel occupies the general, uneven turning point between modernity and postmodernity, and as such interrogates each. Neither the amorality of Dan nor the bourgeois humanism of Sello offer viable options for Elizabeth.

Rather than a subject prey to one master narrative, as in psychoanalysis and the traditional *bildungsroman*, *A Question of Power* presents a subject beset by multiple, overdetermined, and sometimes contradictory ideologies, interpellated in ways that may present an impossible choice, yet demanding that the subject retain some kind of unity. These processes are complex and overdetermined due to the nature of the situation. As we are told early in the novel, the fact that some of the conclusions of the journey "were uncovered through an entirely abnormal relationship with two men might not be so much due to her dubious sanity as to the strangeness of the men themselves" (19).[10] Sometimes when the unconscious erupts, things really are amiss, not only with the patient but with the very *situation* itself. Arlene Elder characterizes Elizabeth's mental illness as an "ironically sane response to the social insanity" of apartheid of South Africa (10), but I would add that the "social insanity" implied in the novel extends beyond South Africa as well. Similarly, Coreen Brown notes that Elizabeth's insanity has been characterized "as a valid response to patriarchy" (2003, 91–92). And the novel professes itself to be an "argument," albeit with "the barriers of the sane and normal... broken down" (15). If we read "sane" as premised on psychological, cultural, and political repression, and "normal" as hegemonic and repressive, then these barriers do need to be broken down. What *A Question of Power* gives us is a taxonomic analysis of the ideologies at work on an individual, not abstract but in the day-to-day life of a particularly situated woman. And unlike otherness postmodernism, Head's novel challenges us to look at all the ways of being that are compressed into any given time and place.

Carol Anne Taylor writes that, in Head's novel, the tragedy is found not in the fall of the protagonist-hero, but "in the continued power of a world that mandates entering a state resembling madness and illness—and yet of one's own choosing and making—as the only means to wholeness" (94). The tragedy presented by the novel suggests what may be at stake in our reconsiderations of conceptions of morality. The novel explores how the concepts of good, evil, and morality, have been deployed in various ideologically problematic ways. In the real world, exposure of such past metanarratives have led us on the Left, particularly literary and cultural studies critics, to regard the entire notion of morality as anathema, but the novel shows us that total rejection of the concept may lead us to disregard and undertheorize values we might want to retain as "good" and "moral." Or rather, perhaps what the novel demonstrates in form and content is an ethics of critical reading that can help us articulate ethics for ourselves. What "saves" Elizabeth at the end of the novel is her realization that her choices are not necessarily limited to either bourgeois humanism or postmodern schizophrenia. While the novel does not resolve all these issues—we are told, "Dan was not over. He had not yet told the whole of mankind about his ambitions, like Hitler and Napoleon, to rule the world" (14)—it does end on a hopeful note invoking some possibilities, reconsidering earlier elements, sometimes associated with the various stages. The conclusion of the novel resonates with the insights produced by the undercutting, insightful processes of the text throughout the novel.[11] That is, throughout the novel, the text distinguishes between Elizabeth's point of view (usually in thrall to Sello or Dan) and a critical evaluation of the pitfalls and possibilities offered by each mode. Toward the end, then, we can recognize the failings of earlier modes while also recuperating or redefining those things we may deem positive.

For example, both Kenosi and Mrs. Jones, although very different, are firmly of the first mode. Kenosi, who is a Roman Catholic, is also "one of the miracles or accidents that saved [Elizabeth's] life" (89). She is "exceedingly beautiful" in her "depth of facial expression, in knowingness and grasp of life" (90). Her constant friendship is one of the anchors in Elizabeth's life, suggesting that the kind of spirituality and kindness associated with the first mode is not limited to the problematic and controlling forms it takes when wielded for exploitative ends. Similarly, Mrs. Jones, who is "full of platitudes after the style of Jesus Christ" and "earnestly [sees] herself walking in the pathway of Christ" (170), is not dismissed by the novel. Although she is monologic and problematic in a number of ways, her desire to help others is genuine. During a mental breakdown, Elizabeth lashes out against Mrs. Jones and the first mode she represents, saying, "Don't you know? You make your children prostitutes" (173). The controlled, obedient students are likened to objects manipulated for the ends of the divine teacher. Later, while Elizabeth is recovering, Mrs. Jones tells her, "I'm going to show you all that love overcomes hatred" (188), and when Elizabeth apologizes, Mrs. Jones tells her, "You must not be afraid of evil" (196). That is, the notions of love, compassion, and spiritual courage can be reimagined, distinct from the problematic ideologies and structures that have deployed them; that is, we might reclaim or retheorize these concepts not in a post-ideological sense but as part of a liberatory, nonrepressive ideology. As Carole Boyce Davies has pointed out, the novel suggests that some ancient traditions, including those associated with growing food and tending children, can heal modern crises like social alienation. Similarly, the character of Eugene, although problematic, is also not characterized as wholly negative, and Elizabeth's work on the cooperative farm in Motabeng, although not in an ideal world, remains valuable and contributes to the eventual peace she strikes with herself and her community.

Cynicism does not necessitate that we cede the ground of morality or ethics to those who would use it for exploitative and reactionary purposes. We can try to learn from Head's example to more fully analyze and possibly rethink morality and ideology not in terms of a Eurocentric psychoanalysis or otherness postmodernism, but with a critical attitude that, while utilizing the insights of poststructuralism and psychoanalysis, keeps an open mind to other epistemological and ethical possibilities.

Concluding Notes

Today, even if the term "postmodern" is passé, the fundamental ideas associated with postmodernism—radical social articulation, the racial/cultural Other as unknowable sublime, the privileging of difference and heterogeneity for their own sakes—permeate progressive cultural studies. Take, for example, a conversation in the 2005 issue of *PMLA*. Bill Brown and his students rightly opine that Jameson greatly overestimates the cognitive unmappability of the Hotel Bonaventura in Los Angeles; according to many, it is actually a very boring building. But the crux of his critique hinges on the similarity of Jameson's Marxist faith to Dante's Christian one. In other words, the problem with Jameson is not that he dehistoricized the aptitude for cognitive mapping of a particular group of people at a particular point in time, that he has become dated or stodgy, or even that he was simply wrong, but rather that he appeals to a universal metanarrative and tries to incorporate into it that which is actually unassimilable. It is yet another manifestation of the same rhetorical moves that we see ad nauseum.

Even more problematic is the roundtable that follows the essay. The various critics seem amazed that religion and fundamentalism are powerful ideas in today's political life the world over. Rey Chow writes, "what if the problem is that we have completely underestimated the potency of such stupidity?" (875). By "stupidity," she refers to the successful ideological manipulation of people by right-wing fundamentalists. Chow is making the case for why notions of the subject, morality, and religion are important for the left, but the way she puts it, in a kind of free indirect discourse mouthing the general chorus of progressive cultural critics, testifies to how myopic and condescending the postmodern Left can be. But as she herself argues, poststructuralism's undermining of referentiality limits its challenge to the structures of social-political life; there are structures, discourses, and realities outside the realm of otherness postmodernism that demand that we "reopen" the conversation.

Although this book focuses on otherness postmodernism in readings of key postmodern texts, here I would like to turn to the ways in which some of its assumptions and logics have moved well beyond the confines of Left-identified cultural studies. The logic of otherness postmodernism is modular and flexible; it can and has been appropriated by various political ideologies for the purposes of "reading" the world in certain ways. For example, despite its critique of the logic of signification, otherness postmodernism shares fundamental assumptions with the kind of liberal multiculturalism prevalent in the United States and other Western countries today. Both otherness postmodernism and multiculturalism rely on the false binaries between sameness and difference that ironically flatten both concepts. Liberal multiculturalism, with the best of intentions, posits the "Sameness" of a monocultural society against the "difference" of multiculturalism. This "you-taste-my-food-I'll-taste-yours" form of multiculturalism is untenable because it casts each cultural group as "Same," or homogenous, and does not account for power differences between and within groups. Seyla Benhabib points out that such "strong" or "mosaic multiculturalism" is impossible because the constituent groups are not clearly delineated and identifiable (7–8). Multiculturalism, also like otherness postmodernism, exalts "difference," or incommensurability. While multiculturalism may not be postmodern in its assumption of the homogeneity of each group, it does rely on a sameness/difference binary. In other words, multiculturalism and otherness postmodernism both juxtapose an oppressive unity against a liberatory heterogeneity. Both otherness postmodernism and multiculturalism fail to engage issues of evaluation, mediations (within and between groups), and efforts toward collaborative articulations of common values, and they both fail to account for structures of power—particularly global capital—that create racial and different human groupings.

E. San Juan, one of the most trenchant critics of both postmodernism and multiculturalism, describes liberal multiculturalism as a fantasy in which "plural cultures of ethnicities [coexist] peacefully, without serious contestation, in a free play of monads in 'the best of all possible worlds'" (6). The multiculturalist or cosmopolitan arena is "a bazaar for anyone who can buy," although some goods not as valuable as others (6); this "mode of appropriation," San Juan argues, "fetishizes and commodifies others" (7). He argues that multiculturalism's rhetoric of difference actually destroys difference; "retrograde" multiculturalisms celebrate otherness and fossilize them, flattening distinctions of race, class, gender, nationality, and various other antagonisms (7). Some versions of multiculturalism may "grant cultural autonomy but *hide or ignore structural inequalities under the umbrella of a refurbished humanist cosmopolitanism*" (7, my emphasis).

Postmodernism, moreover, can be as useful to the Right as the Left. The Right's utilization of postmodern concepts can highlight some of the flaws in and dangers of the postmodern Left's ideological fantasy of articulation and privileging of negativity. Some neoconservatives now claim to agree about the impossibility of fixing signification and universals, the importance of privileging "local" contexts and genealogies, and the necessity of being pragmatic and strategic. But it is telling to examine their actual intentions, interests, and actions. The new neoconservative strategic postmodernists constantly rearticulate and change the terms of the discussions as it suits the interests of power, repudiating older notions of ideology, but they ultimately *act* according to the perceived necessities of institutional structures. For example, claims for "equal representation" of creationism or "intelligent design" in the United States rely on the notion of cultural pluralism, although it belies the Christian fundamentalism that does *not* recognize the relative equality of religions or ideas.[1] Stanley Fish writes about the appropriation of the rhetoric of postmodernism, multiculturalism, and Gerald Graff's notion of "teaching the conflicts" by intelligent design proponents. The Right's appropriation of this discourse is effective because it "takes the focus away from the scientific credibility of intelligent design . . . and puts it instead on the more abstract issues of freedom and open inquiry" (70)—and, it may be added, pluralism and diversity. But such arguments are, of course, strategic; the Right's tactical use of postmodern and multicultural logic does not mean they believe them. Rather, the appeal to "multiculturalism" or equal representation is a strategy within a particular historical-political situation; conservatives know that many people in the First World, wanting to think of themselves as basically good and fair, have imbibed the tenets of multiculturalism and the underlying postmodernist notions of cultural relativism and even social constructionism. Fine, the conservatives say, let us pretend to agree that knowledge is constructed by the ideological state apparatus of schools (although perhaps not with those words) under the ideological hegemony of Western science or liberalism. This approach could be thought of as "strategic postmodernism."

One of the most blatant examples of strategic postmodernism can be found in the concept of "Postmodern Empire." Robert Cooper, a senior British diplomat and one of Tony Blair's chief advisors, called for a new postmodern imperialism in the April 2002 issue of the *Observer*.

Cooper's essay was then reprinted in the humbly titled volume *Re-Ordering the World* (2002). Cooper describes "post imperial, postmodern states" as those that "no longer think of security primarily in terms of conquest," and which are characterized by "the rejection of force for resolving disputes and the consequent codification of self-enforced rules of behaviour" as well as "the growing irrelevance of borders." For such states, "security is based on transparency, mutual openness, interdependence and mutual vulnerability." States still stuck in the modern and premodern modes—primarily in the Third World—threaten the postmodern world. In such a climate, Cooper writes, the West needs to stop worrying about universalism:

> The postmodern world has to start to get used to double standards. Among ourselves, we operate on the basis of laws and open cooperative security. But, when dealing with old-fashioned states outside the postmodern continent of Europe, we need to revert to the rougher methods of an earlier era—force, pre-emptive attack, deception, whatever is necessary to deal with those who still live in the nineteenth century world of every state for itself. ("Why We Still Need Empires")

In recognition of the unilateralist aggression of the Bush administration, Cooper notes that the United States is "reluctant" to enter the postmodern world, although he nevertheless includes the United States in the postmodern.[2]

Cooper's claims constitute a thinly veiled justification for neo-imperialism. His division of the world is based on a progression without consideration of interlinked histories—for example, the ones depicted in Ngugi wa Thiong'o's scathing novel *Devil on the Cross*—and his actual criteria for modernity is power. Underlying his postmodern/premodern schema is the "clash of cultures" rhetoric that draws on multiculturalism's notion of various cultures. But Cooper's acceptance of the progression from modernity to postmodernity ("Post-Modern State" 12), and his embrace of the term postmodern again raise the fundamental question of evaluation. How do we differentiate Cooper's claims from that of progressive postmodernists? How do we know that, as Tariq Ali puts it, Cooper's statement is hypocrisy dressed up at postmodernism?

Another example of strategic—or perhaps, in this case, earnest—postmodernism can be seen in the curious fate of what is known as the "Washington consensus"; this case exemplifies the easy appropriation of postmodern ideas by neoliberals as well as neoconservatives. In foreign policy and economics circles, the Washington consensus refers to the general agreement—at least in Washington, D.C.—that international stability and prosperity can only be achieved through the twin tenets of neoliberalization and democracy. In common usage, "neoliberalization" refers to privatization, free trade, economic regulation, and the like, while "democracy" refers specifically to free elections, constitutional reform, rule of law, and so on. Washington consensus is sometimes used synonymously with "market fundamentalism" and "neoliberalism" (Williamson, "What Should" 252), and it certainly informed the G.W. Bush's administration's desire to spread "freedom": "As the Bush Administration's 2002 National Security Strategy pre-emptively puts it, in case anyone begins to think differently, there is only one 'single sustainable model for national success: freedom, democracy, and free enterprise' " (Grandin). The term was first presented by economist John Williamson at a 1989 conference of the Institute for International Economics, and then explicated in a 1990 essay titled "What Washington Means by Policy Reform." In that essay, Williamson outlines ten basic guidelines for policy reform, what he calls "the lowest common denominator" of policy reform prescribed by Washington for Latin American countries.[3] Williamson meant this term to refer to an "intellectual convergence" informing reform policies, the result of decades of debate about economic development. In other words, he did not see these reforms as the imposition of American will; his emphasis was on the "consensus" rather than the "Washington." Later, he would observe that comparable terms such as "universal convergence" or "one-world consensus" might work better (251). But in 2000, Williamson surveys the use of the term and finds that it has been hijacked. His original purpose, he points out, had been to identify practical, useful policy reforms against extremes of Reagonomics (market fundamentalism) when it was on the decline, but now the term is often used to refer to the extremest form of market fundamentalism. He cites Joseph Stiglitz, former chief economist of the World Bank, as one of the misusers (256). Moisés Naím, editor of *Foreign Policy* magazine, concurs that during the 1990s, "The world was under the impression that a clear and robust consensus existed about what poor countries should do to become more prosperous" (87).[4]

The theoretical moves Williamson uses to grapple with what he sees as the mutation of his term will be familiar to postmodernists. Because "the battle of economic ideas . . . is fought to a significant extent with rhetoric," he wants to examine "the semantic issues involved" in the debates about the Washington consensus (252). So he shifts the conversation from fundamental economic principles to issues of discourse and articulation. He relinquishes ownership of the term and implicitly acknowledges polysemy: "I had naively imagined that just because I had invented the expression, I had some sort of intellectual property rights that entitled me to dictate its meaning, but in fact the concept had become public property" (252). By the phrase "public property," he means that different constituents of the social sphere will struggle over it. In this context, Williamson justifies his use of the concept by its emphasis on a *specific* context: "the Washington Consensus as I conceived it was in principle geographically and historically specific, a lowest common denominator of the reforms that I judged 'Washington' could agree were needed in Latin America as of 1989" (254). Of course, he adds, the basic principles would not have been that different applied to other parts of the Third World, that is, Africa and Asia. Nevertheless, he implies that he was referring to a specific context and did not mean that the term should be thought "valid for all places and at all times" (255). Debates about social terms should focus on localized meaning; debates about universals are specious, he argues, because "there is little merit in attacking abstract, undefined concepts that are interpreted to mean whatever the author momentarily decides they mean. It is better to spell out those concepts that are being criticized and debate policies on the basis of their merits" (262). Therefore, he concludes that the problem with the usage of the term is that people were trying to totalize from his local, specific use: "My qualifications about the Washington Consensus being an agenda for a specific part of the world at a particular moment of history were quickly forgotten, as the search for a new ideology, to endorse or to hate, was perceived to have succeeded" (256). He also points out that the utilization of the term, and particularly the emphasis on economic liberalization was a *strategic* negotiating tactic: "the staffs of the Bretton Woods institutions perceived themselves as storming the citadels of statism, which led them as a negotiating ploy to demand more in the way of liberalizing reforms than they really expected to achieve" (256). Finally, what he *calls* for—aside from actual meaning—is *post-ideology*:

> Admittedly my suggestions do not answer the pleas for a new ideology that would more adequately reflect the goals of the multilateral development banks and that might thus increase the chance of establishing local ownership of the sort of economic policy stance conducive to rapid and equitable growth. Let me plead in defense that I am not a suitable person to launch an ideology, inasmuch as Naím (2000) characterizes ideology

as a thought-economizing device and I actually believe that thinking is more desirable than economizing on thought. (262)

In sum, Williamson recommends "post-ideological" or antifoundationalist approaches, giving up "the hopeless quest to identify a consensus where there is none" (262). In other words, Williamson's experience with polysemy makes him decide to embrace and utilize that semiotic negativity.

Other economists agree with Williamson about the inability to reach consensus. Tim Geithner, former CEO of the Federal Bank Reserve of New York and current Secretary of the Treasury, claims, "I don't think anyone believes that there is some universal model that can or should be imposed on the world—Washington consensus, post Washington consensus, or not" (qtd. in Williamson 261). Economist Ravi Kanbur concurs, "local realities matter and a broad approach as captured in one consensus or another is bound to be problematic if applied across the board," and warns against making "blanket statements" (2). Moreover, Kanbur emphasizes that "intellectual analysis" must recognize "the conditional nature of the original policy prescriptions" (3). Moisés Naím agrees that there is more of a "Washington Confusion" than consensus. These economists recognize that the Washington Consensus had been used as, in Laclau and Mouffe's terms, a "nodal point" to fix the field of signifiers, but that no such overarching articulation can be permanent or wholly consistent. Naím writes, "the Washington Consensus became an ill-suited and temporary substitute for the all-encompassing ideological frameworks that millions of people had come to depend on to shape their opinions about affairs at home and abroad, judge public policies, and even steer some aspects of their daily lives" (90). What helped the illusion of a coherent ideology, Naím writes, was the term's "self-assured tone ('the consensus'), its prescriptive orientation, its directional message, and its origin in Washington, the capital of the victorious empire" (90). But that consensus was as illusory, he claims, as that of communism, so new postideological, strategic, and local solutions must be found to "develop" the Third World.

Naím's solution, likes Williamson's, is that the international economic structure must embrace country-specific policies and institutions: "The solution is not to wait for a new 'global financial architecture' that would eliminate the effects of the international economic cycle" (97). There are "no preordained solutions," and ideologies must not be imposed from outside due to "a general uneasiness about the policy direction of the last ten years," or an overemphasis on a unified ideology of neoliberalization (Naím 100–101). Rather, the Third World needs a unity of specificity and difference; Naím writes, "If developing countries are to buy time to make these reforms work, then they must rely on a shared ideological commitment that emerges from within, not one that is imposed from without" (101).

But these conversations about a post-Washington Consensus occlude the actual processes. As evidenced by the Bush administration's Iraq war, it is not Washington's rhetoric that forces Third World nations to reconfigure their economies or cut their health care and educational services; rather, economic, political, or military pressures produce these outcomes through direct or structural violence. In a sense, then, to refer to either Washington Consensus or Confusion as "free market fundamentalism" is essentially correct because that *is* the system in which we all live; this free market fundamentalism has forced debilitating structural adjustment policies and narrow economic development on third world nations, focusing on exports to richer countries rather than sustainable infrastructures. These theorists ignore that, in practice, the Washington Consensus does describe the policies of economic neoliberalization all over the world in favor of First World economies, all under the banner of "democracy"; the International Monetary Fund and World Bank loans that turned out to be so debated, contested, and problematic in ensuing years, were in fact "conditional on the adoption of [Washington] consensus-inspired policy reforms" (Naím 90).

Furthermore, this Washington consensus has exacerbated ethnic hatred in the world. In the popular *World On Fire*, Yale law professor and former international development worker, Amy Chua argues that United States' naïve promotion of constitutional democracy (primarily in the form of free elections) is dangerous in conjunction with the ethnic and cultural tension created by free-market neoliberalization that favors an ethnic minority. The favored status of what Chua calls "market-dominant minorities" has produced what seems greater ethnic hatred and violence. The actual source of this violence, however, is the continuing unequal distribution of resources.[5] While Chua was initially in favor of neoliberalization, reference to historical events leads Chua to question the Washington Consensus and theorize a reason for racial tensions that does not rely on simplistic, unmediated binaries of sameness and difference.

In other words, the gap between rhetoric and reality can only be determined by notions of reference, ethics, and metanarratives. All elements of the social have to be articulated for us to understand them, and no one can have total and final knowledge, but these ideas themselves are not the key to politics. They are simply descriptions of how things work and hence do not in themselves provide justification and explanation for a Left politics. As Gilroy suggests, we need to go beyond the dichotomies of sameness and difference, but the answer is not to simply privilege heterogeneity or radical articulation. Rather, it is a messy, difficult, ongoing process of finding more information, debating and struggling, identifying the structures of power that shape and move us in particular ways, and then changing them.

The claims of postmodernism neglect structural inequalities that can be traced historically and evaluated. And because otherness postmodernism pervades not only literary and cultural studies (broadly defined) but also increasingly the public conversations about race, ethnicity, identity, and other related issues, recent conversations have tried to mediate between the untenable limits of sameness versus difference and suggest several alternatives. In this last section, I will turn to some of these options. One important argument is that we need to take seriously the notion of critical referentiality, or "truth" with a small "t." A second necessity is to reconsider metanarratives of various kinds. We also need some kind of an ethics of reading literature *and* the world that takes into account both the mistakes of the past as well as the cultural *and* structural elements of contemporary politics.

At this moment in cultural studies, Rey Chow's argument to let referentiality interrupt our theoretical frameworks is crucial. Sandra Harding discusses the possibility for a "strong objectivity," which takes seriously processes of signification and interpretation while also attempting to produce increasingly accurate accounts of the world. An analogy for this would be letting a close reading of a text shape one's arguments about a text; we understand that texts are mediated by language, ideology, subjectivity, form, production and distribution, and many other factors, and these should all constitute part of our understanding of a text, yet we also understand that within these discourses and contexts, we can make arguments about the meaning of a text based on, as we like to tell our students, "what is on the page." Of course, these will not be simple or unanimous; in fact, contention is important—both about the shape and nature of the social structures in which we live and the meta-discourses we use to analyze them.

By the same token, we need to rethink our skepticism about metanarratives, particularly at a time when valuation of difference is as easily embraced by the Right as well as the Left. In the wake of the instrumentalization and fragmentation of the society and the academy, Masao Miyoshi writes,

> Critics, however, can still discern signs among people and organize their findings into an argument and program for dissemination. The academics' work in this marketized world, then, is to learn and watch problems in as many sites as they can keep track of... In fact, far from abandoning the master narratives, the critics and scholars in the humanities must restore the public rigor of the metanarrative. (49)

In other words, we do not have to stay stymied in the false binary of absolute, timeless Truth versus absolute difference. Miyoshi argues not only that we can, but also that we must reimagine comparative, unifying metanarratives.

Likewise, in *The Claims of Culture*, Seyla Benhabib argues that the relativism of Rorty and Lyotard fails because "the very process of individuating and identifying frameworks contradicts the claims of framework relativism" (28). In other words, there must be some common ground upon which the apparently disparate elements are articulated and differentiated. While relativism may have "hermeneutic truth" (34), it is ultimately not a viable model for social democracy. Like Habermas, Benhabib seeks to recast "discourse ethics" through "interactive universalism" (14). Benhabib argues that for political democracies to develop a truly pluralist society, need "universal respect," "egalitarian reciprocity," "voluntary self ascription," or not forcing members into a group, and "freedom of exit and association" with a group (11, 20). While she fails to address the structural inequalities or the will-to-power notions of truth and knowledge—Benhabib's prescription is practical, reasonable discourse—the way she addresses flexibility in these matters is important and, I would argue, if we take into account structures of power, more nuanced than the general postmodernist notion of articulation.

In fact, many of the theorists generally associated with postmodernism and more particularly and accurately with poststructuralism do not disown the notion of "truth." Interestingly, such comments often occur during interviews, when the theorist is posed questions about truths their work has raised. In a late interview, Foucault claimed that "What I try to achieve is the history of the relations which thought maintains with truth; the history of thought insofar as it is the thought of truth. All those who say truth does not exist for me are simple minded" (257). That is, while he denies any absolute or transcendent morality or truth, he does recognize that our collective practices constitute ontology and epistemology. This history of relations, the genealogies that Foucault examines, expose foundationalist or absolute universalist notions of things like sexuality, insanity, or morality, but these histories themselves can be more or less true accounts of human practices. By the same token, in *Limited, Inc.*, Derrida explains that what he means by "text" can be "context," or "the entire 'real-history-of-the-world,'" which "is extremely vast, old, powerfully established, stabilized or rooted in a network of conventions (for instance, those of language) and yet which still remains a context" (136). In other words, as Christopher Norris vehemently argues, Derrida does not reject notions of referentiality and truth; rather, he is interested in better and more accurate understandings of the world we live in (*Derrida*). Žižek, too, argues that his beloved Lacan is not postmodernist or anti-reason, but rather interested in better articulating the conditions and processes through which subjects are formed (*Sublime* 7).

Just as we reconsider poststructuralist theorists, we should also reconsider those methods and areas of study that may have been too quickly dismissed as essentialist, empiricist, or otherwise theoretically naïve. In a 1996 essay, Mae G. Henderson examines the problematic relationship of "black cultural studies," defined as poststructuralism-influenced cultural studies imported from Britain, to U.S. Black Studies. She is "concerned about the uncritical appropriation of British cultural studies as a model for understanding African American culture and experience" (63), particularly when Black studies is dismissed as naïve, simplistic "victim" or "oppression studies" and nationalist, masculinist, and essentialist.

Recovering Black Studies as a model for cultural studies, then, means reclaiming it as a multidisciplinary, cross-cultural, and comparative model of study that places into juxtaposition the history, culture, and politics of blacks in the United States, Caribbean, and Africa. Such a program was meant to challenge the conventional disciplinary boundaries of humanistic study as well as to enlarge our conceptions of culture and its relation to history and politics. By introducing a comparative and historical dimension into its methodologies—and this in spite of its avowed nationalist agenda—Black Studies set into motion a revolution in the academy through its challenge to the ethnocentric Euro-American scholarship that had provided the basis for knowledge claims. (Henderson 63–64)

I agree with Henderson that the specificity of not only African Americans but also *anyone* will be lost if any object of study is uncritically subsumed into a particular methodological or ideological paradigm. Moreover, the assumptions of otherness postmodernism have become so normalized in literary and cultural studies that we tend to reproduce them continually without even realizing that there may be other viable and important ways of dealing with issues of culture, politics, ideology, and art. Henderson suggests that, in addition to British works of cultural studies, "we ought to reexamine some of the works published in the 1960s and 1970s documenting the institutionalization of Black Studies as founding texts of this movement" (66). By the same token, we can revisit the work of cultural theorists who exemplify alternatives from historical materialism, ethnic and postcolonial studies, and historicized psychoanalysis. Just a handful of such theorists include Simone de Beauvoir, Angela Davis, Frantz Fanon, Manning Marable, E. San Juan, Jean-Paul Sartre, and A. Sivanandan.

The reconsideration of referentiality, contexts, and metanarratives are important because they ground a reconsideration of a politics of human rights, or perhaps a critical humanism. There is much discussion these days about the problems with human rights discourse, but the problematics of the discourse does not render all uses and forms of human rights problematic. In fact, universal human rights is an important notion that can offset the politics of difference *and* explain why different, unequal, exploitative, and/or abusive structures for different people are wrong. Žižek concurs with Benn Michaels and others that "politics today is increasingly a politics of merely negotiating compromises between different positions" ("One Measure"), but rather than simply calling for us to abandon the discourse of identity and difference, he argues for notions of critical, human-produced universality. Žižek argues that "true universality" is not a priori or fundamental but forged through practice and through common struggle, and that human rights as universal can be the basis for attacking exclusionary humanisms:

> Far from being pre-political [fundamental, essentialist], "universal human rights" designate the precise space of politicization proper; what they amount to is the right to universality as such—the right of a political agent to assert its radical non-coincidence with itself (in its particular identity), to posit itself as the "supernumerary," the one with no proper place in the social edifice; and thus an agent of universality in the social itself...At the very moment when we try to conceive the political rights of citizens without reference to a universal "meta-political" human rights, we lose politics itself; that is to say, we reduce politics to

a "post-political" play of negotiation of particular interests. ("Against Human Rights" 131)

In other words, it is not merely the difference claimed by otherness postmodernism that can ground a radical politics; it is also the *sameness* of human beings that can help explain why, in Rey Chow's terms, the exclusion of X is wrong. As opposed to his emphasis in *Sublime Object* that the impossibility of signification forms the basis of political analysis, in such later essays Žižek seems to approach the subject and the social field more dialectically.

By the same token, Gayatri Spivak also grounds the potential for agency in notions of reason, accountability, and even freedom. She has said that:

...identity claims are political manipulations of people who seem to share one characteristic and therefore it is a sort of roll-call concept.
Now it seems to me that agency relates to accountable reason. The idea of agency comes from the principle of accountable reason, that one acts with responsibility, that one has to assume the possibility of intention, one has to assume even the freedom of subjectivity in order to be responsible. That's where agency is located. (*Selected* 294)

Implicit in her discussion of agency is a notion of the human subject with the capacity for reason, responsibility, obedience or resistance, honesty or deception. Both Spivak and Žižek balance the political particularities produced by the inequities of this world, or a politics of difference, with the ethical and transformative power of a notion of the human, or a politics of sameness.

The false unmediated binaries between totality and difference, sameness and otherness, and foundationalism and skepticism can be broken down by examining how they actually interplay in the world. Religious fundamentalists will strategically utilize the liberal multicultural politics of difference if it suits them; postmodernists (self-proclaimed or not) often rely on implicit notions of justice and human rights. When such ossified structures of thought prevent us from actual engagement with the complex dynamics of the world we live in, it helps maintain power structures. If we bracket off the ugly, messy complexities of social reality from debate, we remain in the fantasy that we can break out of ideology without changing those social realities. The texts I discuss in this book demonstrate the best ways to read the world— literature, signification, identity, social formations, all constituted by and constituting that world—and I worry that our failure to rise to the challenge posed by these texts corresponds to our failure to read that world. Fortunately, we have the capacity for constant and ruthless criticisms that can interrogate hegemonic discourses, structures, and processes and our implication in them.

Notes

One   The Ideological Fantasy of Otherness Postmodernism

1. Žižek illustrates this notion of ideology by drawing on Peter Sloterdijk's 1987 *Critique of Cynical Reason*, which explores how cynicism has today become the dominant form of ideology. "Ideology" in the traditional Marxist sense assumes false consciousness, but the notion of "false consciousness" itself can be a bulwark for ideological reality. If the dominant ideology is cynicism, the notion of "enlightenment" or simply providing information is not enough. Sloterdijk reformulates Marx's comment that "They do not know it, but they are doing it," as "They know very well what they are doing, but still, they are doing it" (qtd. in Žižek, *Sublime* 29). Sloterdijk calls this a kind of "enlightened false consciousness," in which you know what you are doing but you keep doing it because of circumstantial necessity; he writes, "To act against better knowledge is today the global situation in the superstructure; it knows itself to be without illusions and yet to have been dragged down by the 'power of things'" (6). Cynicism becomes predominant "with the passing of defiant hopes," when we are left with only "detached negativity that scarcely allows itself any hope, at most a little irony and pity" (Sloterdijk 6). The most obvious example would be a leftist academic who nevertheless lives the typically overconsumptive life of the United States; the justification, according to Sloterdijk, is the sense that "at least I am not as bad as someone else might be." I do not exempt myself from this paradox; I am not advocating an anarchic voluntarism or the idea that we can simply pluck ourselves out of structures. My point is that the overreliance on an ideological fantasy is never enough. Nevertheless, this "knowing better" is the axis of political solidarity that the otherness postmodernism identifies as the new radical democratic attitude.

2. As compelling as Žižek's work is—particularly his recent work—what I would call his Lacanian fundamentalism is frustrating and reflects the problems of the theorists that he critiques. While Žižek means to puncture the notion of false consciousness as superstructural (i.e., not enforced by structures, believed rather than lived), for him, essentially the "false consciousness" that constitutes a subject is the belief in and desire for

signification. For the Lacanian Žižek, the fundamental purpose of the ideological fantasy is to hide the fact that, despite our desire to know what the Other wants so we can fulfill it, every attempt to affix a signifier's identity will fail. This leads Žižek to conclude that "the real aim" of ideology is to justify its own form: "the real goal is the consistency of the ideological attitude itself . . . that we continue to walk as straight as we can in one direction, that we follow even the most dubious opinions once our mind has been made up regarding them" (*Sublime* 84). As such, Žižek argues that we must recognize a fundamental state of misrecognition as unavoidable and formative. He argues that not only must we recognize the surplus of the Real beyond symbolization, we must recognize that lack as the driving force of signification: "it is this surplus of the Real over symbolization that functions as the object-cause of desire" (*Sublime* 3). To Žižek, this driving force means not a field of the Real beyond our ability to understand, reach, and articulate, but rather "a fundamental deadlock ('antagonism'), a kernel resisting symbolic integration-dissolution" (*Sublime* 3). Psychoanalysis, for Žižek, offers the best understanding of this process because it explains how and why responses to the central "empty signifier" proliferate.

But here we begin to see a nonessentialist, antifoundationalist drive beginning not only to echo itself as its own assertion, but also superseding admittedly provisionally, historically articulated but nevertheless real, experienced political-social problems. For example, one of Žižek's examples of a fundamental, impossible antagonism is gender relations, for which he says there is no final resolution, "and the only basis for a somewhat bearable relation between the sexes is an acknowledgment of this basic antagonism, this basic impossibility" (*Sublime* 5). While a fundamental difference or nonbreachable chasm may exist ontologically and discursively between not only men and women, but also between different groups of women and men, and between individual men and men and women and women—while such difference may be true ontologically, what insight does this offer us into protecting against sexual harassment in the workplace or preventing the exploitation of third-world women's labor in free-trade zones? At such moments, the line between description of ontology and exaltation of fundamental nonidentity becomes problematically blurred. Žižek runs the risk of degenerating into a rhetoric of difference, the central assumption of otherness postmodernism, and perpetuating the ideological fantasy that he himself points out and names, and which actually enables patriarchy and gendered exploitation to continue. For further discussions of Žižek's work, see Sharpe and Bellamy.

3. For examples of such controversies, see Aronowitz; Butler et al.; Connery; *On Left Conservatism*; Pollitt; Proyect; Robbins and Ross; San Juan; Sand; Sivanandan; and Sokal.

4. The movement toward poststructuralist ethics is promising, but even the best attempts ultimately do not move beyond the sameness-difference

binary. Poststructuralist ethics in the vein of Emmanuel Levinas and Drucilla Cornell is premised upon the notion that engagement or recognition of the Other can only take two forms: cooptation and cultural imperialism, or the recognition of the impossibility of knowing the Other. See Cornell, *Philosophy of the Limit*, and Butler, "Poststructuralism and Postmarxism."

5. Gilroy writes, "Neither the mechanistic essentialism that is too squeamish to acknowledge the possibility of difference within sameness nor the lazy alternative that animates the supposedly strategic variety of essentialism can supply keys to the untidy workings of diaspora identities. They are creolized, syncretized, hybridized, and chronically impure cultural forms" (*Against Race* 129).

6. The discussions of these categorizations and histories are too numerous to provide any kind of comprehensive or even adequately representative list, but the following sources provide a sample range: Benn Michaels; Callinicos; Foster; Hassan; Hogue, "Postmodernism" and *Race*; hooks; Hutcheon, *Poetics* and *Politics*; Huyssen; Leitch; Lyotard; Mohanty; Nicholson; and West.

7. See also Eagleton, *Illusions* and *Figures*; Katz; Norris; Wilson; and Wolin.

8. Jameson, Harvey, and Eagleton are the best known critics of postmodernism as a cultural form and mode of production deployed by advanced global capitalism; see also Hennessy.

9. For examples of how such cross-pollinations may work, see Shen.

10. Other theorists have also articulated means for knowing the world around us. Satya Mohanty suggests a "post-positivist realism" for evaluating between different interpretations of the world, and while I agree with his argument in spirit, I also think he underestimates the structures of power that make rational and truthful discourse extremely difficult. That is also the weakness of Seyla Benhabib and Jürgen Habermas; while their hopes for a public discourse and ethics is laudable and necessary, they underestimate structural (political, economic, psychic) pressures on subjects as well as plain old disingenuousness, selfishness, and fear.

11. Tied to such readings of experimental texts by marginal writers is the tendency to read *all* texts by ethnic writers as transcriptions—in content or form—of experience and subjectivity. As Frederick Luis Aldama points out, in readings of texts by marginal writers, quite often "the anthropological has subsumed the literary" (2). And because such literary texts are identified with reality, both the aesthetic form of those texts and the complexities of reality are underread; Aldama continues, "By confusing aesthetics with ontological fact, we risk committing acts of romantic racialism that fail to address the real issues of real oppression and exploitation in the world" (40). Gina Caison also refers to the tendency to confuse aesthetic text with ontology—particular the marginal writer's life—as "autobioethnography."

Two   Theresa Hak Kyung Cha and the Politics of Form

1. On narrative, see Guarino-Trier; on translation, see Bergvali; on dictation, see Min; on collective identity, see Lee; and on reading and writing, see Frost, Twelbeck, and Shih, "Nationalism and Korean American Women's Writing."

2. I do not mean to conflate or homogenize the broad areas of postmodernism, the historical avant-garde, and modernism. Rather, in this essay I will use "postmodernism" and "experimental art" as a shorthand for the kind of art that rejects the conventions of mimetic realism in literature, film, and other arts, as ideologically problematic. Furthermore, although there are obviously many differences between film, literature, and visual art, I discuss these things together as forms of art similarly impacted by politically progressive theories of formal disruption.

3. Because the subject is so vast, this list is by no means complete, but for further discussions of the politics of Western avant-garde art in the twentieth century, see Adorno; Brecht, "Against George Lukács"; Bürger; Harvey, *The Condition of Postmodernity*; Huyssen; Jameson, *The Political Unconscious* and *Postmodernism*; and Lukács.

4. In this chapter, unnamed page numbers in parentheses refer to the anthology, *Apparatus: Cinematographic Apparatus*, edited by Cha.

5. In *Apparatus*, these essays include Jean-Louis Baudry, "Ideological Effects of the Basic Cinematographic Apparatus," 25–37, "The Apparatus," 41–62, and "Author and Analyzable Subject," 67–83; Thierry Kuntzel, "*Le Défilement*: A View in Closeup," 232–47; Bertrand Augst, "*Le Défilement* Into the Look," 249–59, and "The Lure of Psychoanalysis in Film Theory," 415–37; and Christian Metz, "The Fiction Film and Its Spectator: A Metapsychological Study," 373–409.

6. Maya Deren, "An Anagram of Ideas on Art, Form and Film," in Cha, *Apparatus*, 94, 112.

7. Also in *Apparatus*, these include the simultaneous pieces by Gregory Woods, "A Work Journal of the Straub/Huillet Film, *Moses and Aaron*," and Danièle Huillet, "Notes on Gregory's Work Journal," 147–231; and Danièle Huillet and Jean-Marie Straub, "Every Revolution Is a Throw of the Dice," 329–54.

8. In *Apparatus*, the Vertov essays gathered under the heading, "The Vertov Papers," include "The Man with the Movie Camera (A Visual Symphony)," 7–9; "From Kino-Eye to Radio-Eye (The Kinoks' ABCs)," 10–14; a 1930 interview, 14–17; and "On Organizing a Creative Laboratory," 17–20. The anthology also includes Vertov's "Film Directors: A Revolution," 85–90. For further discussions of these texts and their contexts, see Michelson (305) and Petric (206).

9. For one discussion of the politics of audiences' resistance to the ideological work of cinema, see Stewart.

10. Furthermore, she is not only the "inverted double" of the viewer and photographer but of the grandmother in the picture as well. She is the "negative" of the grandmother, who "is a massive figure in the foreground,

a dark mass with a white head," while "the maid is a slim figure in the background, a white mass with a dark head." She is also the "repetition" of the grandmother because she is like the figure of the mother (in another photo in the memoir), and because she is "a figure positioned as a *reclame*, in the technical sense of the term." Vernet has a good time with the variations on this term, which in music indicates "the response that is repeated after the versicle," and in typography "is a mark placed in the margin of the text, indicating the point at which the composition or the reading is to be picked up and continued" (359). In a further felicity for an essay centering on "the difference between the sexes and fetishism in film and cinematic apparatus," Vernet "cannot pass up the opportunity to point out this happy coincidence provided by the French language"; *reclame* is not only the musical response and a punctuation mark indicating where a reading is to stop and be taken up again, but "in falconry, *le reclame* is the signal used to call the bird of prey back to the lure" (359).

11. See Sontag (*Reader* 99, 102). Susan Sontag was another significant influence on Cha. It is interesting that, in her most recent book, *Regarding the Pain of Others*, Sontag criticizes the postmodernist emphasis on depthless "spectacle," pointing out that many people "do not have the luxury of patronizing reality" (111). So, in a sense, her approach has shifted toward a more complex ethics of reading, even to the point of explicitly arguing against claims she made in the 1970s.

12. In "Commentaire," blank white pages are 262 and 276–7, and blank black pages are 260, 287–8, 294–5, 313–7.

13. For further discussions of white space, see Dodson, Caminero-Santangelo, and Hill.

14. One of the most striking examples of the remnants of essentialist readings of the text is the tendency to assume a singular narrator in *Dictee* and to identify that narrator with Cha. Sometimes even character-speakers or unidentified voices in the text identify with Cha. For a further discussion of this issue, see S. Kim.

15. In his study of "downtown fiction," *Suburban Ambush*, Robert Siegle writes that the introductory section "works well to foretell the effects of the narrator's schooling as a threatening encounter with a powerful educational establishment determined to regularize students' thinking and writing" (238–9).

16. See also Nahm and Choy.

17. For further discussion of epistemic content of identity and emotions, see Mohanty.

Three   Not Three Worlds But One: Thomas Pynchon and the Invisibility of Race

1. Important exceptions include Young, Rothberg, Caesar and Takashi, and Lynd. Criticism of *Mason & Dixon*, of a different historical moment, tends

less toward otherness postmodernism and, as the very syntax of the novel demands, grapples with our historical responsibilities, in a variety of ways; see Daniel Punday's thoughtful essay.

2. See Bové (657) and Tanner (75).

3. Joseph Tabbi uses the Kantian sublime to describe the failure to comprehend "technological structures and global corporate systems" (ix); he calls this the "technological sublime" (1). Although he accepts Lyotard's "elevation of the notion of the unpresentable" and Baudrillard's "description of the technological culture as mediated through and through" (Tabbi 28), Tabbi disagrees with the rejection of all truth claims and the ethically and politically transformative potential of literature (28).

4. It's often amusing and not a little surreal to see these two branches converse—or more weirdly, not converse—with one another.

5. For a discussion of the difference between the postmodern schizophrenia and the desire of paranoia to "reassert coherence," see Rosenfeld 362–3 and Baudrillard, "The Ecstasy of Communication" in Foster, 126–34. For more discussion along these lines, see Apter and Rushing.

6. I would include Katje Borgesius to this list, but there is insufficient room here to discuss the particular developments of her character.

7. Both the form and content of the novel encourage paranoia on the part of the reader, as well. In *The Fictional Labyrinths of Thomas Pynchon*, David Seed notes how the text disrupts the 1944–45 period of the novel, using anachronisms to push the reader to apply to the contemporary Nixon era. The novel is not limited to the postwar era, but tries to extend its analyses to the present and all of us in it.

8. In his study of postwar cultural representations of jazz by white and black writers, Jon Panish argues that white writers romanticized, appropriated, and dehistoricized African American cultural forms such as jazz and bebop. Panish explores how texts by white writers tended to use minstrel-like caricatures of black speech, romanticize jazz musicians' experience, stereotype jazz heroes, dehistoricize/decontextualize the historical development of the music, particularly attributing it to some primal or innate "primitive" nature (136), and emphasize "competitive individualism" over community.

9. In *On the Road*, Sal Paradise "wishes" he were a "Negro," "Denver Mexican, or even a poor overworked Jap" (Kerouac 180). As Maxine Hong Kingston writes in her skewering of masculinist literary ego-trips, *Tripmaster Monkey*, "Shit. Bumkicked again…Et tu, Kerouac" (69–70). The Beats' disillusionment with being a "white man" takes the laughable form of wanting to become an Other that they do not really see.

10. Ralph Ellison discusses how black characters in American literature are seldom complex, often depicted as "an image drained of humanity," an "oversimplified clown, a beast, or an angel" (Ellison 25, 26). African Americans in fiction are "counterfeits," projections, and because they ring so false, they must serve some psychological function as a "symbolic

ritual" (27). The individual creates clichés by reading into them: "The prejudiced individual creates his own stereotypes, very often unconsciously, by reading into situations involving Negroes those stock meanings which justify his emotional and economic needs" (27).

11. For example, Ned Polsky's *Hustlers, Beats and Others* describes racial conflicts among the Beats, including limited roles for Black Beats and opposition to their relationships with white women (Polsky 181, 184, and Panish 36).

12. For more information about Pynchon's development of this chapter, see Seed, *Fictional Labyrinths,* and Herman and Krafft.

13. But again, the text betrays ambivalence. In particular, technology and paranoia start to become important considerations. Mondaugen's paranoia about "the truth" of the stories he is being told and the reader's "paranoia" about what the real story is. Also, Mondaugen's job as engineer starts to constitute his reality, but outside forces suggest that his technologically constituted, paranoid reality is not necessarily all there is. Mondaugen becomes the voyeur who dreams/revisits Foppl's experiences as a young soldier in von Trotha's army, because his job, as engineer, is to listen; he begins to feel invisible, which becomes an ontological question: "if no one has seen me then am I really here at all; and . . . if I am not here then where are all these dreams coming from, if dreams is what they are" (*V.* 258). It is impossible to distinguish which narrative level is the "true" one. In the text, Mondaugen's narrative is told by Stencil to Eigenvalue the psychodontist (who treats psychological problems through dentistry), who breaks into the middle of the story to question its authenticity. Furthermore, during Foppl's story, neither the reader, narrator, nor Mondaugen are sure if Foppl narrates it or if Mondaugen voyeur-dreams it (like *Gravity's Rainbow*'s Pirate Prentice, who can invade Other people's dreams). Mondaugen thinks, "if dreams are only waking sensation first stored and later operated on, then the dreams of a voyeur can never be his own" (*V.* 255). Perhaps Godolphin, another 1904 survivor, tells the story, but because another character, Vera Meroving, has initiated a "program of indoctrination" on him, "there was no way to say for certain, later, whether Foppl himself might not have come in to tell tales of when he'd been a trooper, eighteen years ago" (256). The passages of memory/story of 1904 (*V.* 256-7, 258-9, 261-5, 266-74) are not introduced or set off from the Mondaugen-at-Foppl's narrative in any way.

But if the point of view is indeterminable, the events described and their effects—on both the murderer and murdered—are not. Recovering later from scurvy, Mondaugen discovers that "his voyeurism had been determined purely by events seen, and not by any deliberate choice, or preëxisting [*sic*] set of personal psychic needs" (*V.* 277). That is, the conditions for his watching, and his watching itself, are determined by the things he sees, both in 1904 as well as in the "present." Listening on his antennae,

a Lieutenant Weissman (another German nostalgic for 1904 who will figure centrally in *Gravity's Rainbow*) insists on helping Mondaugen break
what appears to be a code of some sort being transmitted through the 'sferics. They pick up the letters "DIGEWOELDTIMSTEALALENSWTASNDEURFUAL-
RLIKST" (*V.* 278). Every third letter spells "GODMEANTNUURK," which is an
anagram for Kurt Mondaugen. The remaining letters read "DIEWELTISALL-
ESWASDERFALLIST," which is the opening line of Wittgenstein's *Tractatus*,
"The world is all that the case is" (*V.* 278). The line "mak[es] it appear,
almost literally, a universal principal gathered from beyond the limits
of the Earth and at the same time a complete nonsense" (McHoul and
Willis 9). But juxtaposed with Mondaugen's realization, the "message"
seems to be ironic. On one level, Mondaugen's realization appears to place
meaning in "events seen," not in narrative sedimentations or language
games. On another, the "world" seems to be the case at hand, the world
outside the walls of Foppl's fortress that, like the Red Death, cannot be
kept outside.

14. See Sale, Plater, and Seed, "Pynchon in Watts." Pynchon's only work of
journalism, the article makes its case "basically through rhetoric" rather
than presentation of facts, since the article does not present any new information (Seed, "Watts" 59).

15. In this chapter, unnamed page numbers in parentheses refer to *Gravity's
Rainbow*.

16. The liberal Slothrop, however, is contrasted to the overtly racist and sexist
Major Duane Marvy, an American pursuing the Zone-Hereros, and who
speaks like this: "Not enough we have to worry about Russkies, frogs,
limeys...Now we got not just niggers you see, but *kraut* niggers. Well,
Jesus. V-E Day just about everyplace you had a rocket, you had you a
nigger" (565). Marvy eventually is castrated (609), while a different fate
awaits Slothrop.

17. Early in the novel, we're told that a Pavlovian scientist, Dr. Jamf, experi-
mented with an "Infant Tyrone," who is conditioned to have an erection at
the sound of a bomb. But *then* we learn that Jamf himself may be a fiction
for Slothrop's peace of mind, and that some of the stars are false. It doesn't
matter; "There never was a Dr. Jamf," suggests "world-renowned analyst
Mickey Wuxtry-Wuxtry," "Jamf was only a fiction, to help him explain
what he felt so terribly, so immediately in his genitals for those rockets
each time exploding in the sky...to help him deny what he could not possibly admit: that he might be in love, in sexual love, with his, and his
race's, death" (738).

18. Although, Weisenburger notes, Malcolm X did not work there as a shoeshine boy until 1940 (*Companion* 45).

19. Although Slothrop's newfound ability draws from the Beat romanticization of African American cultural forms, I would argue it is not just
about the redemption of the white man. Symbolically and formally, it indicates one of the implicit choices of the novel. Slothrop's rediscovery of the

harmonica follows a section in which two characters, the composer Gustav and the counterfeiter Saüre, continue their long-running debate over "who is better, Beethoven or Rossini. Saüre is for Rossini" (440). The debate echoes a larger struggle between empathy/the importance of friendships and aloneness/the alienation of genius. The former is the Italian Rossini, who stands for warmth, simplicity and unsophistication, irrationality, organicism, comedy, and an emphasis on melody, and the latter is the German Beethoven, who symbolizes coldness, complexity and erudition, rationality, mechanicalness, tragedy, and an emphasis on harmony (Weisenburger 205–6). Against this framework the blues is projected: "Blues is a matter of lower sidebands—you suck a clear note, on pitch, and then bend it lower with the muscles of your face. Muscles of your face have been laughing, tight with pain, often trying not to betray *any* emotion, all your life. Where you send the note is partly a function of that" (643). In Other words, the form of the blues depends on the content, particularly the emotion derived from the political/social situation of the music-maker. So in this sense, it "sees deeper" into Kerouac and Mailer by incorporating the history and the anger involved in the creation of form, which Panish noted that postwar writers ignored, in the form and content and juxtaposed with Slothrop's disintegrating self. It also is an indication of "choosing" empathy, community, and organicism over the cold logic of *V.*'s late-stage colonialism.

20. The first sentence translates as "I have dreamt a nightmare," while the second translates roughly as "he was shining in my dream as if he were alive" (Seed, "Herero" 37–38), presaging Enzian's paranoid visions.

21. While in Pynchon's earlier works, the "colonial zone is distant from the metropolitan center," in *Gravity's Rainbow*, "the Zone is in the center of Europe, in the remains of Germany" (Ivison 138). And in the Zone, Pynchon's Herero are the ultimate Displaced Persons because they are permanent exiles bearing the superimposition of colonizers and their languages; the Hereros have to learn not only German but also the language of the new imperials, English (Seed, "Herero" 43). History is recalled and worked into the use of Herero language in the novel.

22. Enzian's mother died long ago after following Samuel Maherero on the "great trek across the Kalahari" into Bechuanaland (323). Khama, the king of the Bechuanas by whom Bessie Head was so fascinated, sends supplies and assistance. The first refugees are told to only drink a little water at a time, but the later ones arrive when everyone is asleep, and "they drank till they died" (323), Enzian's mother among them. Enzian is also called "Oberst Nguarorerue" (732), a name or title meaning "one who has been proven" rather than "leader" (316; Seed, "Herero" 40).

23. The leader of Empty Ones is Josef Ombindi. *Ombindi* is from the Herero word *ombinda*, meaning "pig" (Seed, "Herero" 41).

24. For more information on the origins of Tchitcherine, see Weisenburger, "Origin."

Four   Analyzing the Real: Bessie Head's Literary Psychosis

1. In arguing this, I do not mean to, as Peter Nazareth cautions, "idealize [Bessie Head] and every scrap of her writing"; I do not think that the novel's insights have to be judged by the author (217). I do, however, take seriously the comment of a "well-known professor," cited by Nazareth, to the effect that the canonization of Head's work is inextricably intertwined with readings that privilege *A Question of Power* over her other work because it seems to correspond to the concerns of Western feminism and poststructuralism (217). My goal is to use some of the insights of such readings while also bringing attention to the novel's analysis beyond Eurocentric paradigms.

2. Lacanian psychoanalysis posits the Real as brute reality outside human access that is felt only as pressure on Imaginary and Symbolic orders. In using the term real, I am not arguing that we can have unmediated access to reality. Rather, I am drawing on Fanon's notion of the political "reality" that may be contradictory to a subject's ideological symbolic order. That is, while acknowledging the possibility of absolute and unmediated access to a brute reality, I argue that we can acknowledge partial, historically situated processes in which a situation that is more factually accurate is repressed as an untenable "real" and that returns to haunt the represser. The best example of this political real would be structural economic inequalities for someone who insists that everyone in the United States has the same opportunities in life.

3. In this chapter, unnamed page numbers in parentheses refer to *A Question of Power*.

4. In *Black Skin White Masks*, Fanon explains that the Oedipal drama primarily applies to European or "civilized" countries because "the family is a miniature of the nation"; he describes "the white family" as "the agent of a certain system," "an institution that prefigures a broader institution: the social or national group," and "the workshop in which one is shaped and trained for life in society" (148–9). In any "closed society," or a society "protected from the flood of civilization," Fanon believes that "the characteristics of the family are projected onto the social environment" (*Black Skin, White Masks* 142).

5. This also shows the limits of the premodern/modern/postmodern categorization, in my usage and in general. The market has always been global, but the "globalization" of postmodernism as a particular phase of capitalism suggests that these global relations are new. For example, the development of a particular export commodity in Botswana is in the interests of capital, whether in its national/imperial stage (modern) or its global stage (postmodern). But within the country, the technological demands and the rhetoric being invoked and inculcated would be consistent with modernity. What is new are the technologies, the organization of capital, and the extreme flexibility and mobility of capital today. As David Harvey points

out in *The Condition of Postmodernity*, different experiences of being, including space and time, linked to different modes of production, can coexist at the same moment and even, as *A Question of Power* demonstrates, conflict and transform.

6. Although, as de Beauvoir points out in *The Second Sex,* myths about woman are so contradictory that any concrete woman is bound to lose.

7. In the influential 1956 book *Pan-Africanism or Communism*, George Padmore warned of both "the restoration of Western imperialism, as well as the dangers of Communism" (Nwafor 1955, xxxiv). Head described Padmore as a "prophet," "a kind of John the Baptist crying in the wilderness—make ready the way," and she claimed that after reading *Pan-Africanism*, "my whole manner of speaking and thinking and walking changed.... It gave me a new skin and a new life that was totally unacceptable to conditions down there [in South Africa]..." (qtd. in Eilersen, *Bessie Head* 45). Head would later become critical of nationalism or any systematic political philosophy.

8. Head's characterization of Dan resonates eerily with Denis Ekpo's description of African dictators, which in turn echoes Fanon. Ekpo writes, "with these people, tyranny and dictatorship are not instruments of purposive rule; they are a stage show, a scaffold, with which they maintain a semblance of leadership and power when they no longer know what to do for their country or how to retrieve themselves from their ideological dead-end. Excessive stage shows, pomp extravaganza, megalomania and so on characterise rulership in most of black Africa. They need such absurd circus-show splendour to hide from their real ugly selves. From this one can see that the problem of the African leader is not that they are tyrants—since in their situation tyranny becomes an unavoidable, even if provisional mode of rule—their problem is that they are vain power freaks, aborted stage-actors who, having imprisoned themselves in falsities and self-deceit, resort to bloody repression and roguish megalomania as a cloak and a way out" ("Aporia" 17–18).

9. Fanon writes that when the black (man) makes contact with "white world," if his "psychic structure is weak, one observes a collapse of the ego," and instead of "behaving as an *actional* person," the "goal of his behavior" will be the esteem of "The Other" to give him worth, or "self-esteem" (*Black Skin, White Masks*, 154).

10. Taylor writes of the difficulty of Head and other writers, "because they set up very different resistances (or do not) depending on which social meanings take priority and on how those meanings (often given such names as race, class, gender, or sexuality) do or do not cohere for particular (and particularly placed) readers. Because of their complex position and a multivocality that disallows singular or authoritative readings, most of these texts—whether adopted into a sense of a canon or not—are already constituted as controversial" (18–19).

11. I thank Robert Short for his insight that the novel actually deconstructs itself, positing the epistemologies of the two Sellos and Dan as a series of "centers," or transcendental, fixed signifiers, that prove unsustainable.

Concluding Notes

1. For more information on debates around climate change, see Achenbach, Begley, and Oreskes. For more information on the debates around intelligent design/creationism, see Wilgoren and Hedges. For an interesting discussion of the philosophical compatibility of postmodernism and conservatism, see Lawler.
2. For further discussions of postmodern imperialism, see Vernet and Straw.
3. Williamson's tenets included: fiscal discipline; a redirection of public expenditure priorities toward fields offering both high economic returns and the potential to improve income distribution, such as primary health care, primary education, and infrastructure; tax reform (to lower marginal rates and broaden the tax base); interest rate liberalization; a competitive exchange rate; trade liberalization; liberalization of inflows of foreign direct investment; privatization; deregulation (to abolish barriers to entry and exit); and secure property rights.
4. For more information about debates concerning the Washington consensus sparked by financial crises around the world, particularly in Asia and Mexico, see Krugman; Naím and Edwards; and Blecker and Bleecher. For the other side of the story, see *Zapatista*, *A Place Called Chiapas*, and Bacon. See also Held and Wolf.
5. Greg Grandin points out that Chua gives the impression that most of the violence in the world is by "dark-skinned masses against a well-heeled minority." Rather, he argues, "Untold numbers of peasants are driven off their land every year by cheap agricultural imports or by the extension of large-scale commercial crop production. Yet they merit little notice compared with the 3,000 white farmers terrorized by Mugabe. Crime, disease and malnutrition directly linked to neoliberal restructuring kill far more than the epic clash of civilizations now purportedly under way."

Works Cited

Achenbach, Joel. "The Tempest." *Washington Post* 28 May 2006: W08.

Adéèkó, Adélékè. *The Slave's Rebellion: Fiction, History, Orature.* Bloomington: Indiana UP, 2005.

Adorno, Theodor. "Commitment." *New Left Review* 87–88 (September–December 1974): 75–89.

Ahmad, Aijaz. *In Theory: Classes, Nations, Literatures.* New York: Verso, 1992.

Aldama, Frederick Luis. *Postethnic Narrative Criticism: Magicorealism in Oscar "Zeta" Acosta, Ana Castillo, Julie Dash, Hanif Kureishi, and Salman Rushdie.* Austin: U of Texas P, 2003.

Ali, Tariq. "A Political Solution is Required." *The Nation* 17 September 2001. Retrieved on 20 November 2005 from <http://www.thenation.com/doc/20011001/ali_wtc_20010917>.

Althusser, Louis. *Lenin and Philosophy and Other Essays.* Trans. Ben Brewster. New York: Monthly Review, 2001.

Appiah, Kwame Anthony. "Is the Post- in Postmodernism the Post- in Postcolonial?" *Critical Inquiry* 17.2 (Winter 1991): 336–57.

Apter, Emily. "On Oneworldedness; Or Paranoia as a World System." *American Literary History* 18.2 (Summer 2006): 365–89.

Aronowitz, Stanley. "Alan Sokal's 'Transgression.'" *Dissent* (Winter 1997): 107–10.

Attewell, Nadine. "'Bouncy Little Tunes': Nostalgia, Sentimentality, and Narrative in *Gravity's Rainbow.*" *Contemporary Literature* 45.1 (2004): 22–48.

Bacon, David. *The Children of NAFTA: Labor Wars on the U.S./Mexico Border.* Berkeley: U of California P, 2004.

Baker, Jeffrey. "A Democratic Pynchon: Counterculture, Counterforce and Participatory Democracy." *Pynchon Notes* 32–33 (Spring–Fall 1993): 99–131.

Balseiro, Isabel. "Between Amnesia and Memory: Bessie Head and Her Critics." *Emerging Perspectives on Bessie Head.* Ed. Huma Ibrahim. Trenton: Africa World, 2004. 17–24.

Beard, Linda Susan. "Bessie Head in Gaborone, Botswana: An Interview." *Sage* 3.2 (Fall 1986): 44–45.

———. "Bessie Head's Syncretic Fiction: The Reconceptualization of Power and the Recovery of the Ordinary." *Modern Fiction Studies* 37.2 (Autumn 1991): 575–89.

de Beauvoir, Simone. *The Second Sex*. Trans. H.M. Parshley. New York: Vintage, 1989.

Begley, Sharon. "The Truth About Denial." *Newsweek* 13 August 2007: 20–29.

Bellamy, Elizabeth J. "Discourses of Impossibility: Can Psychoanalysis Be Political?" *Diacritics* 23.1 (Spring 1993): 24–38.

Benhabib, Seyla. *The Claims of Culture: Equality and Diversity in the Global Era*. Princeton: Princeton UP, 2002.

Benn Michaels, Walter. "Political Science Fictions." *Is There Life After Identity Politics?* Ed. Bill Albertini, Ben Lee, Heather Love, Mike Millner, Ken Parille, Alice Rutkowski, and Bryan Wagner. Spec. issue of *New Literary History* 31.4 (Autumn 2000): 649–64.

———. *The Shape of the Signifier: 1967 to the End of History*. Princeton: Princeton UP, 2004.

Berger, Roger A. "The Politics of Madness in Bessie Head." *The Tragic Life: Bessie Head and Literature in Southern Africa*. Ed. Cecil Abrahams. Trenton: Africa World, 1990. 31–43.

Bergvali, Caroline. "Writing at the Crossroads of Languages." *Telling It Slant: Avant-Garde Poetics of the 1990s*. Ed. Mark Wallace and Steven Marks. Tuscaloosa: Alabama UP, 2002. 207–23.

Bersani, Leo. "Pynchon, Paranoia, and Literature." *Representations* 25 (Winter 1989): 99–118.

Bérubé, Michael. *Marginal Forces/Cultural Centers: Tolson, Pynchon, and the Politics of the Canon*. Ithaca: Cornell UP, 1992.

Bhana, Hershini. "Reading Ghostly Desire: Writing the Edges of Bessie Head's *A Question of Power*." *Emerging Perspectives on Bessie Head*. Ed. Huma Ibrahim. Trenton: Africa World, 2004. 33–50.

Blecker, Robert, and Robert Bleecher. *Taming Global Finance: A Better Architecture for Economic Growth and Equity*. Washington, D.C.: Economic Policy Institute, 1999.

Bové, Paul. "History and Fiction: The Narrative Voices of Pynchon's *Gravity's Rainbow*." *Modern Fiction Studies* 50.3 (Fall 2004): 657–80.

Boyce Davies, Carole. "African Women Writers." *A History of Twentieth Century African Literatures*. Ed. Oyekan Owomoyela. Lincoln: U of Nebraska P, 1993. 311–46.

———. "*Against Race* or the Politics of Self-Ethnography." Rev. of *Against Race*, by Paul Gilroy. *Jenda: A Journal of Culture and African Women Studies* 2.1 (2002). Retrieved on 23 February 2006 from <http://www.jendajournal.com/vol2.1/cbdavies.html>.

Brecht, Bertolt. "Against George Lukács." *New Left Review* 84 (March–April 1974): 33–54.

———. *Brecht on Theatre: The Development of an Aesthetic*. Ed. and Trans. John Willett. New York: Hill and Wang, 1992.

Brown, Bill. "The Dark Wood of Postmodernity (Space, Faith, Allegory)." *PMLA* 120.2 (May 2005): 734–50.

Brown, Coreen. *The Creative Vision of Bessie Head*. Madison: Fairleigh Dickinson UP, 2003.

Bürger, Peter. *Theory of the Avant-Grade*. Trans. Michael Shaw. Minneapolis: U of Minnesota P, 1984.

Butler, Judith. "Poststructuralism and Postmarxism." *Diacritics* 23.4 (Winter 1993): 3–11.

Butler, Judith, Ernesto Laclau, and Slavoj Žižek. *Contingency, Hegemony, Universality: Contemporary Dialogues on the Left*. London: Verso, 2000.

Caesar, Terry, and Aso Takashi. "Japan, Creative Masochism, and Transnationality in *Vineland*." *Critique* 44.4 (Summer 2003): 371–87.

Caison, Gina. "Dancing the Gap? Cinema and American Indian Autobiography." Unpublished essay, 2007.

Callinicos, Alex. *Against Postmodernism: A Marxist Critique*. New York: St. Martin's, 1990.

Caminero-Santangelo, Marta. "Moving Beyond 'The Blank White Spaces': Atwood's Gilead, Postmodernism, and Strategic Resistance." *Studies in Canadian Literature* 19.1 (1994): 20–42.

Cancel, Robert. "Gestures of Belonging and Claiming Birth Rights: Short Stories by Bessie Head and Ama Ata Aidoo." *Emerging Perspectives on Bessie Head*. Ed. Huma Ibrahim. Trenton: Africa World, 2004. 181–98.

Cannon, Steve. "Godard, the Groupe Dziga Vertov, and the Myth of 'Counter-Cinema.'" *Nottingham French Studies* 32 (Spring 1993): 74–82.

Cha, Theresa Hak Kyung, ed. *Apparatus: Cinematographic Apparatus, Selected Writings*. New York: Tanam, 1980.

———. *Dictee*. New York: Tanam, 1982.

Chow, Rey. "The Interruption of Referentiality: Poststructuralism and the Conundrum of Critical Multiculturalism." *The South Atlantic Quarterly* 101.1 (2002): 171–86.

Choy, Bong-Youn. *Koreans in America*. Chicago: Nelson Hall, 1979.

Chua, Amy. *World on Fire: How Exporting Free Market Democracy Breeds Ethnic Hatred and Global Instability*. New York: Anchor, 2003.

Clayton, Cherry. "'A World Elsewhere': Bessie Head as Historian." *English in Africa* 15.1 (May 1988): 55–69.

Connery, Christopher L. "Actually Existing Left Conservatism." *Boundary 2* 26.3 (1999): 3–11.

Cooley, Ronald. "The Hothouse or the Street: Imperialism and Narrative in Pynchon's *V*." *Modern Fiction Studies* 39.2 (Summer 1993): 307–25.

Cooper, Robert. "The Post-Modern State." *Re-Ordering the World*. Ed. Mark Leonard. [Director of Foreign Policy Centre] London: The Foreign Policy Centre, 2002.

———. "Why We Still Need Empires." *Observer* 7 April 2002. Retrieved on 18 October 2005 from <http://observer.guardian.co.uk/comment/story/0,,680096,00.html>.

Cornell, Drucilla. *The Philosophy of the Limit*. New York: Routledge, 1992.

Coundouriotis, Eleni. "Authority and Invention in the Fiction of Bessie Head." *Research in African Literatures* 27.2 (Summer 1996): 17–27.

Dalsgaard, Inger H. "Terrifying Technology: Pynchon's Warning Myth of Today." *Pynchon Notes* 42–43 (Spring–Fall 1998): 91–110.

Derrida, Jacques. *Limited Inc.* Ed. Gerald Graff. Evanston: Northwestern UP, 1988.

Dixon, Winston Wheeler. *The Films of Jean-Luc Godard.* Albany: State U of New York P, 1997.

Dodson, Diana. " 'We Lived in the Blank White Spaces': Rewriting the Paradigm of Denial in Atwood's The Handmaid's Tale." *Utopian Studies* 8.2 (1997): 66–86.

Dubey, Madhu. *Signs and Cities: Black Literary Postmodernism.* Chicago: U of Chicago P, 2003.

Eagleton, Terry. *Figures of Dissent: Reviewing Fish, Spivak, Zizek and Others.* New York: Verso, 2003.

———. *The Illusions of Postmodernism.* Malden: Blackwell, 1996.

Eilersen, Gillian Stead. *Bessie Head: Thunder Behind Her Ears.* Portsmouth: Heinemann, 1995.

———. "Social and Political Commitment in Bessie Head's *A Bewitched Crossroad.*" *Critique: Studies in Contemporary Fiction* 33.1 (Fall 1991): 43–52.

Ekpo, Denis. "The Aporia of Post-Colonial Anger: Dissidence and Difference in Africa's Contemporary Literary Discourse." *Social Semiotics* 9.1 (1999): 5–22.

———. "How Africa Misunderstood the West: The Failure of Anti-West Radicalism and Postmodernity." *Third Text* 35 (Summer 1996): 3–13.

———. "Towards a Post-Africanism: Contemporary African Thought and Postmodernism." *Textual Practice* 9.1 (Spring 1995): 121–34.

Elder, Arlene. "Bessie Head: The Inappropriate Appropriation of 'Autobiography.' " *Emerging Perspectives on Bessie Head.* Ed. Huma Ibrahim. Trenton: Africa World, 2004. 1–16.

Elias, Amy. *Sublime Desire: History and Post-1960s Fiction.* Baltimore: Johns Hopkins UP, 2001.

Ellison, Ralph. *Shadow and Act.* New York: Random House, 1953.

Espiritu, Yen Le. *Asian American Panethnicity: Bridging Institutions and Identities.* Philadelphia: Temple UP, 1992.

Fanon, Frantz. *Black Skin, White Masks.* Trans. Charles Lam Markmann. New York: Grove Weidenfeld, 1952.

———. *Wretched of the Earth.* Trans. Constance Farrington. New York: Grove Weidenfeld, 1963.

Fish, Stanley. "Academic Cross-Dressing: How Intelligent Design Gets Its Arguments From the Left." *Harper's* 311 (December 2005): 70–72.

Foley, Helen. *The Homeric Hymn to Demeter: Translation, Commentary, and Interpretive Essays.* Princeton: Prince UP, 1994.

Foster, Hal, ed. *The Anti-Aesthetic: Essays on Postmodern Culture.* Seattle: Bay, 1989.

Foucault, Michel. *Politics, Philosophy, Culture: Interviews and Other Writings, 1977–1984.* New York: Routledge, 1990.

Frost, Elizabeth. "'In Another Tongue': Body, Image, Text in Theresa Hak Kyung Cha's Dictee." *We Who Love to Be Astonished: Experimental Women's Writing and Performance Poetics.* Ed. Laura Hinton and Cynthia Hogue. Tuscaloosa: U of Alabama P, 2002. 181–92.

Garrett, James M. "Writing Community: Bessie Head and the Politics of Narrative." *Research in African Literatures* 30.2 (June 1999): 122–35.

Genette, Gerard. *Narrative Discourse: An Essay in Method.* Ithaca: Cornell UP, 1983.

Gilbert-Rolfe, Jeremy. "Blankness as a Signifier." *Critical Inquiry* 24 (Autumn 1997): 159–75.

Gilroy, Paul. *Against Race: Imagining Political Culture Beyond the Color Line.* Cambridge: Harvard UP, 2000.

———. *The Black Atlantic: Modernity and Double Consciousness.* Cambridge: Harvard UP, 1993.

Grandin, Greg. "What's a Neoliberal To Do?" *The Nation* 10 March 2003. 20 January 2007 <www.thenation.com>.

Grice, Helena. "Korean American National Identity in Theresa Hak Kyung Cha's *Dictee.*" *Representing Lives: Women and Autobiography.* Ed. Alison Donnell and Pauline Polkey. New York: St. Martin's, 2000. 43–52.

Guarino-Trier, Jennifer. "'From the Multitude of Narratives…For Another Telling for another Recitation': Constructing and Re-Constructing Dictee and Memory/all echo." *Screening Asian Americans.* Ed. Peter Feng. New Brunswick: Rutgers UP, 2002. 253–72.

Guerts, Kathryn. "Personal Politics in the Novels of Bessie Head." *Présence Africaine* 140 (1986): 47–64.

Habermas, Jürgen. *The Philosophical Discourse of Modernity.* Trans. Frederick Lawrence. Cambridge: MIT Press, 1995.

Haley, Alex. *The Autobiography of Malcolm X.* New York: Ballantine, 1964.

Hall, Stuart. "The Toad in the Garden: Thatcherism among the Theorists." *Marxism and the Interpretation of Culture.* Ed. Cary Nelson and Lawrence Grossberg. Urbana: U of Illinois P, 1988. 35–58.

Harding, Sandra. *Science and Social Inequality.* Urbana: U of Illnois P, 2006.

———. "Rethinking Standpoint Epistemology: What is 'Strong Objectivity'?" *Feminist Epistemologies.* Ed. Linda Alcoff and Elizabeth Potter. New York: Routledge, 1993. 49–82.

Hardt, Michael, and Antonio Negri. *Multitude.* New York: Penguin, 2004.

Harvey, David. *The Condition of Postmodernity.* Cambridge: Blackwell, 1990.

Hassan, Ihab. *The Postmodern Turn: Essays in Postmodern Culture.* Columbus: Ohio State UP, 1987.

Head, Bessie. *A Bewitched Crossroad: An African Saga.* Craighall: Ad Donker, 1984.

———. *The Cardinals with Meditations and Other Short Stories.* Ed. M.J. Daymond. Portsmouth: Heinemann, 1993.

Head, Bessie. *The Collector of Treasures and Other Botswana Village Tales*. London: Heinemann, 1977.

———. Foreword. *Native Life in South Africa*. By Sol Plaatje. Johannesburg: Ravan, 1982. ix–xiii.

———. *Maru*. Portsmouth: Heinemann, 1971.

———. "Notes From a Quiet Backwater." *Drum* March 1982: 33–34.

———. *A Question of Power*. Portsmouth: Heinemann, 1974.

———. *Serowe: Village of the Rain Wind*. London: Heinemann, 1981.

———. "Social and Political Pressures that Shape Literature in Southern Africa." *WLWE: World Literature Written in English* 18 (April 1979): 20–26.

———. *When Rain Clouds Gather*. Portsmouth: Heinemann, 1969.

———. "Writing Out of Southern Africa." *New Statesman* (August 16 1985): 21–23.

Hedges, Chris. *American Fascists: The Christian Right and the War on America*. CITY: Free Press, 2007.

Held, David. *Global Covenant: The Social Democratic Alternative to the Washington Consensus*. Boston: Polity, 2004.

Henderson, Mae G. " 'Where, By the Way, Is This Train Going?': A Case for Black (Cultural) Studies." *Callaloo* 19.1 (Winter 1996): 60–67.

Hennessy, Rosemary. *Profit and Pleasure: Sexual Identities in Late Capitalism*. New York: Routledge, 2000.

Herman, Luc, and John M. Krafft. "From the Ground Up: The Evolution of the South-West Africa Chapter in Pynchon's *V.*" *Contemporary Literature* 47.2 (Summer 2006): 261–88.

Hill, Jennifer. "Unspotted Snow: Arctic Space, Gender, and Nation in the Nineteenth-Century British Imaginary." Ph.D. dissertation, Cornell University, 2000.

Hogan, Patrick Colm. "Bessie Head's *A Question of Power*: A Lacanian Psychoanalysis." *Mosaic* 27.2 (1994): 95–112.

Hogue, W. Lawrence. "Postmodernism, Traditional Cultural Forms, and the African American Narrative: Major's *Reflex*, Morrison's *Jazz*, and Reed's *Mumbo Jumbo*." *Novel* 35.2/3 (Spring 2002): 169–92.

———. *Race, Modernity, Postmodernity: A Look at the History of People of Color since the 1960s*. Albany: State U of New York P, 1996.

Homans, Margaret. "Feminist Fictions and Feminist Theories of Narrative." *Narrative* 2.1 (January 1994): 3–16.

Hong Kingston, Maxine. *Tripmaster Monkey: His Fake Book*. New York: Vintage, 1989.

hooks, bell. "Postmodern Blackness." *Yearning: Race, Gender, and Cultural Politics*. Boston: South End, 1990. 23–31.

Hutcheon, Linda. *The Poetics of Postmodernism: History, Theory, Fiction*. New York: Routledge, 1988.

———. *The Politics of Postmodernism*. New York: Routledge, 2002.

Huyssen, Andreas. *After the Great Divide: Modernism, Mass Culture, Postmodernism*. Bloomington: Indiana UP, 1986.

Ibrahim, Huma, ed. *Emerging Perspectives on Bessie Head*. Trenton: Africa World Press, 2004.

Ivison, Douglas. "Outhouses of the European Soul: Imperialism in Thomas Pynchon." *Pynchon Notes* 40–41 (Spring–Fall 1997): 134–43.

Jameson, Fredric. *The Political Unconscious*. Ithaca: Cornell UP, 1981.

———. *Postmodernism; or, the Cultural Logic of Late Capitalism*. Durham: Duke UP, 1991.

———. *A Singular Modernity: Essays on the Ontology of the Present*. New York: Verso, 2002.

Jeyifo, Biodun. "The Nature of Things: Arrested Decolonization and Critical Theory." *Research in African Literatures* 21.1 (Spring 1990): 33–48.

Johnson, Joyce. "Metaphor, Myth and Meaning in Bessie Head's *A Question of Power*." *Literature Written in English* 25.2 (1985): 198–211.

Katz, Adam. *Postmodernism and the Politics of "Culture."* Boulder: Westview, 2000.

Kanbur, Ravi. "The Strange Case of the Washington Consensus: A Brief Note on John Williamson's 'What Should the World Bank Think About the Washington Consensus?'" Ithaca: Ravi Kanbur, 1999.

Kapstein, Helen. "'A Peculiar Shuttling Movement': Madness, Passing, and Trespassing in Bessie Head's *A Question of Power*." *Critical Essays on Bessie Head*. Ed. Maxine Sample. Westport: Praeger, 2003. 71–98.

Kerouac, Jack. *On the Road*. New York: Penguin, 1955.

Kim, Elaine. "Myth, Memory, and Desire: Homeland and History in Contemporary Korean American Writing and Visual Art." *Holding Their Own: Perspectives on the Multi-Ethnic Literatures of the United States*. Ed. Dorothea Fischer-Hornung and Heike Raphael-Hernandez. Tübingen: Stauffenburg, 2000. 79–91.

———. "Poised on the In-between: A Korean American's Reflections on Theresa Hak Kyung Cha's *Dictée*." *Writing Self, Writing Nation: Essays on Theresa Hak Kyung Cha's DICTEE*. Ed. Elaine Kim and Norma Alarcón. Berkeley: Third Woman, 1994. 3–20.

Kim, Sue. "Narrator, Author, Reader: Equivocation in Theresa Hak Kyung Cha's *Dictee*." *Narrative* 16.2 (May 2008): 163–77.

Knight, Peter. "Everything is Connected: *Underworld's* Secret History of Paranoia." *Modern Fiction Studies* 45.3 (Fall 1999): 811–36.

Krugman, Paul. *The Return of Depression Economics*. New York: Norton, 1999.

Lacan, Jacques. *Écrits: A Selection*. Trans. Alan Sheridan. New York: Norton, 1977.

Laclau, Ernesto and Chantal Mouffe. *Hegemony and Socialist Strategy: Towards a Radical Democratic Politics*. New York: Verso, 1985.

Larsen, Neil. *Determinations: Essays on Theory, Narrative, and Nation in the Americas*. New York: Verso, 2001.

Lawler, Peter Augustine. "Conservative Postmodernism, Postmodern Conservatism." *The Intercollegiate Review* 38.1 (Fall 2002): 16–25.

Lee, Sue-Im. "Suspicious Characters: Realism, Asian American Identity, and Theresa Hak Kyung Cha's *Dictee*." *JNT: Journal of Narrative Theory* 32.2 (Summer 2002): 227–58.

Leitch, Vincent. *Postmodernism: Local Effects, Global Flows*. Albany: State U of New York P, 1996.

Lew, Walter, *Dikte for Dictee*. Seoul: Yeul Eum, 1992.

Ling, Jinqi. *Narrating Nationalisms: Ideology and Form in Asian American Literature*. New York: Oxford UP, 1998.

Lorenz, Paul. "Colonization and the Feminine in Bessie Head's *A Question of Power*." *Modern Fiction Studies* 37.3 (1991): 591–605.

Loshitsky, Yosefa. *The Radical Faces of Godard and Bertolucci*. Detroit: Wayne State UP, 1995.

Lowe, Lisa. *Immigrant Acts: On Asian American Cultural Politics*. Durham: Duke UP, 1996.

Lukács, Georg. *Realism in Our Time*. Trans. John and Necke Mander. London: Merlin, 1962.

Lynd, Margaret. "Science, Narrative, and Agency in *Gravity's Rainbow*." *Critique* 46.1 (Fall 2004): 63–80.

Lyotard, Jean-François. *The Postmodern Condition: A Report on Knowledge*. 1979. Trans. Geoff Bennington and Brian Massumi. Theory and History of Literature, Vol. 10. Minneapolis: U of Minnesota P, 1984.

MacKenzie, Craig. *Bessie Head*. New York: Twayne, 1999.

Madsen, Deborah L. "Family Legacies: Identifying the Traces of William Pynchon in *Gravity's Rainbow*." *Pynchon Notes* 42–43 (Spring–Fall 1998): 29–48.

Mailer, Norman. *Advertisements for Myself*. New York: Putnam, 1959.

Maipose, Gervase S. "Economic Development and the Role of the State in Botswana." *DPMN Bulletin*10.2 (April 2003). Retrieved on 3 September 2005 from <http://www.dpmf.org/>.

Mandel, Ernest. *Late Capitalism*. Trans. Joris De Bres. New York: Verso, 1975.

Manning, Marable. *The Great Wells of Democracy: The Meaning of Race in American Life*. New York: BasicCivitas, 2002.

Mardorossian, Carine M. *Reclaiming Difference: Caribbean Women Rewrite Postcolonialism*. Charlottesville: U of Virginia P, 2005.

Matsikidze, Isabella. "The Postnationalistic Phase: A Poetics of Bessie Head's Fiction." *Bucknell Review* 37.1 (1993): 123–33.

McHoul, Alec, and David Willis. *Writing Pynchon: Strategies in Fictional Analysis*. Urbana: U of Illinois P, 1990.

McKenzie, F.A. *The Tragedy of Korea*. New York: Dutton, 1909.

Mhone, Guy, and Patrick Bond. "Botswana and Zimbabwe: Relative Success and Comparative Failure?" *Globalization, Marginalization and Development*. Ed. Syed Mansoob Murshed. Routledge Studies in Development Economics 28. New York: Routledge, 2002. 233–47.

Michelson, Annette, ed. *Kino-Eye: The Writings of Dziga Vertov*. Trans. Kevin O-Brien. Berkeley: U of California P, 1984.

Min, Eun Kyung. "Reading the Figure of Dictation in Theresa Hak Kyung Cha's *Dictee*." *Other Sisterhoods: Literary Theory and U.S. Women of Color*. Ed. Sandra Kumamoto Stanley. Urbana: U of Illinois P, 1998. 309–24.

Miyoshi, Masao. "Ivory Tower in Escrow." *Boundary 2* 27.1 (Spring 2007): 7–50.

Mohanty, Satya. *Literary Theory and the Claims of History: Postmodernism, Objectivity, Multicultural Politics.* Ithaca: Cornell UP, 1997.

Monaco, James. *The New Wave: Truffaut, Godard, Chabrol, Rohmer, Rivette.* New York: Oxford UP, 1976.

Nahm, Andrew. *Korea: Tradition and Transformation, A History of the Korean People.* Elizabeth: Hollym, 1988.

Naím, Moisés. "Washington Consensus or Washington Confusion?" *Foreign Policy* 118 (Spring 2000): 86–103.

Naím, Moisés, and Sebastian Edwards, eds. *Mexico 1994: The Anatomy of an Emerging-Market Crash.* Washington, D.C.: The Carnegie Endowment for International Peace, 1997.

Nazareth, Peter. "Path of Thunder: Meeting Bessie Head." *Research in African Literatures* 37.4 (2006): 211–29.

Ngugi wa Thiong'o. *Devil on the Cross.* Portsmouth: Heinemann, 1982.

Nguyen, Viet Thanh. "Asian America and American Studies: Aliens, Citizens, and Cultural Work." *American Quarterly* 50.3 (1998): 626–35.

Nicholson, Linda J., ed. *Feminism/Postmodernism.* New York: Routledge, 1990.

Nkosi, Lewis. *Tasks and Masks: Themes and Styles of African Literature.* Harlow: Longman, 1981.

Norris, Christopher. *What's Wrong with Postmodernism: Critical Theory and the Ends of Philosophy.* Baltimore: Johns Hopkins UP, 1990.

———. *Derrida.* Cambridge: Harvard UP, 1987.

Nwafor, Azinna. Introduction. *Pan-Africanism or Communism.* By George Padmore. 1955. Garden City: Doubleday, 1971.

Ogungbesan, Kolawole. "'The Cape Gooseberry Also Grows in Botswana': Alienation and Commitment in the Writings of Bessie Head." *Présence Africaine* 109 (1979): 92–106.

Ogwude, Sophia Obiajulu. "Protest and Commitment in Bessie Head's Utopia." *Research in African Literatures* 29.3 (September 30 1998): 70–81.

Omi, Michael, and Howard Winant. *Racial Formation in the United States: From the 1960s to the 1990s.* 1986. 2nd ed. New York: Routledge, 1994.

On Left Conservatism, Parts One & Two. Special issues of *Theory & Event* 2.2–3 (1998). Retrieved on 24 May 2006 from <http://muse.jhu.edu/journals/theory_&_event>.

Oreskes, Naomi. "Beyond the Ivory Tower: The Scientific Consensus on Climate Change." *Science* 306.5702 (3 December 2004): 1686.

Padmore, George. *Pan-Africanism or Communism.* 1955. Garden City: Doubleday, 1971.

Palumbo-Liu, David. "Assumed Identities." *Is There Life After Identity Politics?* Ed. Bill Albertini, Ben Lee, Heather Love, Mike Millner, Ken Parille, Alice Rutkowski, and Bryan Wagner. Special issue of *New Literary History* 31.4 (Autumn 2000): 765–80.

———. "*Against Race*: Yes, But At What Cost?" *African Diasporas in the New and Old Worlds: Consciousness and Imagination.* Ed. Klaus Benesch and Geneviève Fabre. Amsterdam: Rodopi, 2004. 39–59.

Panish, Jon. *The Color of Jazz: Race and Representation in Postwar American Culture.* Jackson: U of Mississippi P, 1997.

Parsons, Neil. "Economy." *Botswana History Pages.* April 1999. University of Botswana. 19 August 1999. Retrieved on 30 August 2005 from <http://www.thuto.org/ubh/bw/bhp5.htm>.

Pearse, Adetokunbo. "Apartheid and Madness: Bessie Head's *A Question of Power.*" *Kunapipi* 5.2 (1983): 81–93.

Petric, Vlada. *Constructivism in Film: The Man With the Movie Camera, a Cinematic Analysis.* Cambridge: Cambridge UP, 1987.

A Place Called Chiapas. Dir. Nettie Wild. Zeitgeist, 1998.

Plater, William M. *The Grim Phoenix: Reconstructing Thomas Pynchon.* Bloomington: Indiana UP, 1978.

Pollitt, Katha. "Pomolotov Cocktail." *The Nation* 10 June 1996: 9.

Poe, Edgar Allan. *Complete Stories and Poems of Edgar Allan Poe.* Garden City: Doubleday, 1966.

Polsky, Ned. *Hustlers, Beats, and Others.* Chicago: Aldine, 1967.

Proyect, L. "Deeper Complexities of the Sokal Affair." Home Page. 1 June 2007 <http://www.columbia.edu/~lnp3/mydocs/modernism/sokal2.htm>.

Punday, Daniel. "Pynchon's Ghosts." *Contemporary Literature* 44.2 (Summer 2003): 250–74.

Pynchon, Thomas. *Gravity's Rainbow.* New York: Penguin, 1973.

———. "A Journey Into the Mind of Watts." *New York Times Magazine* 12 June 1966: 34–35, 78–84.

———. *Mason & Dixon.* New York: Henry Holt, 1997.

———. *Slow Learner: Early Stories By Thomas Pynchon.* Boston: Little, Brown, and Company, 1984.

———. *V.* 1963. New York: Harper & Row, 1986.

Qazi, Javaid. "Source Materials for Thomas Pynchon's Fiction: An Annotated Bibliography." *Pynchon Notes* 2 (February 1980): 7–19.

Redfield, Marc W. "Pynchon's Postmodern Sublime." *PMLA* 104.2 (May 1989): 152–62.

Robbins, Bruce, and Andrew Ross. "Response by *Social Text* editors." *Lingua Franca* July/August 1996. Retrieved on 7 May 2007 from <http://linguafranca.mirror.theinfo.org/9605/sokal.html>.

Rose, Jacqueline. "On the 'Universality' of Madness: Bessie Head's *A Question of Power.*" *Critical Inquiry* 20 (Spring 1994): 401–18.

Rosenfeld, Aaron S. "The 'Scanty Plot': Orwell, Pynchon, and the Poetics of Paranoia." *Twentieth Century Literature* 50.4 (Winter 2004): 337–67.

Roth, Moira. "Chronology." *Writing Self, Writing Nation: Essays on Theresa Hak Kyung Cha's DICTEE.* Ed. Elaine Kim and Norma Alarcón. Berkeley: Third Woman, 1994. 151–60.

Rothberg, Michael. "Dead Letter Office: Conspiracy, Trauma, and *Song of Solomon's* Posthumous Communication." *African American Review* 37.4 (Winter 2003): 501–16.

Rushdie, Salman. "Thomas Pynchon." *Imaginary Homelands: Essays and Criticism 1981–1991*. New York: Penguin, 1991.

Rushing, Robert A. "Am I Paranoid Enough?" *American Literary History* 18.2 (Summer 2006): 390–3.

Sale, Kirkpatrick. "The World Behind Watergate." *New York Review of Books* 20 (May 3 1973): 9–16.

San Juan, E. *Racism and Cultural Studies: Critiques of Multiculturalist Ideology and the Politics of Difference*. Durham: Duke UP, 2002.

Sand, Patrick. "Left Conservatism?" *The Nation* 9 March 1998. 6–7.

Sartre, Jean-Paul. *Critique of Dialectical Reason: Theory of Practical Ensembles*. Vol.1. 1976. Trans. Alan Sheridan-Smith. Ed. Jonathan Rée. London: Verso, 1976.

———. *Search for a Method*. Trans. Hazel E. Barnes. New York: Vintage, 1963.

Seed, David. *The Fictional Labyrinths of Thomas Pynchon*. Iowa City: U of Iowa, 1988.

———. "Pynchon in Watts." *Pynchon Notes* 9 (June 1982): 54–60.

———. "Pynchon's Herero." *Pynchon Notes* 10 (October 1982): 37–44.

Sharpe, Matthew. "The Sociopolitical Limits of Fantasy: September 11 and Slavoj Zizek's Theory of Ideology." *Cultural Logic* 5 (2002). Retrieved on 20 January 2006 from <http://eserver.org/clogic/2002/sharpe.html>.

Shen, Dan. "Why Contextual and Formal Narratologies Need Each Other." *JNT: Journal of Narrative Theory* 35.2 (Summer 2005): 141–71.

Shih, Shu-mei. "Global Literature and the Technologies of Recognition." *PMLA* 119.1 (January 2004): 16–30.

———. "Nationalism and Korean American Women's Writing: Theresa Hak Kyung Cha's Dictee." *Speaking the Other Self: American Women Writers*. Ed. Jeanne Campbell Reesman. Athens: U of Georgia P, 1997. 144–62.

Short, Robert. "Subject-Object Epistemology & Delusion in Bessie Head's *A Question of Power*." Unpublished Essay, 2009.

Siegle, Robert. *Suburban Ambush: Downtown Writing and the Fiction of Insurgency*. Baltimore: Johns Hopkins UP, 1989.

Sivanandan, Ambalavaner. *Communities of Resistance: Writings on Black Struggles for Socialism*. New York: Verso, 1990.

Sloterdijk, Peter. *Critique of Cynical Reason*. Trans. Michael Eldred. Theory and History of Literature, Vol. 40. Minneapolis: U of Minnesota P, 1987.

Sokal, Alan. "Alan Sokal Replies [to Stanley Aronowitz]" *Dissent* (Winter 1997): 110–1.

Sontag, Susan. *Regarding the Pain of Others*. New York: Farrer, Straus, and Giroux, 2003.

———. *A Susan Sontag Reader*. Ed. Elizabeth Hardwick. New York: Vintage, 1982.

Spahr, Juliana. "Postmodernism, Readers, and Theresa Hak Kyung Cha's *Dictee*." *College Literature* 23.3 (October): 23–43.

Spanos, William. "Thomas Pynchon's *Spectral Politics*." *Contemporary Literature* 44.4 (Winter 2003): 727–36.

Spivak, Gayatri. *The Selected Works of Gayatri Spivak.* Ed. Donna Landry and Gerald MacLean. New York: Routledge, 1996.

———. "Theory in the Margin: Coetzee's *Foe* Reading Defoe's Crusoe/Roxana." *Consequences of Theory.* Ed. Jonathan Arac and Barbara Johnson. Baltimore: Johns Hopkins UP, 1991. 154–80.

Stewart, Jacqueline. "Negroes Laughing at Themselves? Black Spectatorship and the Performance of Urban Modernity." *Critical Inquiry* 29.4 (Summer 2003): 650–77.

Straw, Jack. Interview by John Kampfner. *The New Statesman* 27 September 2004. Retrieved on 20 October 2005 from <http://www.newstatesman.com/People/200409270023>.

Tabbi, Joseph. *Postmodern Sublime: Technology and American Writing from Mailer to Cyberpunk.* Ithaca: Cornell UP, 1995.

Tanner, Tony. *Thomas Pynchon.* London: Methuen, 1982.

Taylor, Carol Anne. *The Tragedy and Comedy of Resistance: Reading Modernity through Black Women's Fiction.* Philadelphia: U of Pennsylvania P, 2000.

Treuer, David. *Native American Fiction: A User's Manual.* Saint Paul: Graywolf, 2006.

Twelbeck, Kirsten. "'Elle Venait de Loin': Re-reading Dictee." *Holding Their Own: Perspectives on the Multi-Ethnic Literatures of the United States.* Ed. Dorothea Fischer-Hornung and Heike Raphael-Hernandez. Tübingen: Stauffenburg, 2000. 227–40.

Van Rensburg, Patrick. *Report From Swaneng Hill.* Uppsala: Dag Hammarsköld, 1974.

Vernet, Daniel. "Postmodern Imperialism." *Le Monde* 24 April 2004. Retrieved on 18 October 2005 from <http://www.truthout.org/docs_03/042903G.shtml>.

Weisenburger, Steven. *A Gravity's Rainbow Companion: Sources & Contexts for Pynchon's Novel.* Athens: University of Georgia, 1988.

———. "Haunted History and *Gravity's Rainbow.*" *Pynchon Notes* 42–43 (Spring–Fall 1998): 12–28.

———. "The Origin of Pynchon's Tchitcherine." *Pynchon Notes* 8 (February 1982): 39–42.

———. "Pynchon's Hereros: A Textual and Bibliographical Note." *Pynchon Notes* 16 (Spring 1985): 37–45.

West, Cornel. "The New Cultural Politics of Difference." *Race, Identity and Representation in Education.* Ed. Cameron McCarthy and Warren Crichlow. New York: Routledge, 1993.

Wilgoren, Jodi. "Politicized Scholars Put Evolution on the Defensive." *The New York Times on the Web.* 21 August 2005. Retrieved on 27 February 2008 from <http://www.nytimes.com/2005/08/21/national/21evolve.html>.

Williamson, John. "What Should the World Bank Think About Washington Consensus?" *World Bank Research Observer* 15.2 (August 2000): 251–64.

———. "What Washington Means by Policy Reform." *Latin American Adjustment: How Much Has Happened?* Ed. John Williamson. Washington, D.C.: Institute for International Economics, 1990. 12–40.

Wilson, Hugh T. *Capitalism After Postmodernism: Neo-Conservatism, Legitimacy and the Theory of Public Capital.* Boston: Brill, 2002.

Winner, Thomas. *The Oral Art and Literature of the Kazahks of Russian Central Asia.* Durham: Duke UP, 1958.

Wolf, Martin. *Why Globalization Works.* New Haven: Yale UP, 2005.

Wolin, Richard. *The Seduction of Unreason: The Intellectual Romance with Fascism from Nietzsche to Postmodernism.* Princeton: Princeton UP, 2004.

Wollen, Peter. *Readings and Writings: Semiotic Counter-Strategies.* London: New Left Books, 1982.

Wong, Sau-ling. "Denationalization Reconsidered: Asian American Cultural Criticism at a Theoretical Crossroads." *Amerasia Journal* 21.1 and 2 (1995): 1–27.

Wong, Shelley. "Unnaming the Same: Theresa Hak Kyung Cha's *Dictee.*" *Writing Self, Writing Nation: Essays on Theresa Hak Kyung Cha's Dictee.* Ed. Elaine Kim and Norma Alarcón. Berkeley: Third Woman, 1994. 103–40.

Young, John K. "Pynchon in Popular Magazines." *Critique* 44.4 (Summer 2003): 389–404.

Zapatista. Dir. Benjami Eichert et al. Big Noise Films, 1999.

Žižek, Slavoj. "Against Human Rights." *New Left Review* 34 (July/August 2005): 115–31.

———. "The One Measure of True Love Is: You Can Insult the Other." *Spiked.* 15 November 2001. Retrieved on 7 January 2006 from <http://www.spiked-online.com/Articles/00000002D2C4.htm>.

———. "The Ongoing 'Soft Revolution.'" *Critical Inquiry* 30.2 (Winter 2004): 292–323.

———. *The Sublime Object of Ideology.* New York: Verso, 1989.

Index